OWLS
MATE
FOR
LIFE

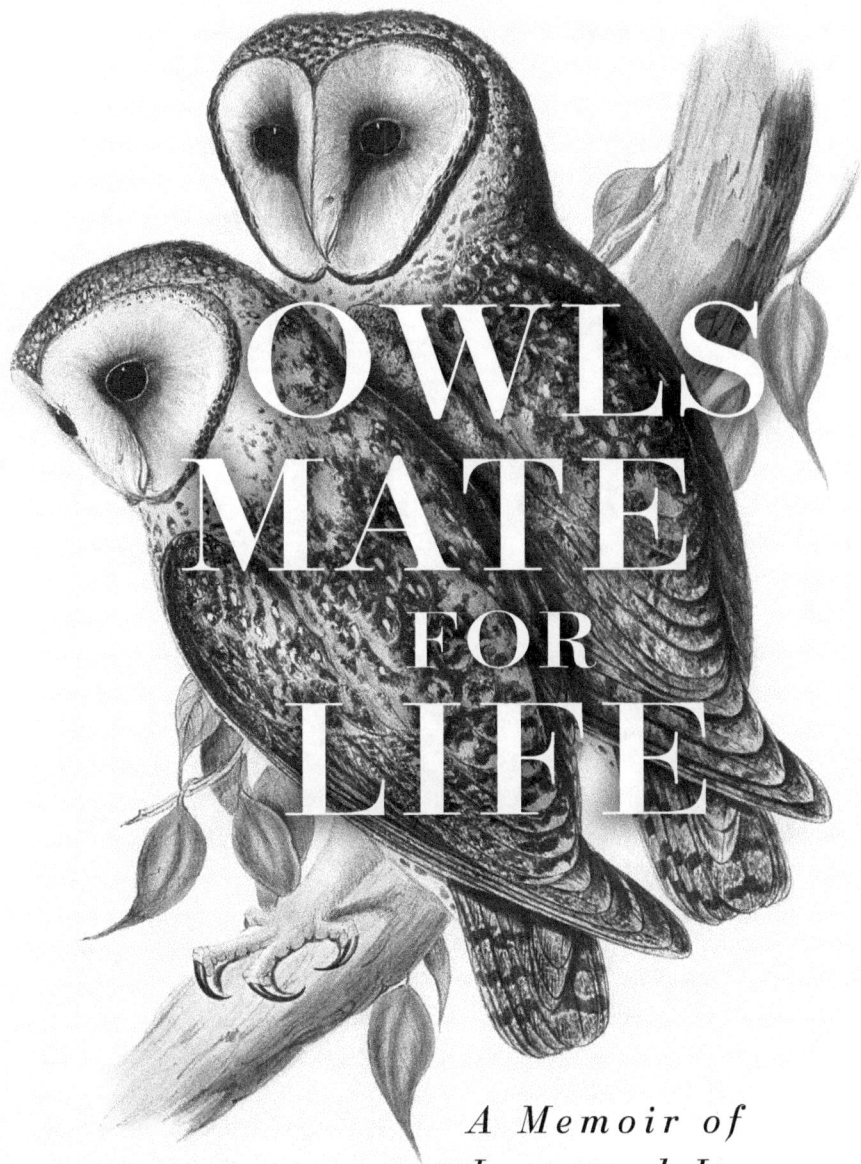

OWLS MATE FOR LIFE

A Memoir of
Loss and Love

JAMES PAAUW

credo
house publishers

INTRODUCTION

"I will exalt you, LORD, for you lifted me out of the depths . . ." So begins Psalm 30, a psalm of David. Our family calls this "Liz's Psalm." It is a psalm of Thanksgiving.

On January 8, 2016, the day of my wife's accident, I began a journey of understanding what David meant when he wrote "weeping may stay for the night, but rejoicing comes in the morning."

For the next seven months Psalm 30 would become our family's story.

CHAPTER 1

My pager was driving me nuts. I was struggling to place a particularly difficult "blind" feeding tube, as it kept going off. Then my cell phone started to ring. Since I keep my phone in my pocket, and I was wearing vinyl gloves for the procedure I was doing, I couldn't check it. That it was ringing at all at work was somewhat unusual. When it rang for the third time, I knew that something extraordinary was up.

I was working that afternoon on 4 Heart at Spectrum Health Butterworth Hospital, Surgical Critical Care with a patient who had recently been removed from a ventilator and was unable to safely swallow—hence the feeding tube. A blind feeding tube is one that our Nutrition Support Service places without benefit of fluoroscopy (moving X-ray) guidance, a modality we usually reserve for mechanically ventilated patients. This particular procedure had been more difficult than most due to the patient's profound swallowing deficit, which meant that his efforts to help me with a swallow instead tended to direct the tube into his airway.

When I finally finished the procedure, I washed up and left the patient's room to check my pager and phone. There were about five or six pages, indicating that I should call my daughter Jackie and our close friend Gary. My phone also recorded several missed calls from both of them, but for some reason I hadn't received any texts. I would find out later that the reason for this was what I had imagined at the time: people feel more comfortable notifying you of bad news directly rather than by text.

As I tried to call my daughter back, I could feel a growing sense of anxiety in the pit of my stomach. There was no answer, so I called Gary.

"Your wife's been in a pretty serious accident," he told me. "Liz is down in the trauma bay in the ER, but I think she's okay. Some broken bones maybe. Jackie and Brek should be down there already. They're trying to get ahold of you—you'd better get down there."

It was only a short walk to the "megavator" that would take me down to the Emergency Department, but I paused to decide what I should do about the white lab coat I was wearing. For a moment I felt conflicted as I tried to grasp the reality of suddenly changing roles from being a physician to becoming a family member of the patient. This would certainly not be the last time I struggled with the nexus of those two positions in the journey I was about to undertake. With resignation I removed my lab coat, placing it over the back of the computer chair in which I had been sitting, and headed for the megavator.

I think this was the moment when I began the torrent of prayer for my wife's recovery and wellbeing that continues to this very day. When my wife and kids told me that I exhibit obsessive-compulsive traits, I've always maintained that I'm the very definition of normal, though they know I'm being a bit facetious when I state that. A friend who treats OCD clients once told me that we all have some degree of those tendencies within our psychological makeup. Compulsive behavior can be crippling, so I don't by any means want to be insensitive to those who daily struggle with this disorder. However, I have found that, in at least one area in my life, I have managed to turn compulsiveness in a positive direction (which a friend calls functional obsession); that's in my prayer life.

As a Christian I believe in a sovereign God, who not only created this world but controls every action or turn of events at every moment. God has directed us to come to him in prayer for all things and, in fact, ordains those prayers. Why would I not avail myself of the opportunity to go to that Creator at every opportunity? I confess that I'm a compulsive prayer; my wife calls me a prayer warrior, but I think she's being generous. So, it was only natural for me to begin what has become an ongoing stream of requests, coupled with gratitude for God's incremental blessings of healing for my wife.

Since my work takes me all over the better part of two hospitals but calls for me to be in the Emergency Department only a few times a year, I had to ask to be directed to the trauma bay once I arrived. The nurse I approached seemed to be surprised at someone suddenly appearing in the middle of her department and asking for directions, but once I explained the circumstances a look of understanding passed over her face, and she walked me over to the room where I could find my wife. I could hear a lot of conversation coming through the curtain that shielded Liz from me. Offering a final prayer that things would go well on the other side of that curtain, I lifted it aside and edged into the cubicle.

About a dozen clinicians of various disciplines—physicians, nurses, aides, and a phlebotomist—surrounded a stretcher whereon lay my wife, covered with only a modicum of decency by a hospital gown. Our daughter, Jackie, eight months pregnant, stood there watching. She and her husband, Brek, had beaten their mother's ambulance to the hospital by a few minutes. Since only one family member at a time was allowed in the trauma bay, Brek sat out in the Emergency Department's waiting room.

Liz was in obvious pain, but when she saw me her face lit up with a bright smile. In that moment I saw something in her that I had not really noticed before but that I would identify often throughout our ensuing ordeal. Her face relaxed into an expression of relief—of almost peace—now that her husband was present.

Through the coming events and even during the worst of times, if I were present by her side Liz would relax and seem to believe that everything would be alright—her husband was there taking care of her. Of course, I knew how foolish this perception was, but I encouraged it because it brought serenity when her mind—and body—were troubled. In trying moments I have often told her, "I'm here; you know I'm taking care of you." Almost always her response has been a smile and an "I know."

In truth, Liz knew that the calm my presence brought was itself only a manifestation of the knowledge that I was literally praying for her without ceasing—and more, marshaling all the other prayer support for her that I could possibly arrange. I believe the tranquility she felt whenever I was in her room came from an awareness of the many prayers being offered up on her behalf, of which I assured her often. Liz's belief is simple and trusting: a prayer brought to God will be answered, so she could relax in that knowledge and move on.

While we both believe in the omnipotence of God in every aspect of life, my faith is of a more complex, brooding variety. Like my namesake, the biblical patriarch Jacob, I often feel that I must convince God of the validity of my position, even wrestle with him. Some might pin that onto a lack of trust in a loving God or a certain degree of arrogance that presumes to change God's mind, but I think it simply reflects the anxiety that accompanies obsessive-compulsive behavior. Better men than me have wrestled in prayer with God— Abraham, Moses, and David, to name just a few.

Looking around Liz's room in the trauma bay, I saw a lot of familiar, now sympathetic faces of clinicians who staffed the trauma service and with whom I worked on a near daily basis. I noticed several residents from the general surgery residency program with whom I had done procedures at some time over the past few years. It felt awkward to be there as a patient's family member and not as a colleague; for some reason I felt as if I had to be careful when I spoke, that I might say the wrong thing.

The staff gave me just a moment to say a few words to Liz and to kiss her before she was taken down to Radiology for CAT scans of her chest and abdomen.

"Everything is going to be alright," I told her with a voice that cracked.

I struggled with my emotions, as much from the sympathy and love I felt from my friends around me as from the sudden shock of seeing Liz in this situation. She told me that her right foot was hurting a lot, and then she was gone, wheeled off for her X-rays. I felt self-conscious standing there, surrounded by the remaining members of the trauma team. It felt wrong somehow to ask clinical questions because I was not a physician in this setting, but the team filled me in on what they knew so far. Due to my emotional state, most of that briefing went right through my brain without leaving much of a trace, something I am told is not unusual for family members of trauma victims. It wasn't until later that evening that I first began to be aware of the injuries Liz had sustained.

A care manager for the Trauma Service introduced herself to Jackie and me and steered us down the hall to a consultation room, where, along with Brek, we could exchange information. On the way I found out that Jackie had received a call from the Michigan State Police just as she had gotten home from work at about the same time as Brek, a realtor.

Fortunately, Gary, Jackie's father-in-law and my former college roommate, had been babysitting their two young sons, so he was able to remain on that duty while they rushed to the hospital. I explained to the care manager that my wife had been struggling for a number of years with a rare underlying autoimmune disease.

"She has hypereosinophilic syndrome," I reported.

This rare disease caused her eosinophilic immune cells to proliferate and attack various parts of her body. Over the years she had developed inflammations of the uvea of her eye, her colon, and her bladder, but most typically of her lungs. She had experienced nearly constant pulmonary congestion, with thick mucus production and shortness of breath, leaving her severely restricted in terms of which activities she could tolerate. It also resulted in what physicians would call opportunistic pneumonias, overgrowth of bacteria that would cause an infection in the lungs because of Liz's underlying immunosuppressed state, complicated by the burden of the mucus in her airways.

"She can usually tell when she has pneumonia because her symptoms get worse," I explained. "For the past week she was saying that she had one on her left side. She had an upcoming appointment with her pulmonary doctor scheduled for this afternoon. We were hoping we could baby her along until she went to that appointment."

Yes, that is a doctor thing and maybe exhibits a degree of arrogance. Neither of us knew just how serious her condition really was.

That day, as was our custom, Liz had agreed to pick me up at the hospital to take me to lunch, but she had called me late in the morning to tell me she felt exhausted. She said she was so tired she couldn't keep her eyes open, so she thought she'd better take a nap. I had told her that that was fine but to remember to get up in time to make it to her appointment at Dr. John Cantor's office at 2:00 that afternoon.

After mentioning this appointment, the care manager looked perplexed.

"Your wife had a head-on accident and was likely going around 55 miles per hour," the care manager said. "Ionia County emergency services responded to the accident."

Now it was my turn to be perplexed. Ionia County was the next county over. I had never heard of the roads the case manager stated to fix the location of the accident for us. The case manager mentioned the town of Lake Odessa, which is well east of Grand Rapids and truly a rural area. Since Liz was coming from our home on the west side of Grand Rapids, she had to have traveled at least thirty miles past her doctor's office in East Grand Rapids to the point of the accident.

"That can't be right," I told the care manager. "She's never been down that way in her life. Not that I'm aware of, anyway. I don't think she could find her way there if she tried."

The care manager attempted to establish relationship to that area for Liz, but there was nothing. She simply had driven miles past her destination to the middle of nowhere and been involved in a high-speed, head-on motor vehicle collision.

It was true that many in our family had noticed a very gradual change in Liz's personality over the past few years, but we had attributed that change to the effects on her mind of the hypereosinophilia. Her memory had slipped a bit, and she had trouble understanding more complex concepts. In short, her mentation seemed simpler. Other than taxing our patience at times, these changes had not brought much hardship to our family.

Much more alarming to us had been a more marked, less gradual progression of, for lack of better terms, general lethargy and sleepiness, most notably over the two months just prior to this accident. Maybe the latter had been evolving more gradually over time and was related somehow to the original, longer-term changes we had noticed in Liz's personality, but it had become a concern for our family in the most recent two months.

Just a week or so before the accident, my daughter-in-law Laura had dropped her three kids at our house for Liz to babysit while she went to lunch with some friends. Laura was shocked when she picked them up to find a lethargic mother-in-law on the couch, difficult to arouse. This was a serious matter to Laura, as one of her kids was just 14 months old, while one of her older twins was an autistic boy who needs special attention.

Later that night her husband, our second son, Tim, had expressed his concerns to me. Even though he is fiercely loyal to his mother, Tim said that he and Laura didn't feel it was safe to leave their children with Mom any longer. He expressed his fear that there was something physically wrong with his mom and stated that, until we figured out what that was and how to fix it, he and Laura didn't feel comfortable using her as a babysitter anymore.

I told Tim that I was upset as well. I had been aware of the mental changes, but whenever I brought up the matter to Liz she was adamantly resistant to recognizing a problem. Nevertheless, I had again questioned Liz, with more than a slight degree of frustration, about why she couldn't have stayed awake long enough to care for her grandkids. She had to be getting plenty of sleep—after all, it seemed as though she slept all the time these days.

Now there was this: an auto accident that had happened well beyond her intended destination. Clearly there was something going on mentally that had contributed to the accident. It broke my heart to think of my wife—lost, confused, and driving mile after mile out of her way until she was involved in an accident. I began to feel deeply regretful that I had not decided to pick her up and bring her to her appointment that afternoon.

My wife was admitted to room 4819 on 4 Heart, ironically the very floor I had been working on when I was notified of her accident; Jackie, Brek and I reached the room at about the same time Liz did. My son Tim, the principal of Jenison Christian School, had immediately left school after having been notified of the accident by Gary. He arrived in room 4819 not much later than his mom.

My third son, Tom, had worked the previous night shift in his position as a nurse at nearby Mercy Health St. Mary's, a hospital a little over a mile south of Spectrum Health Butterworth. Tom was still sleeping, but we had been able to contact his wife, Emily. They both arrived in Liz's room at about the time he would have started his scheduled work shift for that evening, which he had asked off.

We had been told that my wife had sustained a concussion, but she was awake and conversant that evening, even laughing through her pain at our light-hearted comments. Dr. CJ Gibson, a recent graduate from our General Surgery residency program and now the Critical Care fellow—and a close friend—came to see us and fill us in on Liz's injuries.

"She broke both bones in her right wrist, as well as in her right lower leg," Dr. Gibson told us. "She also broke numerous bones in her right foot. Her right chest sustained blunt force trauma, resulting in nine fractured ribs and a large pulmonary contusion."

The chest CAT scan he showed us revealed that Liz also had pneumonia in the left lower lobe, confirming what she had been telling me for the past week. Unfortunately, the fact that the rib fractures and lung contusion were on the opposite side of the chest as the pneumonia meant that my wife had two damaged lungs now, a point that would come back to haunt us some time later. Liz was also receiving several blood transfusions at that time, although this was not unexpected, given the extent of her fractures and lung injury.

Dr. Gibson asked if he could speak with me privately outside her room, which was the last room at the south end of that hallway. As we stood by the window that looked south down the hill at St. Mary's, I was worried that he might be holding back worse news, but this was not the case.

"Jim—you know we treat all of our patients with the best care we can, but I just want you to know that your wife is a VIP here."

After telling me this, he embraced me and then walked away. I stood there weeping, overcome with emotion. (Forgive me for using the term "weep" instead of "cry," but for some reason it has always sounded more acceptable to me for a man to weep than to cry). Weeping had not been a reaction I was personally disposed to exhibit, but that would change on this night. Soon I found myself more and more prone to emotional lability and weeping.

CJ's comments and embrace were the beginning of a tremendous degree of support I received from an overwhelming number of colleagues at my workplace. Physicians, nurses, aides, dietitians, therapists, unit secretaries, environmental service workers—daily they rallied around me and encouraged me, often with expressions of their prayers (more about that later).

I believe that the Nutrition Support Service on which I work is an important part of hospital care, but we are quite often a relatively inconspicuous slice of that care. One afternoon a week or so after the accident, I hung out on the fringes of the Critical Care service as they conducted their daily rounds outside my wife's room. Impressed

with their efficiency and coordination of care, I complimented Dr. Betsy Steensma, the Critical Care attending surgeon that day, on how excellently and seamlessly the Critical Care/Trauma services performed patient care. She brought tears to my eyes by her response.

"Well, you're one of us too, you know."

Even now, several years later, a day does not go by without one, two, or several friends at work asking me how my wife is doing and offering expressions of support and encouragement. Believe me, there is not much more that will absolutely make you love the place you work than an experience like this.

My family and I needed this support and encouragement, especially considering the waves of psychological trauma we were about to endure for the next seven months.

As I returned to Liz's room, Tim was calling his brother Jamie to fill him in on the news. The oldest of our sons and a physician himself, Jamie was our only out-of-town child. Four months earlier he had moved from Kansas City to join an ophthalmology group in Lynchburg, Virginia. Although this was not an immediate matter of concern, we thought that his newness in that practice might make it difficult for him to break away and help care for his mother.

Compounding this was the fact that Jamie and his wife, Halle, also had three very busy young children: a six-year-old son and two three-year old daughters whom we call "accidental twins" because they had been born only three weeks apart and had been adopted into our family at the same time. Jamie and Halle had no family support around Lynchburg and were just getting to know a new church and neighborhood friends. We were able to tell Jamie that there was no urgency for him to travel to Grand Rapids. Mom had sustained significant injuries but was stable and in good spirits despite a fair amount of pain.

The last immediate family member to be called was our youngest son, Mark, at the time in his senior year as a premedical student at Calvin College (now Calvin University), a highly rated liberal arts institution here in Grand Rapids. Calvin College had a school term in January called the interim term, a four-week period that allowed students to take a single class in a more concentrated fashion. Since many of the courses offered during that month were graded as pass/fail and wouldn't affect a student's grade point average, this offered a good opportunity to complete required classes outside one's core group of studies.

It was also not unusual for students to seek opportunities to study abroad at that time, as Mark was then doing. While his major studies were in Biology, Mark was working on completing a minor in Spanish. Part of the requirement for this minor was a semester abroad for something of a Spanish immersion experience. Mark had been looking forward for several years to this month in Mexico, where he would live with a Mexican family and participate in classes and other cultural experiences each day. Although he was nervously anticipating living with a family he would just be meeting, he was excited to improve his Spanish language skills.

Mark had traveled to Mexico to first meet his host family on Tuesday, January 5, just three days before the accident. In the ensuing three short days this had already been a very good experience for him. While several other students had been assigned to live with less privileged families in very modest homes, some with outdoor showers, Mark had landed in the well-to-do family of a physician who lived in an upscale home with all the amenities. Mark's hosts insisted that he call them Mom and Dad, and Mark shared a room with a "brother" roughly his own age.

Moreover, everyone in the family spoke reasonably polished English, which, of course, they tried to refrain from using to enhance Mark's Spanish skills but which made it much more comfortable for Mark to fit in. Mark had had several days of classes with his professor and classmates, who were following a rigorous curriculum. Each student was expected to research an assigned topic and present to the group in Spanish, and Mark's turn would be coming up soon.

Despite all of this, on learning of his mother's accident Mark's first question was not "if" but "when" he should come home. Realizing how much Mark had looked forward to this Mexican experience and to improving his Spanish language skills, I assured him that there was no urgency and that I didn't anticipate that necessity in the future. I explained to Mark that his mother was banged up but stable and doing fine and that we anticipated a relatively quick and uneventful recovery.

Despite my reassurances, Mark felt quite guilty about not coming home to help care for his mother—a manifestation, I'm sure, of the obsessive-compulsive disorder he shares with his dad. I finally managed to convince him that it would be okay for him to remain in Mexico, with the caveat that we would communicate daily to keep him updated on his mother's status. If anything were to change for the worse, which I certainly didn't anticipate, we would work to expedite his return to Grand Rapids. Satisfied with this compromise, Mark hung up to notify his fiancée, Tamara, a student at Kendall School of Design here in Grand Rapids.

Tamara joined us that evening at the bedside of her future mom. Now that all of our immediate family members had been notified, we began to contact our extended families and churches. Liz's and my mothers had to be told, as did our various siblings. We found it convenient to ask siblings to call other siblings, as well as nephews and nieces, and to have pastors send out the notice on the prayer chains of our various churches.

While this seemed at the time to be just the next order of business, I was aware that it was the most important thing we could be doing. I had been convinced of the amazing power of prayer throughout my life and was going to spare no effort to round up as much prayer support as I possibly could through the course of Liz's recovery. I knew that I, as her husband, would be called on to make decisions for Liz's care and that my being a physician would most likely be advantageous in that process (although I was to discover that the latter would not always be the case).

Ultimately, though, I knew that my main role in my wife's care, as I feel it should be with any patient's family member, would be to marshal the prayer support to barrage a merciful God who loves to give good things to his people. Already on that first night expressions of prayer and encouragement began to pour in from all over the country and even outside of it.

As I recall, about seven or eight of us stayed in Liz's room late that evening, to encourage her through the escalating pain she was experiencing in several places but also to allay her anxiety. That anxiety, we soon learned, would grow to have a long-lasting and paralyzing effect on this wife and mother. We decided that evening to try to have a family member stay with Liz throughout each night, at least for the time being. I have already noted that Tim is fiercely loyal to his mother, so it was no surprise that he insisted on staying with her that first night. Before the rest of us left, we held hands as we circled her bed; I remember Tim concluding his prayer with the following:

> "Lord, whatever your plans are in the course you have planned out for our mom, we pray that, above all, they will reflect great glory, honor, and praise to your Name."

It struck me that, of anything he might have prayed for, he had placed the highest priority on God's glorification and honor. What did that mean? I was soon to learn. Tim and I shared the duty of giving my wife a hands-on blessing, a practice I had kept up for many years with our children when they were still living in our home.

As we left room 4819 that evening, I noticed the nurse hanging another unit of blood to be transfused into my wife. Later that night I lay awake for a long time, unused to being alone in our room at night and thinking about that extra blood.

I was worried.

CHAPTER 2

A s I climbed out of my car the next morning to head into the hospital, I thanked God for His providence. It was Saturday, January 9, and I was preparing to start my morning rounds. Our Nutrition Support Service (NSS) is small: myself; my partner, Dr. Jim Veldkamp; and our Nurse Practitioner, Annette Broersma. Because we are a small service, there is not much flexibility; our schedule calls for at least one of the physicians to be physically present on any given day.

On some days both physicians work together, but on days when one of us is off the other one will work with Annette. Monday is the one day of the week when all three of us are usually working together. Jim and I split weekends, during which we are assisted by either Annette or one of four Critical Care dietitians, all of whom are a delight to work with. As the NSS covers the patients at two acute care hospitals in the city of Grand Rapids, Spectrum Health Blodgett and Spectrum Health Butterworth, on weekends the scheduled physician generally starts out his day at the Blodgett campus and catches up to Annette or the dietitian at the Butterworth campus later in the day.

The schedule frequently results in a four-day weekend off for the physicians, which, since there is an extra staff member on Mondays, can easily be stretched into a five-day block to allow for short out-of-town trips as they arise. Jim Veldkamp was on just such an excursion, having gone with his wife to Washington, D.C., for a professional education meeting, coupled with some personal time for sightseeing and relaxation. Normally I would have started my workday at Blodgett, but, providentially, I was scheduled to work with Annette that weekend, and she had immediately volunteered to cover the Blodgett responsibilities so I could spend some pre-work time with Liz that morning before starting my rounds at Butterworth.

Annette, Jim, or I would each do anything to help one of our partners, but besides that, Annette "had some skin in the game"—she is Liz's first cousin, and they had always been fairly close. In fact, it didn't surprise me that Jim Veldkamp texted me later that afternoon to tell me that he was going to come home early. He had heard of Liz's accident from his kids that day, who in turn had heard of it through our church's prayer chain. The Veldkamp and Paauw families live about a mile apart and worship together at Walker United Reformed Church, a modestly sized church on the Grand Rapids West side. Jim and Mary's original plan was to return to Grand Rapids on Monday, January 11; I texted Jim that we were doing okay and that he should stick with his scheduled arrangements.

As I entered Liz's room, Tim sat at her bedside. I could see that he was exhausted.

"How's she doing?" I asked him.

"She's had a hard time sleeping. You can tell she's dealing with a lot of significant pain."

Tim reported that it had been a long night of praying, handholding, and offering comforting words.

As I sat down beside Liz, I noticed several ominous signs. Her blood pressure was on the low side, with a mean arterial pressure

(MAP) of 58. The MAP is not a measured value but is based on a simple calculation involving the usual two blood pressure numbers. Critical care and emergency clinicians routinely use the MAP as a determinant of shock, which is the technical term for blood pressure that is too low to sustain normal organ perfusion. A desirable MAP is greater than 65, the number we use to ensure adequate blood perfusion of vital organs. MAP values progressively lower than 65 indicate steadily worsening under-perfusion of these critical organs, with associated risk of organ damage and even organ failure.

I noticed a bag of blood hanging from Liz's IV pole, along with a few more IV pumps than I had seen the night before. These, I surmised, would most likely be infusing blood pressure-raising medications (pressors), which I found out to be the case when I looked more closely at those bags. Liz was clearly more uncomfortable than the previous night, writhing in bed and moaning frequently.

My son Tom arrived shortly after me, so Tim turned the responsibilities over to him and headed home for a well-deserved rest. Tom settled in at his mom's bedside, ready to take over what was obviously going to be an emotionally exhausting experience. Liz was very fidgety, and her speech was not as clear as it had been the night before. This was worrisome since we had been told that, although she was awake and alert in the emergency department, she had sustained a concussion at the accident scene. I stayed with Tom in the room for a while but eventually felt that I had to get to work. I got ready start my rounds, but my plans were arrested by one of those cardinal moments that comes at you unlooked for but that changes your life forever.

As I slipped on my white lab coat to leave the room, Dr. Richard Hagelberg, the Trauma surgeon to whose care Liz had been admitted the day before, entered room 4819. He and I had spoken the previous night—an upbeat conversation—but now his demeanor was more solemn.

Richard, a good friend of mine, was kind but direct; he felt that Liz needed to go to the operating room urgently that day for an exploratory laparotomy. Richard laid out his reasoning in a calm and orderly way, and when he was done I knew he was right. Liz's CAT scan from the previous day had revealed a modest amount of blood in her abdomen, but she was now receiving the eighth unit of blood since her admission to raise her serum hemoglobin level. Despite those blood transfusions, her hemoglobin hovered a little above 6.0, quite anemic and obviously contributing to the ongoing shock she was experiencing. All that blood was going somewhere. The goal of the surgery was simple: to identify any source of bleeding and fix it.

An operative consent form was prepared for the laparotomy and for the orthopedic trauma surgeon, Dr. Miller, to place an external fixator device on her lower leg and foot to stabilize those fractures until a more definitive surgery could be performed. I signed the consent forms and let Annette know that I was going to be tied up for a while. After almost transforming back to being a physician, I was once again the family member.

Tom and I followed Liz down to a preoperative holding area, where we met Emily and Jackie, who had together come from a cousin's baby shower as soon as they had received my text. Jackie told me months later that she had cried bitterly when she read my text about the planned exploratory laparotomy because she knew it was going to be very difficult for the staff to get Liz back off a ventilator after the surgery.

Jackie had worked as a nurse for a year and a half on this very floor a few years earlier with similarly critically injured patients and knew the ramifications that two marginal lungs would have on ventilator weaning and extubation. She told me later that, after reading my text, she had wondered if this might be the last chance she would get to speak with her mom.

The four of us stood next to Liz's transport stretcher, trying to comfort the very uncomfortable patient. Because it was Saturday, the surgical holding area where we were waiting was short staffed, and the nurse assigned to Liz had felt safe leaving her with light supervision because the four family members present were all medical personnel. Those forty minutes or so seemed much longer as Liz progressed from uncomfortable to restless to downright agitated.

"I can't do this anymore," her weak voice pleaded repeatedly.

It was difficult for us to see her writhing and moaning. We worked hard trying to keep her calm, and I was grateful there were four of us to share that load, as well as the burden of prayer. We reasoned that Liz wouldn't be comfortable until she was placed under anesthesia, so we all breathed a sigh of relief when the operating crew finally came to take her into surgery. After sharing one more moment of prayer together, we went our separate ways.

After several hours of making my rounds, I received a page notifying me that Liz was back on 4 Heart, but now in room 4821, a slightly larger room to accommodate the growing number of IV pumps and other nursing paraphernalia. On entering the room late in the afternoon, I encountered an array of flashing lights from her IV pumps, the number of which had grown again since I had last seen her.

Her blood pressure was "soft," meaning on the low side, which accounted for several of the new pumps that were being used to administer a continuous infusion of pressors. She also now had a bulky metal brace, an external fixator, drilled into her right lower leg in several places to stabilize the fractured bones in her leg and ankle. Liz had been kept sedated and intubated on a mechanical ventilator because of those low pressures, so we were unable to speak to each other, a new and disagreeable experience for me.

Dr. Hagelberg arrived a few minutes later to brief us on the results of the surgery.

"I found a small laceration of the capsule of the liver. It's not the reason she lost eight units of blood, but since it was still oozing, I went ahead and repaired it."

He paused for a moment and then proceeded with his news.

"I also encountered a shrunken and hardened, nodular liver."

Dr. Hagelberg didn't say anything more, but he didn't have to; as a physician I recognized the classical description of liver cirrhosis. To say I was stunned would be a gross understatement. Suddenly the picture became clear, as I thought of Liz's recent episodes of sleepiness and the blood ammonia level of 126 the previous evening, which had perplexed me until I dismissed it as a laboratory error. A flood of emotions overwhelmed me, and I struggled to contain them.

Dr. Hagelberg gave us a few more details about Liz's current condition, including that she would likely be kept on the ventilator for a day or so until her condition stabilized enough to warrant extubation, removal from the ventilator. Liz had undergone a previous gastric bypass weight-loss surgery years earlier, and Dr. Hagelberg also mentioned that he had placed an intestinal feeding tube in the so-called common channel of that configuration. As a specialist in nutrition support, I appreciated his foresight in placing a tube for future feeding access.

The rest of the evening was pretty much a blur to me. Tom and Em showed up immediately after Dr. Hagelberg had left, and other family members drifted in and out of Liz's room. Given the current circumstances, I had to make some phone calls and texts. I was on the Board of Trustees of Westminster Seminary California (WSC) in Escondido and was scheduled to fly out to San Diego the following

Tuesday, January 12, for their semiannual Board meeting. My mother and my sister Joan had been planning to make the drive to Escondido from my mom's home in central California so we could all spend some time together during down moments around those meetings. I had delayed my return flight until Saturday, even though the meetings would be done by Thursday afternoon, to give the three of us a little more time together.

I struggled with the decision to cancel the trip, as I believed Liz would be in reasonably good condition by Tuesday, but it was obvious that she would still be hospitalized and likely in the Critical Care Unit. I texted Joan to let her know that I was canceling and to ask her to notify my mom as well. Joan was very disappointed and asked me if there wasn't yet a possibility I could still go. There wasn't. I also texted Dawn Doorn, the Vice President of Development for WSC, to update her and the WSC community on Liz's course and my absence from the upcoming meetings.

Shock is the word that most closely describes how Dawn and many others I texted or called felt about the news. Dawn expressed concern and promised that the seminary family would be much in prayer for Liz, me, and our family. This was not an insignificant thing to me— or, I believed, to Liz's recovery. Throughout the course of Liz's hospitalization, I received daily texts, cards, and even a few visits from that seminary community, always assuring me of their continued prayers, which I in turn solicited at every opportunity. If the prayers of the righteous are powerful and effective (James 5:16), this was indeed a group whose prayers I coveted greatly. I was already impressed at this early date by how many people from numerous personal associations were lifting up my wife in prayer.

I had begun keeping a journal to record the events of Liz's hospitalization, so that, when she had recovered, she and I could look back together at how events had transpired. Late that evening I wrote, ". . . a small nodular cirrhotic liver?? Ammonia level 126—suddenly all becomes clear. One of the worst days of my life." Tim had returned to the room, and we talked well into the night about the surgical findings; he again volunteered to spend the overnight shift on guard by his mother's side. I appreciated the chance to sleep in my own bed, although I lay awake for some time, my mind plagued with anxiety and loneliness.

I was in the hospital early the next morning to check on Liz and then to complete my patient rounds; Annette was taking care of the Blodgett Hospital patients again. My normal Sunday routine is to get to the hospitals by 5:30 or 6:00 in the morning to finish rounds by 9:00 a.m. and make it to church in time for our 9:30 worship service. Getting done that quickly usually entails a somewhat frenetic pace, but with the help of Annette or one of our dietitians it usually works out well.

This Sunday, however, because of Liz's status, I had determined to spend the day with her after I had finished seeing my patients. Providentially, no patient procedures had needed to be done on our service either Saturday or Sunday, a rare occurrence allowing me to focus on Liz and her care.

As I stood bedside briefly talking with Tim before starting my rounds, Dr. Hagelberg appeared at the doorway in a plaid shirt and blue jeans, looking for all the world as though it were his day off—it was. Richard had come in to personally meet with me and my family to discuss the ramifications and prognosis of his surgical findings and to hopefully answer any questions we might have; he did not want to leave this to whichever of his partners was on call that day.

Tim and I joined Richard in a staff conference room and peppered him with questions. Chief among them was how one who almost never touched a drop of alcohol could develop cirrhosis. I was familiar with the term nonalcoholic steatohepatitis (NASH) but not much more than that. Richard was a picture of empathy and professionalism, yet honest.

"In my experience," Richard told us, "the advanced nature of Liz's liver disease indicates that she is likely to live less than two years."

I felt as though I would vomit. As I sat there reeling with devastation, Tim immediately focused on how we could save her life. As the protector, Tim asked if his mom was a candidate for a liver transplant and if part of his own liver might be acceptable. Richard told us that, due to her underlying diabetes and the extent of her injuries, she would not likely get to the point of being a candidate for a transplant.

After we had thanked Richard for coming in to see us on his day off, and for his compassion and kindness, Tim and I returned to room 4821 in a state of despondency. We exchanged a few words of mutual condolence before I turned away to complete my patient rounds. Tim notified his siblings of the bad news; unbeknownst to us then, this was but one among many dark times yet to come.

Turning my attention later in the day to family arrangements served, to some extent, to take my mind off my grief. I spoke with Mark about coming home from Mexico but encouraged him to stay put for the time being, as his mom seemed to be stabilizing. Mark was torn about this decision, specifically worried that he might not get to see her again, but I assured him that that specter was not at all likely, given her improvement that day.

Jamie was working on flying up from Virginia to help me with medical decisions and to help organize my financial concerns, a task Liz had always overseen. This latter issue would turn out to be a big deal, compounded in part by my lack of expertise—I was familiar with the use of a credit card but hardly knew how to write a check. Jamie was able to repurpose a partial refund from my now canceled ticket to San Diego to arrange to fly up the next day, Monday. I tried to convince him not to come, as he had joined his current practice only a few months earlier, but he was insistent. This was a family crisis, and as the oldest child he was going to be there, no argument; secretly, I was very relieved.

Word about Liz's tenuous status and the shocking news about her previously undiagnosed liver disease filtered out to our extended family, friends, neighbors, and distant acquaintances. Expressions of sympathy, hope, and especially assurances of prayer began to pour in, each one so meaningful to our immediate family. We were just starting the learning process of what the family of God really is.

Our pastor, Rev. Corey Dykstra, and his wife, Jill, came to visit and pray with us that afternoon, the first of many hospital visits he would make on our behalf. Dave and Camille Van Dyk, close friends from church, also popped in for just a few minutes, not wanting to disturb our hospital routine as they left a large wicker basket filled with food, soda, paper tablets, pens, and a variety of other useful items.

They had obviously put considerable thought into this gift, and it became a valuable asset to those of us who would spend extended time in Liz's room. In fact, that basket followed Liz from room to room for several months, as we kept replenishing the goodies in it, which not infrequently provided some of the only food we watchers would have to eat as we took our turns at the bedside shifts.

Tim had to return to his work as a school principal early the next morning, so my son-in-law, Brek, volunteered to stay the night at Liz's bedside, now in room 4821. As I've noted, I believe the staff moved us to this room because it was larger than 4819; I think this was in part to accommodate the family and friends who came to visit

Liz. How these young people managed to get some reasonable sleep in those bedside lounge chairs was beyond me, but Brek said he could sleep fine there.

After arriving home, I felt relieved to once again be in my own bed. But as the hours passed, I lay awake most of the night under a burden of anxiety and grief.

I wondered if I would ever get used to being alone.

CHAPTER **3**

The moment I walked into room 4821 early in the morning on Tuesday, January 12, and saw the look on Tim's face, I knew that something was amiss. Dr. Mosher was filling him on details about Liz.

"Things aren't looking good," my son told me.

This was surprising to hear, since I had woken up with optimism for Liz after an encouraging Monday. Her blood pressures had finally started to stabilize, the pressors were off, and the staff had been able to turn the ventilator settings down to numbers reflecting her improvement. The Critical Care team had told me that she was doing so well that they would have worked on weaning her from the ventilator that day if her orthopedic trauma doctor had not been planning to take her back to the OR the next morning to surgically repair her fractured right wrist.

After arriving back home from Washington, D.C., Dr. Jim Veldkamp texted me on Monday to say that I should take whatever time I needed to care for my wife. As I was scheduled to work with Jim on Tuesday, I had planned to fit my usual clinical routine around time spent in Liz's room the next day, but I appreciated his offer immensely. It was great to have good partners.

Another thing I was grateful for was to have our oldest son back home. Jamie had arrived early the previous evening and had immediately come to see his mom. It was great to have another medically experienced decision maker available. Jamie's personality is characterized by common sense, along with a great sense of humor that would serve to keep us from becoming overly weary during dark moments. *There shouldn't be too many more of those*, I had assured myself; as the staff noted, this seemed to be Liz's golden hour.

The situation, however, had obviously changed for the worse overnight. I arrived at Liz's room ready to sign the consent form for the surgery on her wrist planned for that morning. Tim had spent the night in her room and in a groggy voice explained that he had been awake most of the night, while the Critical Care staff and Liz's nurse struggled with progressively declining blood pressures as Liz slid into shock. After she had become stabilized, Tim had fallen asleep, only to be awakened by staff a few minutes before my arrival. They told him that his mom's health was deteriorating rapidly and that she needed to go immediately to the operating room for an exploratory abdominal surgery to determine the source of her shock.

Since I had arrived at the tail end of that brief conversation, Dr. Mosher quickly updated me. She explained that the bladder pressures they had been monitoring in Liz were now perilously high. Bladder pressures are measured because they are reflective of intraabdominal pressures; in Liz's case, the elevated bladder pressures told the surgeons that something catastrophic was happening in her abdomen, resulting in a dangerously elevated abdominal pressure, a condition called abdominal compartment syndrome. It's dangerous because, as abdominal pressure rises, it begins to restrict blood flow to vital organs in the abdomen, such as the liver, the small intestine, and parts of the colon. As these organs gradually die, so does the patient.

Liz was also experiencing shock and seriously low blood pressure, almost certainly from an infectious source. The most likely origin of this infection was her intestines, which were being compromised by the dangerously elevated intraabdominal pressure. Serum lactic acid levels are used to monitor tissue and organs that are not being perfused adequately with blood. Liz's lactic acid level was well above normal, indicating that the blood flow to her intestines was probably already being significantly compromised.

This was a life-threatening indication for emergency surgery, but the concurrent shock that she was experiencing compounded the risk of this surgery exponentially.

"There is a substantial chance that Liz won't survive this surgery, given her vital signs," Dr. Mosher explained. "But there is a one hundred percent chance of mortality if we don't proceed with it."

I felt as though I were suddenly standing in a fog. My hand felt numb as I signed the consent, while the nurses and aides hurriedly prepared to take Liz down to the operating room. By 7:30 a.m. several members of our family had begun to gather around the room, along with Rev. John Currie, pastor to Tim and to two others of our children and their families. He pulled us together to lead us in reading a passage of Scripture and in prayer. As we held hands and gathered around Liz's bed, Pastor Currie paused and then asked if any of us had an appropriate Bible passage we would like him to read at that moment. With our minds seized with anxiety and clouded by emotion, none of us answered immediately.

"What about Psalm 31?" Joleen, the nurse who had just started at 7:00 that morning, asked the pastor.

The psalm ends with the words, "Be strong and take heart, all you who hope in the LORD." I was impressed by the spiritual maturity of this young Christian woman.

Before they could take her away, I kissed Liz goodbye and whispered to her assurances of my love and prayers. The fact that her ongoing sedation rendered her unaware didn't stop me from talking to her. Her skin had felt cool to my lips.

This might be the last time I ever speak to my wife while she's alive on this earth.

As they wheeled her out of the room on a transport ventilator, I began to weep. Even though Tim was also badly shaken, he consoled me with a prolonged hug. We shared this brief moment before turning to the next task at hand: contacting everybody else.

Tim had already started the process of calling his siblings and other family members and friends to notify them of the decline in his mom's condition and the impending surgery. The first person I called was Mark, knowing that it was very early in the morning in Mexico. I told him he needed to begin working on getting back to Grand Rapids as fast as possible if there were going to be any possibility of his seeing his mother alive.

Although I didn't say it to Mark, I thought it was unlikely that he would, and I think he sensed the same in the tone of my voice. He sounded frightened and specifically asked me several times about the possibility of his not making it in time to see his mom; I finally conceded that the prospect had a high probability. He hung up to begin a long, arduous day of cobbling together flight arrangements and traveling to make his way back home to see his mom.

The Surgical ICU staff allowed us to relocate to a family conference room just outside their unit, a room normally reserved for staff/family conferences where family members would be given condition updates and be able to discuss care decisions with their medical staff. I understood later that there had been a little push-back from several physicians arguing that the room was not available for those purposes that morning, but the nurse manager stood firm in allowing our family to camp out there for several hours. Whether this was professional courtesy because I was a staff physician or just common compassion, I never knew, but we greatly appreciated that kind offer.

We would make great use of that room in the hours and days to come.

By 9:00 a.m. all the family available in town had arrived, those with kids a little later after having made arrangements for childcare. We gathered in what had quickly become a hospitality room: myself, four of my kids (excluding Mark, who was in transit), and three of their spouses, as well as Tamara, Mark's fiancée. Jamie's wife, Halle, had driven from Virginia the previous day to drop off their three children at her mother's home in the Cleveland area and had heroically continued through a blizzard that afternoon of the surgery to arrive in Grand Rapids later that evening.

Our family wasn't alone at the hospital. Also present was Rev. John Currie, pastor of Redeemer Orthodox Presbyterian Church in nearby Ada, where three of my children's families were members and where I attended a weekly men's Bible study. Skip Pylman, an elder at Redeemer OPC and a prominent local attorney, had arrived with his pastor. Not only did Skip come to offer his prayers and support that morning, but later that week he told my son Tim that he would represent us pro bono in any legal matters that might arise from the accident and its financial sequelae. In fact, we did turn to him a few times for his help, which was greatly appreciated.

My own pastor, Rev. Corey Dykstra from Walker United Reformed Church, also joined us. Even though Corey was in his early thirties and probably not much experienced in this type of situation, he demonstrated a remarkable maturity in his prayers and words of encouragement. It was great to have the pastors and Skip there, as they took turns in prayer and Scripture reading with our family. We gathered there, the lot of us, and waited on the will of God, while much in prayer.

Throughout the surgery, the atmosphere in that room varied; I think this would have made for a fascinating psychological study. At times the conversation became heavy and spiritually tinged, interspersed with desperate prayer. At other times it tended toward lighthearted banter and even modest joking. Our moods alternated from emotional struggle, manifested by grief and weeping, to hilarity and laughter; usually, in fact, all of those outlets were present in that room at the same time. I felt as if I were the center of attention in that room, as though family and friends were monitoring me to see if I was okay. At times a comment made or a Bible verse read would trigger an emotional response from me. I struggled to keep from crying, though not often successfully.

I noticed my daughter-in-law Emily peering at me often, as if trying to read my feelings to see how I was doing. Over the course of months I observed this frequently with Em, and I began to recognize it as a manifestation of her training as a medical social worker to determine when a comforting touch or a soft word would bring healing.

Of everyone in that room that morning, I recall that our daughter-to-be, Tamara, took the situation the hardest and wept the most bitter tears. She was the youngest person in the room and was missing her fiancé, Mark, but I also realized that she was mourning the future mother-in-law she already loved deeply. At one point I hugged her and tried to lighten the mood with a comment.

"Well, this is what we do in this family, Tamara," I said. "We welcome you in, and then we hurt you." As soon as I said that I realized it was too close to the truth to be funny. Now we were both weeping.

As the minutes and then the hours ticked by, we did not get many updates from Joleen, who served as our relay from the OR. I found out later that this was because the operative procedure had become a panicked ordeal, a guerilla operation as the surgeons desperately fought to save Liz's life in the face of profound shock and a systolic blood pressure that hovered around 60 milliliters of mercury throughout the case. The shock progressed despite the best efforts of the anesthesiologist, who poured in IV fluids and pressors to keep Liz barely stable enough to allow the surgeons to do what had become a salvage procedure, what they call "damage control." Those of us in the "war room" heard only that Liz was in shock but that the surgery was going well.

At noon Kathy Door, the mother of a friend and former schoolmate of my son Tom, unexpectedly arrived with lunch—trays of sandwiches, chips, fruit, and vegetables to dip, along with a variety of soda to drink, plates, cups, and utensils. There was plenty for all of us in that room and leftovers for later that day. We had been casual friends with the Doors over the years because of the close friendships of our kids, so we were stunned by her kindness and generosity.

Mrs. Door must have been notified by her son Dan of our situation and had taken it upon herself to deliver lunch to our group. She slipped into the room, dropped off the food, and left, not wanting to interfere with our gathering. Her actions reminded me of the exhortation of Hebrews 13:2: "Do not forget to show hospitality to strangers, for by so doing some people have shown hospitality to angels without knowing it." Only in this case the angel was the one offering hospitality.

Dr. Mosher finally entered the room in the early afternoon to detail for us the results of the surgery and of Liz's condition. Upon entering the abdomen, Dr. Mosher had encountered a large contusion of the left colon, and much of the rest of the colon was ischemic (too little blood flow) and nonviable. A nearly total removal of the colon (colectomy) had been performed, leaving only the short portion of the left side known as the sigmoid colon.

"We also found a tear in the small intestine where the feeding tube had been placed during the previous abdominal surgery," Dr. Mosher explained. That hole had allowed spillage of intestinal contents into Liz's abdomen, which had to be cleaned out. The surgeons had made several attempts to repair the hole around the feeding tube by suturing it closed but were unsuccessful because the tissue around the hole was friable (crumbly) and kept tearing each time they tried to place a stitch.

Liz's condition was deteriorating by the minute as she slipped more deeply into shock. The surgeons, under the urging of the anesthesiologist, who was desperately trying to maintain some measure of survivable blood pressure, eventually abandoned the attempt to repair the intestine and moved to damage control, resecting that part of the intestine that contained the hole and leaving the two ends of the cut intestine on either side stapled closed. Dr. Mosher told us that, if she had taken the time to try to connect those two ends back together, Liz would almost certainly have died there on the operating table.

I found out later that the anesthesiologist was maintaining Liz's minimal blood pressure with three different pressure-raising intravenous drugs, as well as massive amounts of resuscitative fluids, basically throwing the proverbial "kitchen sink" at her. Out of time and realizing that Liz would have to be taken back to the operating room later anyway to reconnect her intestine, Dr. Mosher had quickly packed Liz's open abdominal incision with gauze and placed a vacuum dressing over it before sending her back in extremely critical condition to the surgical ICU.

Dr. Mosher explained that, with what little time she had had left, she had been unable to locate what is known, after a gastric bypass surgery, as the remnant stomach in which to place a new feeding tube. Had she been able to find it, she would not have had adequate time to place this feeding tube anyway.

As she gave us her report, Dr. Mosher explained that, although Liz was critically ill, she was hopeful that she might yet be able to survive this period of septic shock. Meanwhile, at bedside the Surgical Critical Care team began the tough battle to stabilize Liz with a balanced treatment of antibiotics, IV fluids, blood transfusions, pressors, and ventilator management.

Those of us gathered there shared a final moment of prayer in the hospitality room before we began to disband, some back to their homes and children and others to hang out by room 4821, encouraging each other and watching the doctors, nurses, and therapists of the critical care team trying to save our wife and mother.

CHAPTER 4

"Has Liz ever made a will?"

The medical social worker serving as our case manager at the time had come Tuesday afternoon to ask me this and other questions. He wondered if Liz had ever expressed an opinion on how far she would want her medical staff to go if she were nearing a situation where such care might be extreme or even futile.

"She doesn't have a will," I replied. "All Liz ever told me was that she didn't need to fill out any paperwork. She trusted me to make any appropriate decisions."

The care manager ultimately wanted to know how far I wanted to go with the current extremely aggressive measures.

"Have you thought about changing your wife's status to 'comfort care'?"

I should have anticipated this question, but I had to admit that it caught me off guard. I thought to myself—and not for the last time—that I didn't want to be "that family" member who won't or can't make the correct decision to switch from aggressive treatment to measures designed to keep a dying patient comfortable. But was it that time yet?

I have seen many family members struggle through this decision-making quandary, which in my experience has caused more family discord than anything else. As clinicians, we have all had to deal with families who can't bring themselves to scale back aggressive therapy in the face of an unsalvageable clinical situation. My brain was telling me now not to be that family member, but my gut and heart were telling me we weren't there yet.

As I worked so closely with the critical care staff on an everyday basis, I didn't want to push them forward into the area of futile care; I felt abashed at even considering the decision to continue aggressive measures. At this time only the case manager had broached the subject, which was, of course, an important part of her job. None of Liz's physicians had yet even hinted to me that we should start to think about exercising comfort measures only. Many months later, however, I would learn how awkward it must have been for these colleagues to have had to contemplate that prospect.

One of Liz's regular nurses, Joleen DeGroot, told my son Tim more than a year and a half later that she was present at a critical care patient care conference early that afternoon at which Liz's condition and outcome were being discussed. As Joleen related to Tim, several critical care and trauma surgeons were asking each other whether they had done all they could to stabilize Liz at that time or whether there was anything they might have been missing. One of the physicians had then quietly turned the conversation to how they could most kindly and gently tell Dr. Paauw that his wife was going to die. Joleen remembered an emotional silence as these experienced professionals somberly contemplated telling one of their own the news they had all hoped they would not have to bring.

As I was questioning my own instincts on the matter of aggressiveness of care, I turned to other family members, who universally voted to continue to move forward with the current aggressive therapies, although my physician son, Jamie, also expressed that it was unlikely his mother was going to survive this episode. With a heavy heart I agreed with Jamie's assessment, but I was relieved by the unanimity among our family members. It helped to move us forward as a cohesive family unit, a characteristic that for the most part continued throughout our ordeal. I think this familial cohesiveness was an outgrowth of the consistent belief among all our family members in the power of God's people earnestly laying their prayers at His feet.

Meanwhile, Mark was enduring an ordeal that had begun with that early morning phone call from his dad, telling him that his mom had taken a sharp turn for the worse and was about to undergo emergency surgery in an attempt to save her life. Mark was the baby of the family, more than seven years younger than his next oldest sibling, and as a result had always had a very close relationship with his mom. This had always made sense to me, as we had experienced a blur of activity with four children within seven years before our life had to some degree slowed down. Mark had appeared as a latecomer another seven years later. Although not an only child, he had enjoyed something of that experience, especially as the older children grew up and became more independent.

Now Mark was in Mexico, a thousand miles away, and the only child not present at her bedside to support his mom. His Mexican "mom" could immediately tell that something was wrong as Mark hung up the phone; she sat down next to Mark on the couch and embraced him. Mark sobbed in her arms for some time as she hugged him and told him things would be okay.

Mark later told me that he had entertained the possibility that his mother might already be dead and that I had told him to come home immediately rather than conveying the truth over the phone. Mark turned to his sister-in-law Halle to help with travel arrangements, as she was still at her mother's home in Ohio that morning and had access to a computer. While Halle wrestled with finding a way to get Mark home, he began to pack and say some rather abrupt goodbyes to his Mexican family.

Mark's two Calvin College professors came to his Mexican home later in the morning to make sure Mark was okay and to express their concern for him. They also prayed with him, which I appreciated immensely. The entire Calvin College community in general was faithfully supportive of Mark and our family throughout our ordeal. One of the deans contacted Mark frequently to make sure he was doing alright and arranged for the school to reimburse him for his unexpected air travel costs to get back from Mexico, since the cost of the trip had originally been rolled up into his tuition for that interim period.

Mark was also contacted by a school chaplain who offered his services if Mark felt the need for counseling. In addition, we heard that the school body was praying for Mark's mom every day in their midmorning chapel services. It was very comforting to know that several hundred students and staff were covering us with prayer each day. I had spent several hours weekly for twenty years serving as a Calvin College Health Center physician; Mark mentioned to me later that, whenever he had opportunity to stop in there after the accident for his monthly allergy shots, the first question he would be asked by the staff was how his mom was doing. The Calvin College community proved to be a very good one to belong to.

Halle, meanwhile, was finding it difficult to plot a way back home for her younger brother. Originally, she found a flight leaving early in the afternoon from the airport in Cancun, that city being as much as three hours away. At first Mark's Mexican "brother" told him he could drive Mark there, but then he began to hedge on that offer; it turned out that he had been having mechanical difficulties with his car and was uncertain it was dependable enough to make it to Cancun and back.

His Mexican mother then suggested that Mark could take a bus or taxi to the Cancun airport instead but warned him they were not always reliable. As it was, Mark would have had just enough time to get to the Cancun airport to catch the flight if everything went perfectly, which, from what his Mexican mom said, was unlikely.

Halle called back to say that she had found a flight to Houston, leaving the local airport there in Merida in a few hours and had been able to book Mark on that flight. As there were no available direct flights from Houston to Grand Rapids that afternoon, she'd had to connect him into Chicago before booking him from there on a 10:30 p.m. flight to Grand Rapids. As his Mexican mother drove him to the airport in Merida, she told Mark how sorry she was that his long-awaited study trip to Mexico had ended so sadly. They agreed that Mark would come down again on his own sometime to visit with this family, to whom he had in so short a time become like one of their own.

Mark has issues with anxiety anyway, and now, on the convoluted journey home, thoughts of never seeing his mom again crowded in on his mind. As he was waiting in a lengthy line to pass through customs in the Houston airport, a middle-aged woman pushed her way into the line in front of Mark. When Mark began to protest, she snapped at him, "Don't even start with me, kid; you can't imagine what kind of a day I'm having." Mark dropped the matter but thought to himself, *My mom's dying today; what's your issue?*

Shortly thereafter Mark was informed that his flight to Chicago had been delayed because of the inclement weather in the Midwest, the same storm that Halle was now struggling to get through as she drove to Grand Rapids from Cleveland. Mark's anxiety level began to intensify as his flight's departure got pushed back several times. When the plane finally boarded that evening, it had become obvious to Mark that he was going to arrive in Chicago too late to catch his Grand Rapids connection and would have to reschedule on another flight to Grand Rapids early the next afternoon. He now was nearly certain he would never again see his mom alive. As he boarded the plane to Chicago, he texted news of the missed Grand Rapids flight to his fiancée, Tamara.

Tamara recruited her dad, Jeff Rosendall, to drive her to Chicago that night through the blizzard to pick up Mark at the airport and bring him back to see his mom. Jeff had agreed to do so without hesitation, glad to be able to help in any way possible. Mark later told me that he had spent that flight from Houston dwelling on the thought that he was the only one of the siblings who was not going to have had the chance to say goodbye to his mother before she died.

Mark finally arrived in Chicago at midnight, Central Time (1:00 a.m. in Grand Rapids), where Tamara and Jeff picked him up and turned around to drive back through the storm to Grand Rapids. Mark finally arrived at his mother's bedside at 6:00 a.m. the following morning, nearly 23 hours after he had first received the desperate call telling him to come home as soon as possible if he were to see his mom alive again. Mark held her hand and wept; she was heavily sedated and unaware of her family around her, but she was alive—and Mark was there.

On Tuesday afternoon after the surgery, family members took turns staying with me at bedside in Liz's room as we prayed and waited on God's will for her. While her life hung in the balance, our family reached out to many different Christian communities to recruit prayers for her. My son Tim had a large Facebook network that he kept updated, a group that continues to grow in number and to this day offers their prayers and encouragement as Tim places posts on her ongoing medical issues and progress.

I began to compile a group of close friends and family members to whom I would text progress reports and matters of special concern as they arose. This list has slowly grown, and this special group has been and continues to be a source of great comfort for me personally. They represent several different churches, schools, and organizations from whom they, in turn, solicit prayers regarding specific concerns for Liz.

On a particularly dark moment late that Tuesday afternoon, as Liz's vital signs began to deteriorate for what seemed like the umpteenth time, I was standing at the end of the hall to get better cell phone coverage, texting out pleas for continued and fervent prayer for Liz. I am embarrassed to admit that, in a text conversation with Liz's sister Maria in Fresno, California, I texted out in desperation my feelings of abandonment: "Where is God tonight? I can't feel him; he's not here."

Maria encouraged me that the God who is sometimes hard to find was indeed there with me now, Maria urging me to please not give up hope. I learned something very valuable over the following days, weeks, and even months—that God is certainly always there, not the least in the presence of his faithful people whom He has wrapped around us like a warm garment. These individuals were indeed God's hands and feet to us, causing me to reflect often on an old Audio Adrenaline song, "Hands and Feet."

It is truly amazing to have experienced what it is like to be in the family of God at a time of crisis. Brothers and sisters in Christ not only pray but recruit others among their associations to pray as well. These Christian societies intermingle with others, the prayer support rippling out to other communities in the area, statewide, across the country, and even internationally. I was and continue to be greatly encouraged by assurances at my workplace from my colleagues and coworkers of their ongoing prayers.

Beyond that, I have been truly humbled by the many communities representing vast numbers of fellow Christians, many of whom I don't individually know, who have faithfully offered prayers and encouragement on behalf of Liz and our family. I am personally aware of many congregations that have prayed for us individually and in corporate prayer, dozens here in Michigan, as well as in Iowa, South Dakota, Minnesota, several other Midwestern states, Alberta, Alabama, Georgia, Arizona, Washington, California, and Mexico, not to mention about a dozen Christian school societies and other Christian organizations. Jenison Christian School, where our son Tim was principal, and West Side Christian School, which our children had all attended, were particularly faithful in cards, letters, and prayers, both private and corporate.

I won't attempt to reference all of the organizations by name for fear of leaving out some, but I have to make special mention of our own church, Walker United Reformed Church; the church of three of our kids—Redeemer Orthodox Presbyterian Church; and Westminster Seminary California (WSC), where I have been on the Board of Trustees off and on for a number of years. We regularly received cards, visits, calls, texts, and meals from members of these churches who walked with us through the valley of the shadow of death.

The staff, board, and students of WSC were kept informed of Liz's course through my frequent texts to Dawn Doorn, Vice President for Development there, and they, in turn, sent many promises of their continued prayers for Liz's recovery. This was especially encouraging to me, as I knew what a godly group of saints these were; it seemed to me that their prayers must have been very near the heart of God.

As God's people prayed throughout the afternoon and evening hours that Tuesday, Liz's condition began to slowly improve, her blood pressure gradually rising and stabilizing. Late Tuesday afternoon, Liz's MAP hovered around the low 60s as the staff gradually weaned her off the intravenous pressors that had been used to elevate her blood pressure through those afternoon hours. A decision was made to take Liz back to the operating room the next morning to clean up any remaining infection and to complete the process of reattaching the two ends of her transected bowel (anastomosis), place a new feeding tube, and close the abdominal incision.

Even though I had full confidence in Dr. Mosher and her team, I was very apprehensive about this surgery. I had seen similar scenarios many times in my years of practice, and I knew they didn't always play out well in the end. The surgeons could run into any number of complications, including abscess (infected fluid), more dead bowel, or even tears in the bowel.

After such surgery, especially in a patient in shock with "soft" blood pressures (pressures that are only marginally adequate), there is also an ongoing risk of intraabdominal infection and poor wound healing leading to other postoperative complications. When the abdominal incision doesn't heal well, there is a possibility of the wound coming apart, a process called dehiscence, which in turn can allow the intestines to spill out (eviscerate). Poor healing of the intestinal anastomosis can allow a leak of intestinal fluid, with catastrophic consequences.

With these concerns weighing heavily on my mind, I turned to a close friend of our family, Dr. Randy Baker, a surgeon who attended Redeemer OPC with our children's families and with whom I had become friends when he was completing a surgical critical care fellowship at Butterworth Hospital many years earlier. Randy had gone on to become a staff critical care surgeon for the Spectrum

Health system before serving as the Chief of the Critical Care service there for several years.

Eventually he had developed an interest in obesity management and had gone through further training in bariatric (weight loss) surgery, leaving the world of surgical critical care to establish a bariatric surgery practice. I reasoned that Randy's experience in both critical care and bariatric surgery made him highly qualified and experienced for exactly the surgery Liz was about to undergo.

I texted Randy to ask if he would be willing to join Dr. Mosher in the surgery the next day, telling him that I would understand if he didn't feel comfortable doing so for reasons of not wanting to appear to be "stepping on the toes" of Dr. Mosher. Randy immediately called to tell me that he would be available the next morning and felt that he would be a beneficial addition to Liz's surgery team. Although he committed to participating in the case the next morning, he also asked me to take steps to minimize any potential hard feelings on the part of Dr. Mosher for sharing the procedure with someone she might see as an interloper.

Surgeons are a special breed, and being a surgeon necessarily requires a firm confidence in one's own training and skills; I'm sure any surgeons reading this narrative would realize that a request to have another surgeon join the case might easily be perceived as a breach in a patient's trust in one's abilities. Randy rarely worked at Spectrum Health any longer, performing almost all of his cases at nearby St. Mary's Hospital. I thanked Randy profusely, overcome once again by emotion born of the ready willingness of a friend to go beyond his routine for the sake of my wife.

Hanging up from talking to Randy, I immediately sought out another close friend, Dr. Marc Hoeksema, the surgical critical care physician who would oversee Liz's care that evening. I explained to him that I had recruited Randy Baker to participate in Liz's reconstructive surgery the following morning. I asked whether he had access to Dr. Mosher that evening and would be willing to inform her of Randy's involvement and smooth over any hard feelings Randy's participation might precipitate. I knew I was asking a difficult task of Marc and was relieved when he readily agreed to the request. He replied that he would take care of the matter and that I was not to worry about it.

I appreciated Dr. Hoeksema's calm and steady demeanor in this exchange and came to appreciate his personality over the next few weeks. He was not only an excellent critical care surgeon but the epitome of how any physician should interact with patients and family members. His quiet efficiency had a way of inspiring confidence in the care being administered but also of imparting a measure of calmness to those with whom he dealt.

I have been in practice many years, but I personally still learned some valuable lessons about bedside manners from Dr. Hoeksema over the weeks he cared for my wife. While I certainly would not wish this situation upon my physician colleagues, I do feel that the experience of being the family member to a hospitalized patient could be a useful learning experience in caring for one's own patients.

True to his word, Dr. Hoeksema intervened with Dr. Mosher that evening to prepare her for Dr. Baker's participation in her case the next morning. To her credit, if she had any hard feelings about Dr. Baker's inclusion in the surgery, Dr. Mosher never revealed them and assured us that she was quite willing to accept his assistance in the operation.

Dr. Mosher impressed me with her professionalism in this matter, later assuring me that she would never entertain personal jealousy in the face of caring for a patient. To Dr. Mosher, securing the best patient outcome was paramount, and any measure that might promote that was acceptable to her. As for Randy, he had no idea what he was getting into!

On Tuesday evening we received the first of numerous meals arranged by Jill Dykstra, our pastor's young wife, who is greatly blessed with the gift of hospitality. In fact, these meals often became the only wholesome food I might eat in a day. At one point very early in Liz's hospitalization, a care manager rounded up those of us on watch at her bedside that afternoon to lecture us about taking care of ourselves as well. She instructed us about the importance of making sure we ate well and got plenty of rest.

Her counsel was that, at this difficult time, there was no such thing as a bad calorie, became somewhat of a mantra for us, almost a standing joke among our family members as we used it as an excuse to eat whatever we wanted. Several weeks later I recall my oldest son, Jamie, texting out a warning to us: "No such thing as a bad calorie is a lie! I've gained 15 pounds!" But as days of terrible anxiety, fear, and stress piled up, eating became less of a priority and sleeping less of a necessity.

I was the worst offender, rushing through my work by day to spend afternoon and late evening hours by my wife's side. Often, I would skip meals altogether and simply live off whatever was currently stocked in the famous wicker basket brought by our friends the Van Dyks. This could be anything, including fruit, crackers, chips, candy, soda, juice boxes—mostly junk food, but usually tasty. The nutrition training in me balked at this unhealthy practice, but the practical side of me just shrugged it off and munched away. I do recall surreptitiously sliding that basket behind the easy chair in the room whenever one of my dietitian friends came to offer their support.

I remember late one evening that Pastor Corey and Jill came to visit and pray with me. I had an open Diet Coke on the floor by my chair, and they caught me red-handed with my arm almost up to my elbow in a family-sized bag of peanut M&Ms. They couldn't hide the surprise on their faces as they stared at me with my mouth full of those delicious candies, truly some of the most delectable food in the world. When Corey asked me somewhat incredulously, "What are you eating?" I had nothing; all I could say was "Dinner."

Months later my children confirmed to me what I had gradually begun to suspect, that they had formed a conspiracy among themselves to get me to eat more regularly. Despite their concerns I found that, maybe because of all the junk food I consumed, when I finally weighed myself several months later I had lost only about seven or eight pounds.

Tim stayed with his mom that Tuesday evening, continuing a family agreement that we would not leave Liz's bedside unattended at any time, at least at this point. I returned home late that evening and was reassured by the fact that Jamie and Halle were staying in our house now. Although it still felt odd to be going to bed alone in my room, their presence in the house was comforting. The three of us stayed up later than we should have, well past midnight. Given my compulsive nature, my evening devotions tend to be rather lengthy anyway, as I obsess over matters relating to my family, friends, and church, among others.

On this particular night my prayers focused heavily on my wife; they were desperate prayers for her survival but also grateful prayers of thanksgiving that she was yet alive and stabilizing after what had amounted to a near-death experience.

CHAPTER 5

When I entered the kitchen early the next morning, I found a breakfast of pancakes ready and waiting for me. Our friend Gary Schutten was just flipping the last one before he began to clean up the kitchen. Gary is a former college roommate of mine with whom we've had a lifelong friendship, sometimes quite close and at other times less so as we've became preoccupied with raising our individual families. Liz and I even share grandchildren with Gary, as his son Brek is married to our daughter, Jackie.

The origin of that relationship goes back a number of years to the time I organized a church youth group service trip, including my high-school aged daughter, to a ministry in British Columbia. Knowing Gary's experience with providing meals for large service projects here in Grand Rapids, I had asked him to accompany us on the trip as our "chef"; he had agreed to do so on condition that Brek could join us. The rest, as they say, is history.

At one time Gary had been a successful homebuilder, constructing large, upscale homes in the Grand Rapids area, but due to a market downturn he had eventually closed that business and become involved in several other positions over the years. As he had sustained injuries to his shoulders and developed arthritis in his hips and knees, however, he had become unable to find steady employment.

After having gone through a divorce, he had moved into our basement. In exchange for room and board, Gary helps around our house with all manner of assistance, including shopping, cooking, cleaning, laundry, yard maintenance, and any number of other tasks to make himself useful. Friends familiar with our "Gary arrangement" have asked me more than once if they could borrow Gary to live in their basements for a while. Gary has a knack for perceiving ways to be helpful around our house, and on this particular morning I was grateful to have a warm breakfast waiting for me.

Liz's surgery was scheduled for 10:00 a.m. When I arrived at 7:00, I found Mark and Tamara already in room 4821, having arrived an hour earlier after their harrowing trip back from Chicago through the blizzard. I couldn't remember a time when I had seen Mark look so exhausted, so I chased these two youngsters out of the room to allow Mark a chance to go home and rest for a few hours. As they left, I breathed a sigh of relief.

Now we're all here.

As Drs. Randy Baker and Jamie Mosher took Liz back to the operating room later that morning, our family gathered once again in the hospitality "war room" with our pastors. This time we were also joined by Rev. Charles Williams, a young pastor intern at Redeemer OPC whom I knew quite well, as he was currently leading the Tuesday evening men's Bible study I attended. I was glad to have the prayers and support of yet another pastor in the room that morning, along with Pastors Corey Dykstra and John Currie once again. Those of us present started out in a lighter mood than on the previous day, although an air of anxiety still hung heavily over the room. Again, our conversation varied from lighthearted banter to emotion-choked exchanges, interspersed with prayer and Scripture reading.

We had a conversation about how many other Christian brothers and sisters around the country and beyond were lifting up Liz that morning. As we compared our individual notes, the list of known supporters grew quite lengthy and was truly amazing.

The first of the weeklong meetings of the seminary Board of Trustees was beginning at almost the same time as Liz's surgery, and it was a great comfort to me that those godly brothers and sisters were fervently lifting up Liz and our family in prayers at that very moment. I continued to pester Dawn Doorn with regular updates on my wife's condition, as well as with specific prayer requests to be passed on to the staff, students, and board of WSC.

I realized full well that the most important service I could contribute to my wife's care was to continue to recruit as much prayer support as possible. This had become an obsession for me. I had learned long ago that, while one may not be able to eradicate compulsive behavior, one can certainly focus it in positive directions—and this was one of those instances.

While my text list of the people I updated and solicited for specific prayer grew gradually longer, our kids were busy placing updates on their Facebook accounts to get the word out that their mother needed prayer. I know how effective a communication device Facebook can be; in particular, some of Tim's posts would generate more than several hundred replies guaranteeing prayers. (I have my own specific reasons for not being on Facebook myself, which I don't always feel comfortable discussing—whenever anyone asks me about this, I just tell them that if I ever decide to commit a crime, I don't want to make it easy for the police to catch me.)

Although we had been told to expect the surgery to last at least two hours, it stretched to three, then four, and finally to five and a half hours. We were happy to have a large supply of leftovers from the food brought by Mrs. Door the previous day. I don't recall even one of us leaving the room to find lunch in one of the hospital's food venues; we had plenty as it was. But as the length of the procedure extended, so did a somber mood in the hospitality room. Texts and calls began to trickle in to the people gathered in that room from outsiders looking for updates on the results of the operation, with the reply "Still in surgery" going back out on a regular basis.

We did eventually begin to get regular reports from the operating room to let us know of progress, all of which sounded positive: ". . . the small bowel was reconnected . . . an ileostomy was formed . . . a feeding tube was being placed in the remnant stomach . . . only thing left is wound closure." I'm sure these reports were meant to reassure us as the time of surgery stretched out, which they did, though we had been through a lot already and weren't about to take anything for granted.

Finally, there came a knock on the door, and Randy was standing there, his surgical scrubs covered by his white lab coat. As he addressed all of us, he kept his eyes on mine. The operation had gone very well, he reported, and Liz had been returned to the surgical ICU in stable condition. Randy explained that he had pulled the closed proximal end of the remnant colon over to the right side of the abdomen and tucked it there near to the ileostomy to make future possible reconnection of these two pieces of bowel a possibility. Although Liz would not even be aware of the ileostomy for several weeks, this information became a source of hope that it might someday be taken down.

Randy patiently answered several questions from family members and encouraged us all again with reassurances that Liz was doing well. Before he left, I reached out and embraced Randy, wondering at the time if it was okay to hug your surgeon. It didn't matter; he was my friend. I told him he was a hero to our family, something that became even more true as Liz progressed through her hospital course.

Back in room 4821 Liz remained sedated on a ventilator, but her blood pressure was better than before the surgery, with a MAP in the low 70s. The mood in her room, as family members rotated in and out, was certainly not as grim as it had been on the previous day—the truth was that we were even a bit giddy. Joleen was Liz's nurse again that afternoon, and having her there was a real blessing to our family.

Joleen was one of four nurses—the others being Anna, Kari, and Lauren—who took care of Liz as a primary assignment while she spent four weeks in the surgical ICU. My understanding is that these dear Christian women each agreed to take Liz as their primary assignment (along with a second patient each shift) during that time, as opposed to rotating around the unit, as would normally have been the case. While we had many other excellent nurses in that unit whom I would hate to slight by omission, the four who took her as a primary assignment were a tremendous benefit to Liz and to our family through the continuity of care and communication this provided, in addition to the prayers they offered.

In my notes I wrote, "Somewhere this week we met Joleen, Anna, Lauren, and Kari—special Christian nurses—so comforting." Of those four, I see three regularly to this day, two who continue to work as nurses on that unit and one who has gone on to become a nurse practitioner on the medical intensive care staff. It is always a pleasure for me to share a moment with them, and each interchange is prefaced with "How's your wife doing?" Special indeed. These nurses were also our heroes. In fact, we began to realize how many heroic hospital staff members there are, tenaciously dedicated to the wellbeing of their charges.

Liz continued to do well throughout the rest of that day, and our family was finally able to breathe a collective sigh of relief. Grateful texts and phone calls, as well as prayers of thanksgiving, went out from our family that evening. I had the special pleasure of being called that evening by Rev. Joel Vander Kooi from Iowa and Rev. David Klumpenhower in Phoenix, the two previous pastors from my own Walker United Reformed Church, to assure me of their prayers and those of their churches. Joel even reported to me that the members of the church he had just transferred from in Calgary, Alberta, were also lifting us up, even though none of them had ever met Liz. I was coming to realize more and more how close the family of God is.

That afternoon Jamie and Halle began the tedious task of sorting through Liz's and my finances, a task that Liz had owned until the day of her accident. She had resolutely refused to share this burden with me, even though I had frequently offered to help, as I sensed she was overwhelmed by it. I rarely picked up the mail from our box and even less commonly opened it, but I saw enough to realize that we were regularly receiving late notices and bank overdraft fees. I am embarrassed to admit that, twice, we'd had to drive down to the municipal water department in the stealth of darkness to drop a check in the mail slot to keep our water from being cut off due to delinquent bills. I couldn't understand this because, as a physician, I am reasonably well compensated. However, we had always committed to paying Christian grade school, college, and some graduate school tuition for our kids, which had quickly eroded those paychecks.

As Jamie and Halle waded through a 14" x 14" x 14" basket full of bills, notes, and unopened mail, they began to realize how disordered our finances were. I think the degree of the disarray revealed, at least to some extent, the encephalopathy resulting from liver disease that Liz had unknowingly been struggling with for some time. I feel bad to this day that I had not been firmer about stepping in and doing more to relieve Liz of what she later admitted had been a terrible ongoing stress in her life.

The darkest item Jamie and Halle found was a $10,000 Capital One debt of which I was unaware and on which Liz had been paying interest only (30%) for several years. Her embarrassment over this debt, Liz later admitted to me, was the reason she had so heatedly refused to allow me to assist her with our finances.

For many years I had received a yearend bonus from Spectrum Health, which she had used to pay part of our annual tuition obligations. When the bonus were somewhat abruptly discontinued one year, she had been caught off guard. As it happened, she had mailed in a loan application from Capital One that afternoon, which she had eventually used in place of the bonus to make a tuition payment, having established no contingency plan to pay it back.

Thereafter she had made periodic interest payments, and as the debt gradually grew she was reticent to let me know of this financial quagmire. On the bright side, I heard Jamie one evening shout, "Hey, I found my Christmas present!" Sure enough, there at the bottom of that muddled basket Jamie had found a $100 check made out to him two months earlier by Liz, with the notation "Christmas gift" written at the bottom.

Jamie and Halle slowly organized and prioritized our bills, created fiscal files for different entities, took me through the establishment of automatic debit payments from my checking account for certain recurring payments, and finally created a master financial spreadsheet on my computer. Part of this organization included setting up a separate tithe checking account by which I was able to make our giving much more orderly; this has been a source of satisfaction for both of us. When Jamie and Halle returned to Virginia at week's end, our financial ship was on the way to being righted, although it would take another six months to finally work out all the kinks.

Throughout that Wednesday afternoon and into the evening, Liz rallied as her blood pressure steadily improved, allowing the ICU staff to gradually wean back her intravenous pressors and her ventilator settings. In fact, she was doing so well that evening that a decision was made by the orthopedic trauma surgeon to schedule Liz the following morning for the reconstructive bone surgery on her right arm that had been postponed the previous morning because of her abdominal catastrophe.

As the family members there that evening texted out this favorable news, we began to receive several excited replies, rejoicing with us at God's faithful answers to our prayers. This was the first time in that ordeal that we experienced this phenomenon: the strengthening of the faith of our prayer partners as their petitions on our behalf were being graciously granted. This was a wonderful feeling for those of us who were firsthand witnesses to the ongoing mercies of a faithful God in sparing Liz's life. The roller coaster ride had bottomed out during the past 24 hours, and we were now nicely cruising up the next hill.

CHAPTER 6

On Thursday, January 14, Liz was stable enough to be taken back to the operating room for surgical repair of the broken bones in her right wrist. Although the surgeon could not repair the ulnar fracture because the bone was too soft, he was not overly concerned because of the nondisplaced nature of this break. The radial fixation went well; Liz sailed through the surgery and returned to room 4821 in stable condition.

She remained sedated on the ventilator afterward, but we spent an uneventful day. We knew we might just be in the "eye of the hurricane," but it felt good to relax a bit and not feel overwhelmed by the constant threat of Liz's dying. For a brief time in the middle of a very hectic week, we enjoyed a momentary respite. Unfortunately, that was to change the following day.

In my notes for Friday, January 15, I wrote, "Our first of many 'ordinary' scares." Our family gradually began to differentiate between ordinary and extraordinary threats. An extraordinary threat could be identified as one akin to what we had been through earlier that week, a situation in which Liz's survival seemed unlikely or was at least questionable. An ordinary alarm was also a threat to her wellbeing and even to her survival but one that passed by relatively quickly, without materializing into a full-blown crisis.

Such was the case this day; the trouble was that, when the alarm was first being sounded, we didn't know how serious the situation would become. Either way, we would text out and send Facebook requests for prayers regarding a specific problem, relying on our growing cohort of prayer warriors to help carry us through yet another crisis. This day began with Liz experiencing fever and shock once again, with the medical staff working strenuously to counter the shock before any organ damage could occur. They also began the process of trying to localize the source of the fever and eventually ordered a CAT scan of Liz's abdomen and pelvis to rule out another intestinal leak or abdominal abscess.

I think that any surgeon would tell you this is one of their greatest fears, especially in the face of three recent abdominal operations. It is technically very difficult to go back a fourth time so soon afterward to try to deal with an intestinal leak. These types of surgeries are fraught with complications, among them abnormal channels (fistulas) forming between adjacent loops of intestine or between intestine and the skin, often becoming chronic issues that prevent patient healing. There was also a risk of short bowel syndrome, a situation in which not enough viable bowel is left after surgery to maintain adequate absorption of nutrients and fluid for survival, necessitating long-term intravenous feeding (TPN), something I deal with frequently in my practice. Liz would be at significant risk for this syndrome because of her previous gastric bypass surgery and her recent colon and intestinal resections. At least an abscess might be amenable to being drained nonsurgically by an interventional radiologist, avoiding the need for another surgery.

Our family discussed all of these possibilities with the critical care team that day and was told that a leak or abscess would be catastrophic at this point in Liz's hospital course. It would truly be a life-or-death situation for her. We had many people praying for favorable results from that scan, and when the results were available they showed only the normal and expected changes in anatomy following the previous surgeries Liz had undergone—no evidence of leak or abscess. We phoned and texted out these results and received many replies praising God for his mercy once again. The moment passed, and Liz's condition gradually stabilized under the watchful eyes of the Critical Care doctors and nurses.

At the same time, however, the skin site of the previous feeding tube (now removed), as well as the lower end of her abdominal incision, began to leak copious amounts of the clear yellow fluid characteristic of advanced liver disease, known as ascites. This fluid forms in the abdomen when pressure from the scarring of cirrhosis restricts normal blood flow through the liver and causes it to back up into accessory veins that carry blood around the liver. It was assumed that this ascites leak might have been the cause of the new fever and shock.

This fluid leaked for weeks, although it eventually switched from those sites to leaking around the new gastric feeding tube (G-tube) site. When abnormal fluid builds up in the abdomen, eventually the pressure will find a way out, and that was now happening—up to four liters per day, overwhelming all efforts to control it with gauze dressings, which in most cases became saturated soon after they were placed. My notes reflect that this didn't stop for five weeks, the protein loss seriously compromising the efforts of the clinicians to restore her nutritional status (nutriture).

In hospital patients, and especially in a critical care setting, adequate nutriture is essential to several recovery processes, chief among these being wound healing and proper functioning of the immune system to prevent infections. When these functions are significantly compromised, sepsis and septic shock result, often leading to a poor clinical outcome and even the death of the patient. Small wonder that over the course of her hospitalization Liz was prone to frequent infections, at times with organisms that are not commonly aggressive enough to cause infections in a healthy person.

In my opinion, the delays and interruptions in providing consistent nutrition, which are often characteristic of a critical care stay, coupled with the large leak of ascites fluid week after week, almost certainly compromised Liz's recovery over her extended hospital course. Many months later I learned at a medical conference that patients with cirrhosis who develop a spontaneous leak of ascites have a mortality rate of between 40 and 60%, in large part because of intraabdominal infection. I suspect that number would be even higher in patients like Liz, who have had a recent major abdominal surgery (or three).

Complicating the nutrition picture, as well as her overall recovery, Liz began to bleed from her new ileostomy the next day, Saturday, January 16. This was almost certainly from large vessels on the lining of her intestine having become swollen from the backpressure caused by her damaged liver. Around that time an ostomy nurse specialist came to assess Liz's new ileostomy and was surprised by what she saw.

"Does she have liver disease?" she asked me.

I responded in the affirmative but wondered how she knew that from looking at the ileostomy. This nurse pointed out to me the enlarged varicose veins on the external surface of the ileostomy, known as caput medusae, characteristic of advanced liver disease. (The name originates from the apparent similarity to Medusa's head in Greek mythology, which had living, venomous snakes in place of hair). This was a great discouragement to me.

Throughout Liz's tenuous hospital course, with its varied ups and downs, hung the grim specter of advanced liver disease and its associated poor prognosis. But I recognized that I could go crazy worrying about it and that there was not much we could do to clinically address it, so it became a matter we commended to our prayer partners for special attention. The ileostomy bleeding continued for about five weeks and necessitated multiple blood transfusions, which, in themselves, pose a risk of depressing the body's immune system, exposing the patient to opportunistic infections—infections that a healthy immune system would prevent.

On the following day, Sunday, January 17, ongoing efforts to wake Liz began to take on a more urgent nature, as she continued to rest unresponsively like some sort of modern-day Sleeping Beauty, even though all sedation had been discontinued several days earlier. The doctors and nurses came in every hour or so to try to get her to open her eyes or move a finger—anything to show evidence that there was some awareness behind those closed eyelids. Yet throughout Sunday, nothing; "unresponsive to commands" was being charted repeatedly.

I tried to stay composed and be the supportive husband who didn't interfere in the work of the clinicians, but my medical side was getting the best of me. The staff tried to calm my worries by noting that my wife's unresponsiveness was not yet out of the realm of normal variation for the time it might take sedating medications to wear off, especially in one whose liver function was so compromised. Unfortunately, my obsessive nature belied their attempts to allay my fears, as did something I eventually realized was a characteristic of that nature.

Throughout Liz's hospital course, whenever her condition began to veer from normality, my medical mind would filter through every possibility and latch on to the most frightening option. Whatever terrible alternative I imagined was a reality in my mind until proven otherwise. Over the course of Liz's hospitalization, I think this characteristic proved to be a major consternation for my family, but equally so for her medical staff. Unfortunately, at times I was right.

This Sunday the possibility of a catastrophic brain injury, such as a large intracranial bleed or one resulting from lack of blood flow (ischemia) when she had been in such profound shock, began to loom large in my mind. My stomach was tied up in knots, and my anxiety level skyrocketed. Eventually I began to realize that I wasn't the only one apprehensive about this possibility, as the staff did not merely brush me off when I brought up these concerns. My family began to share my fears, and we began to discuss what decision we might make if our worries were confirmed.

Those medically trained among us shared a consensus that, given all the other insults Liz had sustained, if she had indeed experienced a disastrous brain injury it would not be meaningfully survivable, forcing us to change her medical care to just keeping her comfortable. Tim, who is always quick to tell staff "I'm the nonmedical one," saw it otherwise. As the son who had grown up always being called "Timmy the Tenderheart," he lived up to his nickname and could not bring himself to agree with that decision. He reminded us of the power of prayer and the miraculous recovery his mom had already made. Hard to argue with that.

Late in the afternoon Dr. Marc Hoeksema, Critical Care doctor that day, finally consented to order a head CAT scan for Liz. I suspected that this was more than anything else for my sake after my persistent haranguing. He probably felt a weighty measure of compassion for the burden of anxiety with which I was struggling. I don't think the CAT scan constituted an expense without medical necessity, given its potential to affect medical decision-making, but I know it was medically necessary for me at that point.

Jamie and Halle had planned to leave later that afternoon to spend the night at her mother's house in Cleveland before returning to Virginia with their children the next day. Given the momentous nature of the CAT scan and the decision it might force, however, they altered their plans to stay another night in Grand Rapids. Jamie's partners graciously told him to delay returning to work until Wednesday— longer if necessary—once they were notified of the tenuous situation in Grand Rapids. Of course, we all understood what the "longer if necessary" part meant; funeral plans are not made overnight.

Once again requests were sent out to what was probably now approaching a thousand warriors to pray specifically for favorable results from the test that evening. A knot of family members yet again gathered in desperate prayer in room 4821, along with other family members in their homes. I don't know how many saints around the country and beyond joined in prayer vigil that night, but out of that desperation was born a sense of peace for those of us in that room as text after text, as well as numerous Facebook posts, poured in bearing a one-word response: "Praying."

Late that evening Dr. Hoeksema, never one to show a lot of emotion, walked into the room with just the hint of a smile on his face to tell us the words we had been praying so fervently to hear: "Everything looks fine."

It became evident that Liz's mental unresponsiveness was almost certainly just a result of delayed clearing of the sedating medications and would wear off given more time. We celebrated as if our team had just won the Super Bowl ("or even better, the Stanley Cup," as my Canadian pastor would say). We offered up grateful prayers of thanksgiving and spread the news to family members and beyond.

Initially we had been reluctant to send out late-night texts with medical updates in real time, worried that we might be disturbing those trying to sleep (other than those who were three hours behind us in California). Gradually we had gotten bolder in this regard, as we received responses from night owls who, we imagined, seemed to be waiting up just to reply to texts. Judging from the number of morning responses we received, though, most people who are trying to sleep leave their phones on silence or in the bathroom overnight, replying to our texts at a more civilized hour. But the large number of late-night responses sharing our excitement surprised us. We were impressed—people really were beating down the doors of heaven for Liz.

Through it all, as we faced ongoing setbacks and threats, we continued to be surprised—even overwhelmed—by the support of our brothers and sisters in Christ who manifested that support and their love with an untold number of cards, calls, visits, and other expressions of care from all over the hospital and elsewhere.

I was back to work the next day, Monday, January 18, when Jessica, a nurse friend on 5 North, brought tears to my eyes. "Our whole floor is praying for you," she told me.

I heard then, and continue to hear to this very day, numerous expressions of support and promises of prayers from many of my coworkers at Spectrum Health. At the risk of being redundant, our family was also aware of the abundant prayers of Walker URC, our former West Leonard Christian Reformed Church; Redeemer OPC; West Side Christian School; Jenison Christian School; and a host of other coworkers, churches, schools, and innumerable individuals.

At the close of this first week in the hospital, I also was quite mindful of the love and intercessions on behalf of Liz and myself by our brothers and sisters at Westminster Seminary California as they met for the semiannual Board of Trustees meeting and associated educational conference. I learned that the attendees were praying for us during the meetings, at the associated luncheons, and during a special time of prayer for us at the beginning of the Thursday Board meeting itself. My notes reflected that I couldn't help thinking, *They're great.*

CHAPTER 7

Einstein was right: time is a relative measure. I discovered that, when my wife was in the middle of a crisis, time crawled along ever so slowly while I kept impatient watch on whatever clock was on a nearby wall. But in less eventful weeks, weeks when one wouldn't think time might drag slowly along, it flows by in a blur instead.

The following week was one of the latter. I returned to my clinical duties as Liz was finally stabilizing, at least to the point that we didn't think she might die on any given day. Our family lived in mortal fear of sepsis and its evil stepsister, shock. We were all now very aware that, given Liz's underlying liver disease and her fragile condition, recurrent sepsis was always a possible, if not a probable, occurrence, and if it did come it would carry a high risk of mortality. The specter of sepsis kept us from fully enjoying a week marked by slow but steady progress.

Late on Monday afternoon, I was around the hospital when Mark texted me.

"You need to come see this."

Mark and Tim had been sitting in the corner of Liz's room when Tim thought he saw her open her eyes and look in their direction. In great excitement, they had rushed to her side to find her opening her eyes and even responding with head nods and hand squeezes. I hurried to Liz's room and found her responsive to me for the first time in nine days—responsive enough to return my kiss and hold my hand. Sleeping Beauty had awakened.

Despite Liz's newly returned consciousness, the staff had difficulty making progress to remove her breathing tube (extubation) and get her off the ventilator. Two days after she awoke, on Wednesday, January 20 (hospital day number twelve), Dr. Gabby Iskander approached me with the suggestion that we proceed with a tracheostomy for Liz to facilitate getting her off the ventilator. I knew the trauma/critical care surgeon because we shared office space across the street from the hospital.

The suggestion did not surprise me; indeed, I had been expecting it for several days as the staff struggled to make progress toward her extubation. The procedure was performed in room 4821 later that afternoon under sedation, and Liz's breathing advanced dramatically after that, allowing her to be taken off the ventilator two days later, on January 22. Little did we know at that time how long Liz would be dealing with that tracheostomy.

After the tracheostomy, the nurses began to allow Liz to take very limited amounts of ice chips, which, although a minor thing, vastly improved her outlook on her current existence. In fact, Liz began to fixate on those ice chips and seemed to do quite well with swallowing despite her recent tracheostomy. Her pleading for more couldn't help but touch the hearts of those of us who sat at her bedside, and, having found the ice machine in a utility room across the hall from room 4821, I'm sure we gave her many times more than she was technically approved to have.

After a day or so of this, we took to surreptitiously sneaking in some Crystal Light to flavor the ice chips—which, of course, made Liz crave them even more. Thankfully, the Speech-Language therapist tested her swallowing the next week and began to liberalize her diet. Throughout the remainder of her ordeal, though, flavored ice chips proved to be a significant means of comfort for her.

I have mentioned earlier that I had attended for a number of years a midweek evening men's Bible study through Redeemer OPC, the church attended by the families of three of our children. Over those years the venue had changed periodically, along with the leader. At the time of Liz's accident our group had been meeting on Thursday evenings with a young associate pastor from that church, Rev. Charles Williams, at his small house adjacent to the church.

That Thursday evening, January 21, at around 6:30, as I stood at Liz's bedside, I was surprised to see two of my Bible study brothers, Duane Bras and Paul Fields, walk into room 4821.

"What are you guys doing here? Don't you have Bible study tonight?"

"We came to visit you and your bride," Duane responded, "and to take you to dinner. Tim tells me you're not eating regularly."

"I'm eating enough to stay alive," I joked. "Besides, I'm not big on cafeteria food."

Duane smiled. "That's okay. We've got something better for you."

The two men pulled me down the hall and directed me into the hospitality "war room" where our family had huddled during Liz's intense abdominal surgeries. I was stunned to see Charles and about a dozen other members of that group with a smorgasbord of food and beverages they had set up there. A delicious smell wafted from a slow cooker with meat that Charles had been cooking for the last 24 hours. We spent about an hour and a half in some of the sweetest fellowship I have ever enjoyed over those delicacies.

While much of the conversation focused on Liz and her progress, we also updated each other on family and job issues, as we always did. It was great to step away from the constant stress of the hospital milieu for a time and to just enjoy regular guy stuff again. I can't put into words how much I needed and enjoyed that brief respite, or how much I loved those thoughtful Christian brothers who gave up an evening with their families to bring solace to a friend.

As I ambled back to Liz's room later that evening, I reflected on their generosity. *Honestly—this has to be a foretaste of heaven.*

This was the same day I began to speak with a couple of close friends of mine, Kristen Duthler and Sue Taylor, both nurse liaisons at Spectrum Health Butterworth from Mary Free Bed Hospital, about where Liz might transition after she had left the ICU. Mary Free Bed is a world-renowned freestanding rehabilitation hospital accepting patients from all over the country; we are blessed to have it in our backyard.

It sits adjacent to Mercy Health St. Mary's Hospital, with which it is connected by a corridor, a little more than a mile or so down the hill from Butterworth. In fact, from the south-facing window at the end of the hall containing Liz's room, where we often went to pick up better cell phone coverage, we could easily see Mary Free Bed Hospital. As Liz's stay on 4 Heart began to drag on, our family members would look out at that building and long for the day when Liz would be there, a transition that would signal to us that her recovery was finally well on the way.

Kristen and Sue spent a lot of time doing "paperwork" and readying Liz for the day she could make that eagerly awaited move. In conference with Liz's caregivers, a plan was gradually formulated to ready Liz for transfer to Mary Free Bed late the next week. This was a great encouragement to me and our family, although Liz experienced a fair amount of anxiety about the pending move. She had become very close to, and even dependent on, this nursing staff that had been so kind and compassionate to her. But for me, Thursday, January 21, was indeed a red-letter day.

We continued to have a family member present in Liz's room 24-7 until Saturday night, January 23. That schedule would have gotten more difficult to maintain on the Monday when Jamie and Halle said goodbye and headed home by way of Cleveland to pick up their kids. It didn't, thanks to the arrival of Jorge Moreno, our "fifth son."

For several years my wife had been involved in the area Healing-the-Children chapter, a program that places overseas children for extended times with local host families while those children undergo their needed surgeries. The surgeons' time and the hospital facilities are donated, as are the sponsorships of the host families. Several of these children who spent lengthy stays as guests in our home continue to count as family to us, often calling us on Mother's Day or Father's Day. At one time we hosted an older teenager from Mexico for facial reconstruction, and when Luis returned to Mexico we somehow inherited a friend of his for a year or so as an exchange student, followed by his friend's older brother, Jorge, for a year after that.

Jorge had lived with us for the better part of a year and had developed a strong family relationship with Liz (especially), me, and our kids, whom he counted as brothers and sister. Our families have remained close. The summer before Liz's accident, I had planned a road trip out West with my son Mark and his college roommate Spencer. Almost at the last minute, Jorge's sixteen-year-old son Jorgito had come to spend some time with our family and practice his English. Arriving just before our trip, he threw in with us and spent the next 12 days taking in the sights in Colorado, Utah, and Arizona.

Jorge arrived late on Wednesday afternoon and immediately went to Liz's room. Although she was confused, Liz's face lit up when she saw her Mexican son. She clung to Jorge's hand and, at least for a

time, let up on the incessant "Help—help—help" from her lips that
had characterized that week. Jorge sat by his other mom's side for that
entire evening and then through the night. Liz had been restless the
past two evenings when I left to go home, but on this night she merely
accepted my kiss and offered me a smile when I left.

Jorge stayed in town for about a week and often spent the
overnight period in Liz's room, a source of encouragement for Liz
during those times when her anxiety tended to be at its worst. We
were sad to see Jorge back off to Mexico at the end of that time, but
Liz had continued to stabilize, and Jorge had a family and business to
attend to.

Liz's disorientation and anxiety, however, though typical of
patients who experience an extended critical care stay, seemed to be
worsening as time went on. She had developed the annoying (at least
to me) habit of perseverating on the word "help," sometimes repeating
it over and over again for an hour or longer. Her tracheostomy was
uncapped, allowing her nurse to place a tube bringing extra oxygen to
the end of the tracheostomy, using devices known as a "t-piece" or a
trach cuff, which ordinarily should have restricted Liz's plea for "help"
to just a whisper.

She had somehow figured out how to push air up past the
tracheostomy, however, enabling her to vocalize in a hoarse but
relatively loud tone. This, of course, made the persistent "help" even
more annoying than the whisper it rightfully should have been. I
soon realized that it was fruitless to try to address this with her, yet
I could not bring myself to stop doing so. I spent a lot of time and
effort reasoning with her that yelling "help" was meaningless unless
she coupled it with something she wanted "help" with. I ran through
examples for her of what this might constitute, such as ice chips or a
blanket or repositioning, some of which suggestions she would take

me up on. But mostly she would listen, as though attentively, to my scolding and then immediately resume her "help" mantra.

During one particularly persistent episode, I am sorry to admit that I raised my voice with her: "Yelling the word 'help' is pointless and aggravating, unless you tell me what you want help with. So, either tell me what you want help with or stop saying the word!"

Liz looked at me contemplatively for a few seconds; then I saw a hint of a smile on her face.

"Help!" she brashly called out yet again.

I could only laugh. Could this behavior be excused because of her traumatic brain injury and her "ICU psychosis," or was this rationally intentional on her part? I suspected the former, but knowing her (at times) devious personality, I couldn't discount the latter.

Possibly more annoying than her persistent "help" was the frequent shaking of her bed rails to get the attention of her nurse or a family member. Because Liz had tended to abuse the nurse call button, even when family was in the room, the staff and family had taken to placing it out of her reach when one of the family members was present in the room. In retaliation, I think, she progressed into her rail-shaking behavior, although it continued even after we returned her call button. We had created a monster. At one point a nurse came into the room and firmly told her she had to stop the rail shaking. Liz defiantly looked the nurse in the face and even more vigorously shook those rails.

Months later, as she recalled that instance, Liz told me that at the time she was determined not to let "that woman" tell her what to do. Her only regret about this whole episode was finding out all those months later that there was a nurse call button built into the railing itself, which she realized much too late she could have been using to get her nurse's attention.

At about this time Liz began to pick at the splint protecting
her recently repaired right wrist, to the point that she eventually had
to have soft wrist restraints placed. When we reminded her of that
behavior months later, she remembered it very clearly and said she had
been unhappy with what she had perceived as a dirty splint, recycled
from another patient—or so she thought. At the time this had made
sense to her.

CHAPTER 8

On Monday morning, January 25, Liz was again evaluated by the Speech-Language therapist and was advanced from a clear liquid diet to a surgical soft diet that basically allowed her to eat almost any food. The dietitian managing Liz's tube feedings arranged to have them "cycled"—that is, running just during the nighttime hours in order not to impact her appetite during the day as she worked on resumption of eating.

Despite that and custom ordering a dinner for that day, Liz ate only a few slices of a mandarin orange that evening, which she obviously enjoyed. Her diet was restricted and advanced in various ways after that. It would be five months before Liz finally graduated from supplemental tube feeds and many more months after that before she was able to discontinue daily protein supplements through her feeding tube.

Over the past week her wakefulness and social interactiveness had improved steadily, allowing her to be much more participatory in her care. One major issue for Liz was—and is—pain control. She endured a lot of pain from her various injuries and surgeries, but worst of all was the pain she experienced from what the wound nurse specialist called a "deep bruise" that developed over her tailbone, a source of much discomfort for her for a number of months, as it would begin to heal and then recur. It was not called a pressure sore yet, mainly, I suspect, because that diagnosis counts as a black mark against a nursing unit and can affect hospital reimbursement.

To this day Liz claims that sore on her bottom was one of the worst things she had to endure during her long hospitalization. She uses the words "horrible" and "terrible" to describe that pain and says she now realizes that, as a nurse herself in her younger years, she had underestimated the pain a pressure sore could cause. Liz says that she would wake up with excruciating pain for which nothing would help—not pain meds, dressing changes, or changing positions.

She was using a lot of pain medications, and our family began to sense that she was overstating her pain at times, so we took steps to try to moderate her use of these medications. This was difficult to achieve as the sore on her bottom caused her a lot of misery, for months necessitating turning her on a very frequent schedule. It broke my heart to see Liz suffering so much, and I often wished I could take her place, but all I could do was offer her compassion—and lots of prayer.

They say that confession is good for the soul. Whether that's true I don't know, but the time has come for me to bring out a very dark and difficult acknowledgment, lest I unduly present myself as some kind of hero husband who only ever had his wife's best interests at heart. The secret I must reveal here has caused me a lot of pain and regret for the terrible effect it had on the one person I love most in life. It is pertinent to this story, though, especially as I address the pain and suffering my wife went through.

A little less than a week before Liz's accident, Gary, our downstairs boarder, finally became concerned enough over Liz's altered mental status and sleepiness that he convinced her to get evaluated in the Butterworth Emergency Department. As I was at work at the time, he volunteered to bring her there himself; Gary texted me as he was leaving with Liz to let me know he was bringing her to the Emergency Department. I am very ashamed to say that I was panicked by the thought of her coming into my workplace, picturing a confused woman with some kind of mental disorder who would likely tell inappropriate tales. I thought how terribly that would reflect on me and my—what I now see as completely baseless—pride.

I'll say it flat out: I was embarrassed of the one who has meant and continues to mean the most to me in my life.

At that moment I made a horrible decision and called Liz on her cellphone. I asked her how she was feeling and whether she really needed to be seen that day. Liz told me she was abnormally tired no matter how much sleep she got, that something was wrong, and that she was worried about it enough to have agreed with Gary to go to the Emergency Department. And here's where my intimate knowledge of Liz came into the conversation, like a snake slithering into the Garden of Eden. I knew she carried in that large purse of hers an extensive array of medications that she juggled for congestion, chronic back pain, and several other ailments. I also knew that she was very defensive of her purse.

"You know, one of the first things they're going to do if you get admitted is restrict your use of those meds you have in your purse," I pointed out. "You're not going to be able to take any of your own meds once you get here."

Of course, Liz became alarmed over losing control over her medications, just as I knew she would. She plaintively asked me what I thought she should do and if I thought she needed to be seen since she was already halfway to the hospital. Coincidentally, the husband of Sue Host, our neighbor and one of Liz's closest friends, had been admitted to Butterworth the night before with a heart attack and cardiac arrest, miraculously surviving after a prolonged course of CPR performed by Sue.

"Well," I replied, "it's up to you, but if you don't want to lose control of your medications you could just skip Emergency and come visit Bob Host."

She decided to take my suggestion, and I told her I would come see her when she arrived. Deep down I was relieved now that she would not be presenting to my colleagues in the Emergency Department. The staff physicians there would almost certainly have been astute enough to order the appropriate laboratory studies to determine the cause of Liz's lethargy and make the proper diagnosis. I am well aware that, had the diagnosis of liver-related encephalopathy been made that day, Liz would not have been driving herself to the doctor a week later. I had set in motion a terrible course of events that culminated in my encephalopathic wife driving out into the middle of nowhere and having a head-on collision that brought her great pain and suffering and nearly cost her life.

At one point in her hospital course, I explained all of this to Liz, and, although she doesn't understand the depth of the guilt I feel, she forgave me for any part I'd played during events leading up to her accident. Still, it is a hard thing to realize that, while there may have been several circumstances that combined to result in her accident, I don't have to look too far to see a proximal cause of it.

When Liz became aware of what I was doing the night I was recording this sad part of our story, she literally forbade me to write it, but I feel it is essential to do so if it might prevent someone else from behaving in the selfish manner I had. She already knew the answer when she asked me that night if I was still ever embarrassed of her. How could I ever again be embarrassed of the person I love most dearly, who has become the greatest hero of my life? I would never betray that love a second time; she indeed is a hero, and I am proud to be known as Liz's husband!

CHAPTER 9

The date to move Liz to Mary Free Bed Hospital was originally set for Wednesday, January 27, but was pushed back to the following day since I had it off. I appreciated the flexibility of the care coordinator to accommodate my schedule, knowing the transition would go much smoother if I could be present. I also appreciated the staff not moving us to a different floor at Butterworth earlier that week, since this would have meant moving Liz twice within 48 hours. She was quite uncomfortable with pain from numerous fractures; recent abdominal surgeries; and, of course, that intense pain from the wound on her bottom. Moving her once would be ordeal enough.

Our family became more excited as the day approached that signaled a major step forward in Liz's recovery process, but Liz's increasing anxiety made it difficult for her to share in that excitement. I spent the better part of that week trying to convince the Orthopedic Trauma service to complete their work on Liz's smashed right foot and ankle. Dr. Miller had told me on the day of Liz's admission that her fractured talus bone was very unlikely to heal properly if he tried to repair it. His plan, in addition to repairing some of the fractures in her foot, was to fuse her right ankle with a bone graft two to four weeks after the accident to stabilize it. I remember thinking initially how terrible it would be for her to lose the flexibility of her ankle joint and that this would certainly be the worst sequela of the accident.

That had been since proven quite wrong, and I had come to more readily accept the plan to fuse her ankle. It was almost three weeks since her accident, and I was desperate to have that ankle surgery done before Liz's transfer to Mary Free Bed to avoid a return trip to Butterworth for that operation. Whether they thought it was too early to do the surgery or were just simply too busy to get the ankle surgery scheduled before her transfer day, it did not get done despite my persistent pestering. As it turned out, this decision was to have a long-lasting effect on Liz's recovery process.

Thursday, the 28th, dawned as a bright, crisp January morning— moving day. This was the first room change since we had "settled in," and there was a lot of work to be done to get ready for the short ambulance ride to Mary Free Bed, not much more than a mile away. As I surveyed the room to see what I needed to address, my eyes settled on Liz's half full bag of liquid tube feeding solution, a bag that should have been full. I discovered that the feeding, which was being cycled over 12 hours at night to allow Liz to eat during the day, was actually running at a 24-hour rate. This meant that it was supplying only one liter, half the nutrition intended. Since she was taking only minimal amounts of her ordered oral diet during the daytime, she was being significantly underfed, not conducive to normal healing. Apparently, the mistake had only been going on for three days, but I was determined to correct that at Mary Free Bed.

When the ambulance attendants arrived at noon, I hurriedly collected everything I had packed and stuffed as much as would fit around the stretcher onto which she was being moved. I had to leave several bags to pick up later, including a bag of clothes that disappeared and mysteriously resurfaced in my office across the street two weeks later. We pushed Liz onto the megavator, just down the hall from her room, and rode down to the ambulance bay, where she was loaded into one of those big, boxy e-units. I have to say I was a little excited to be riding along, as this had been one of those silly lifelong dreams we harbor that turn out to be much less dramatic than anticipated. My dad had driven an ambulance during a year off from college and had filled our heads with romantic stories of "making runs."

When I was a boy, I spent my free time roaming the neighborhood with my one-year-older brother, Don, and a younger neighbor, Glen Parker. The summer that I turned nine years old I was kept inside for several weeks with a particularly nasty case of mononucleosis. My two buddies carried on happily without me until one day, when Glen fell off a log crossing a creek and injured his ribs. Don ran to a nearby house to get help and became an instant neighborhood hero, even getting his name in the paper. Worse for me, Don got to take my dream trip in an ambulance as he rode with our friend to the hospital. For several months afterward I had to listen to memories of how cool that trip had been.

My notes from my own experience on that Thursday, January 28, weren't as enthusiastic:

"My first trip in an ambulance—way overrated!"

For starters, it was uncomfortably warm. There were no windows, and the driver took the scenic route. I tried to explain to him that Lafayette Ave., a block to the east, ran in a straight line all the way down to the corner of Wealthy Street, where sat Mary Free Bed Hospital. The driver, however, seemed married to his GPS, which was telling him to take the circuitous route through town, a route that involved about eight turns. Each turn caused Liz a fair amount of discomfort, and I found myself holding tightly to her to keep her from being tossed around on her stretcher.

Sometime later we rolled into a beautiful room on the third floor of Mary Free Bed; the hospital had been remodeled only a year earlier and was very clean and updated. On the bed was a piece of paper that upset me. Liz had an appointment the following week with the Spectrum Health orthopedic trauma surgeon at his office on the east side of Grand Rapids to determine a time for her ankle surgery. This would mean loading Liz back up into an ambulance and taking her across town just to determine when we could schedule her operation. Receiving this notice when we had been there on 4 Heart only a half hour earlier was quite frustrating.

I immediately started to think about what our options might be at Saint Mary's, adjacent and physically connected to Mary Free Bed. This would certainly be a lot easier on Liz. I asked Dr. Sam Ho, our rehabilitation doctor, to investigate consultation with a Saint Mary's orthopedic surgeon for Liz. Dr. Ho mentioned Dr. Geoff Sandman, and I immediately concurred. Geoff had gone to medical school at Michigan State University and had trained in the citywide orthopedic program in town; he had an excellent reputation as a skilled surgeon, particularly with traumatic injuries.

But before all of that, Geoff, then a student at Calvin College, had worked as an assistant in a research lab a few blocks from Butterworth Hospital under the direction of Alan Davis. Alan is an expert in research design and clinical statistics and has filled various roles for the Michigan State University presence in Grand Rapids for more than three decades. Alan and I have been longstanding friends and colleagues; at one time he served on my PhD graduate committee, and I did my laboratory doctoral work in his lab down the road from Butterworth Hospital on Michigan Street.

It was there that I first got to know Geoff Sandman, a very bright mind beneath a quiet demeanor. Our paths had crossed multiple times over the years since that time we had shared lab space, and I was delighted when Dr. Ho mentioned his name. We were to schedule an appointment to see Dr. Sandman the following week, either in our Mary Free Bed room or in his office a short journey by walkway across Lafayette Ave.

A second frustration quickly came to light. Liz's diet had been transcribed incorrectly, and she was now ordered to be on a mechanically soft diet instead of a surgically soft diet. This may not sound like a big deal, but there is a world of difference between the two diets. A surgical soft diet varies between institutions ("no seeds, peels, or skins," I had learned at one time) but basically allows normal food.

A mechanically soft diet, on the other hand, consists of visibly unappealing ground and pureed foods pressed into unrecognizable shapes. I'm not sure how much difference this made, as Liz was taking by mouth almost exclusively ice chips anyway, but she would not even look at the pureed stuff. Also, Liz no longer had any intravenous fluid running, as her IV had been "heplocked" (capped off) that morning before the transport to Mary Free Bed. I expressed my concern about Liz's hydration to the hospitalist who came to see Liz that afternoon.

This physician was difficult to communicate with, as his command of English was underwhelming, and his apparent youth did not instill confidence in me. He turned out to be 28 years old, younger than most of my kids and young to have already finished a residency. He encouraged Liz to drink more fluids and did not order intravenous fluids to be started, but he assured me that he would be checking some bloodwork in the morning to keep an eye on her hydration. Apparently that satisfied me at the time because my notes just say, "Met young hospitalist."

That same day the Head of Nursing and the floor nurse manager stopped by to welcome us and to offer their contact information in case we found we needed anything. I didn't know if this was standard operating procedure or if Liz was being given a bit of VIP treatment, but I was impressed and appreciated their kindness. Liz had a few sessions of various therapies later that afternoon, mostly in her bed because of her generalized deconditioning. Several therapists did manage to slide Liz over onto a stretcher that transformed into a recliner, the first time she had been sitting up in four weeks.

We had intended to watch a movie together that evening from the Mary Free Bed entertainment menu, but the long day had exhausted her, so she fell asleep immediately after "dinner." I stayed for a few hours munching on Peanut M&Ms from the famous Van Dyk treat basket that had followed us over from 4 Heart.

Lying in bed later that night, I had my usual awareness of how strange it felt to be there alone. I began to estimate when Liz might be coming home. *Maybe four to six weeks.*

This was a very comforting thought.

CHAPTER 10

As I was in the middle of a four-day weekend off, I was back to Liz's room before 8:00 the next morning; her daily schedule called for breakfast at that time, following which she would embark on a full day of therapy. Excluding an hour to get cleaned up and dressed after breakfast, Liz was to have about four or five hours of mostly evaluation, although she did engage in some light physical and occupational therapy that day as well. Included in the evaluative sessions was time with a psychologist, who was tasked with determining the extent, if any, of residual manifestations from Liz's brain injury.

I had brought along a laptop computer to occupy myself with financial matters and to work on a lesson for the adult Sunday school class I lead at Walker United Reformed Church. Pastor Corey had offered to have someone fill in for me in that class, but our class had been working through a study of the book of Job for several years, and I was determined to complete that study by the time our season ended in the spring. Before the accident I had been involved in several activities at that church, but because of the large amount of attention I had to pay to my wife's recovery I was unable to keep up with some of those. My very busy three-year term as an elder had finished up the

Sunday before Liz's accident, taking a lot off my plate and speaking, I think, to the perfection of God's timing.

I was also in the middle of my fifteenth year as a leader of our church youth group, Adverse City, a group I loved dearly. The group meets every second Sunday, and at the time I was preparing lessons for every other meeting, about monthly. This preparation had always been time consuming, taking about ten hours to complete a lesson, but it was a labor of love. My younger colleagues—Kraig and Jenna Zemaitis (in their forties) and Nick and Jessica Kortman (twenties)—were outstanding leaders and readily able to fill in for my responsibilities, but I missed that group immensely.

They had been such a wonderful part of my life for many years, and now I realized that my time with them was almost certainly finished. I grieved that separation, a sense of loss I took a long while to get past. But Adverse City (as well as the rest of Walker church) faithfully held up Liz and me in prayer throughout our ordeal. When I finally was able to reconnect with those youth at their annual chili cook-off several months later, it was a very warm and emotional homecoming.

Liz's hospitalist saw her early in the morning but didn't have much to say other than to encourage her to try to increase her oral intake. I was still particularly concerned about Liz's hydration, as she was not yet eating any part of her meals, and her liquid intake consisted predominantly of ice chips. I tried unsuccessfully to encourage her to drink more liquids and to get her diet changed back to surgical soft, also to no avail—because she had been admitted on a mechanically soft diet, she had to be reassessed by a Mary Free Bed speech therapist before being allowed to advance back to the surgical soft foods.

Other than once first thing in the morning, Liz did not urinate until that evening, which was in itself concerning. I was working on my laptop late in the afternoon when several therapists came by to place Liz in a stretcher chair and possibly take her on a tour of her unit. Almost immediately upon being placed in the chair, however, Liz began to feel lightheaded, and her blood pressure dropped precipitously. The therapists quickly moved her back into bed, but her pressure did not respond, remaining significantly low.

The nurses got an order to run a "fluid bolus," essentially the equivalent to the patient's chugging a pitcher of water but given intravenously to quickly rehydrate the patient. The order was for 500 milliliters of fluid, the equivalent of about a pint. I thought this was certainly less than a generous amount under the circumstances. After the fluid bolus was given, continuous IV fluid was started at 75 milliliters per hour, which is basically a maintenance amount—also not very generous. I would have favored at least a liter of fluid bolus followed by an IV at at least double the rate that had been ordered, but I was reluctant to speak up lest I be seen as "that" family member—a choice I would come to regret.

As Liz's blood pressure hovered in a potentially dangerously low range, I asked her nurse if I could see her lab values from that morning. I was dismayed to see that her blood urea nitrogen level, which had been 20 at Butterworth the previous morning, had doubled to forty 24 hours later, with a creatinine level of 1.2. Even though at that time Liz still experienced a continued ooze of blood from the varices around her ileostomy, her serum hemoglobin had risen 1½ grams per deciliter in those 24 hours, indicating that her red cells were circulating in a significantly smaller volume ("hemoconcentration"). The morning numbers were strongly indicative of dehydration or what is called "volume contraction," and now we were 12 hours farther from when those labs were drawn down the path of persistent inadequate fluid intake. In my mind she was clearly in hypovolemic shock—dangerously low blood pressure caused in Liz's case by inadequate blood volume.

My fragile emotional state began to crumble as I once again began to fear the worst for my wife. I immediately called my trusted friend and go-to advisor, Dr. Randy Baker, and quickly explained the situation to him, reading him the morning lab numbers. As I spoke to Randy, our young hospitalist physician arrived carrying new lab data; the BUN had risen to 80 over the course of the day, an extreme rise.

I explained to the physician that I was on the phone with Dr. Baker, the former director of critical care at Spectrum Health with whom he seemed familiar. I assumed that this was because Randy worked regularly at St. Mary's those days. The young hospitalist readily agreed to take the call when Randy asked me to pass the phone over, and he listened intently, making note of Randy's suggested course of treatment and monitoring. To his credit, the young doctor did not express any resentment at the counsel from the more experienced physician but readily put Randy's plan into action.

I was relieved a few moments later to see Liz's nurse turn up her IV rate to 200 milliliters per hour. In the meantime I began to make renewed prayer requests via family phone calls and text messages indicating that Liz was once again in a threatening condition. I always felt a measure of peace in knowing that many others were now sharing my prayer burden. Liz's blood pressure began to respond over the next few hours, and I felt comfortable enough to go home around midnight to sleep in my own bed. Despite the late hour, I lay for a while with a knot in my stomach, much in prayer on behalf of my wife.

The next morning, January 30, was a Saturday, a somewhat quieter day with regard to planned therapies, but I was there early to check on how my wife was doing. The short answer to that was not good. She still appeared to be significantly dehydrated and in need of both fluids and blood transfusions, her previously concentrated hemoglobin level having dropped as she was undergoing rehydration through the night.

Unfortunately, the IV catheter in her arm had been inadvertently dislodged when several therapists had moved her from her bed into a chair. A new IV was able to be placed, but as she was receiving some medications through it in addition to fluids, a second IV catheter was needed to allow Liz to get the needed blood transfusions. Several nurses tried to place an IV in various locations without success. Finally, an experienced nurse was called over from the St. Mary's Hospital emergency department, but after numerous attempts, including several in her foot, the nurse admitted defeat and left.

It was very difficult for me to see Liz suffer through that plethora of painful pokes, with which I'm sure many readers who have had their own such personal or family experience can identify. I wished often that morning that my daughter, Jackie, had been at the bedside that day. In her position as a sedation nurse for endoscopy procedures (gastrointestinal scopes), she had become known as a "vein whisperer," one of those elite nurses who seems to have near-mystical talents at securing IV access.

To make matters worse, I was alone in the room with Liz a short while later when she began to complain of intense, almost unbearable pain in her bottom from her pressure sore (yes, now that she had transferred hospitals, it could officially be labeled as such). In an effort to alleviate her pain, I grabbed the sheet on one side of her bed and shifted her body to take the pressure off that ulcer. To my horror, the remaining IV catheter popped out as I did so. Now she had no IV access at a time when she sorely needed it. Needless to say, I felt awful, but there was no way I could fix it. I wished that I could just put in a central venous catheter, as I frequently did in my own practice.

It was now 6:00 p.m. on a Saturday, long after the interventional radiologist at St. Mary's Hospital had left for the day. I discovered that the IR department at St. Mary's is smaller than at Spectrum Health and operates on a shorter daily schedule. Consequently, we had to take Liz over to that hospital's emergency department, where a very kind young physician was willing to place a central venous catheter but wanted their "top gun" nurse to try first. She was able to get an antecubital IV catheter placed (at the crook of the inside of the elbow), not the most desirable location, but it would work as long as Liz kept her elbow straight with the aid of an arm-board. Once the IV was in place, Liz began to receive the first of two units of transfused blood.

When we learned that Mary Free Bed wouldn't take Liz back since they didn't have the nursing staff to properly care for her, we had the choice to be transferred back to Spectrum Butterworth or to be moved to a medical floor at St. Mary's. Since we were anticipating ankle surgery with Dr. Sandman soon, we opted for St. Mary's. I had a gut feeling that I wanted Liz to stay as near to Mary Free Bed as possible; Mary Free Bed had always seemed to be that one-step-from-home place we wanted to be in.

Liz was very alert and interactive that evening in the emergency department. To date I had not informed her about the terrible fact of her liver disease and the accompanying cirrhosis, and we had all taken pains not to speak of it in her presence. During our conversation that night, our discussion turned to what it would be like to finally be healed and go home to live a normal life. My heart was heavy, but I knew the time had come for her to be informed of our dark family secret, a secret that had hung over all of us like a black cloud. I thought of several different ways to tell Liz but realized the best and most honest way was just to be direct.

"Liz, there's something I haven't told you . . ."

I proceeded to relay to her this fearsome news as gently and lovingly as I could. I expected a reaction bordering on hysteria, but Liz lay quietly for a moment before finally speaking.

"I don't want to die . . . I want to enjoy my grandkids."

At that she turned her face to the wall (much as King Hezekiah had) and wept quietly. I did the same.

A short while later Tim found us there, deep in prayer. He had hurried down to sit with us after getting his kids to bed. We heard that Liz was assigned to a room on 8 Main, but it took a long time for that floor's nursing staff to be ready for a late-night admission. Tim finally convinced me to go home and rest while he stayed to look after his mom. They finally reached the room at 2:00 a.m., and Tim spent the rest of the night at bedside to help calm the profound anxiety Liz was experiencing from the room change coupled with this terrible news.

I lay awake a long time with my own anxiety, texting Tim and Randy half the night, worrying about the liver disease and wondering how Liz was handling that news. I appreciated that Randy was still answering my texts at 2:00 a.m. and thanked God for that faithful friend. I was especially concerned that Liz's need to have blood transfusions represented a new "occult" (hidden) source of blood loss that might be ongoing and undetected. As I have noted before, having medical knowledge is not always a helpful thing.

My brain rummaged through possible blood loss sources and finally settled on bleeding esophageal varices, a not uncommon occurrence in patients with advanced liver disease. Of course, once that thought popped into my mind, my obsessive-compulsive nature fanned the flame of possibility into reality. I texted my fear to Randy, who tried to calm me while at the same time scheduling Liz for an early Sunday morning emergent upper endoscopy (EGD) in the endoscopy suite at St. Mary's Hospital.

The next morning that EGD showed a healthy esophagus, immediately relieving my fears; I was immensely grateful to my friend for interrupting his own Sunday morning routine to ensure Liz's wellbeing and my own peace of mind. I texted family and friends the favorable information and received numerous replies reporting encouragement from answered prayers.

Sunday tends to be a quieter day in most hospitals, with tests and procedures at a minimum. Liz spent the rest of that day settling into room 836, receiving IV fluids and blood transfusions, and was in surprisingly good spirits, given all that had transpired the day before. I went to her former room at Mary Free Bed to pick up her things to bring to her new room. In her former room was a bag of handmade clothes that had just arrived from Fresno, California, sent by Liz's sister.

Jean is practically a wizard at designing and sewing clothes, and when she heard that her sister had a new ileostomy she had immediately set about creating clothes specifically designed to accommodate that device. That bagful of clothes was a result of Jean's efforts, although Liz had not yet had a chance to try on any of them. A nurse manager assisting me with collecting and moving Liz's belongings volunteered to store that bag until Liz was able to come back to Mary Free Bed, a kindness I readily accepted. Little did I know that this decision would lead to a humorous moment much later on.

Through all this turmoil Liz's anxiety was sky-high. I stayed with her until late Sunday evening, but she still called me in the middle of the night and again when I was at work on Monday morning. By the time I received the second call, I realized that I could not alleviate her anxiety by phone, so I decided to leave Butterworth to come and sit with her for about five hours until our kids came down to take over later in the day. I was very thankful to my partners, Jim and Annette, for covering for me.

Earlier that morning, February 1, Dr. Sandman saw Liz and scheduled her for a surgical repair of her shattered right ankle on

Wednesday, February 3. Moreover, he told Tim, who was there that morning on his birthday, that rather than fusing it—the thought of which had so horrified me four weeks earlier—he felt confident that he could repair the ankle using "micro-plating," although it would necessarily be a rather lengthy procedure.

Our family was quite excited about this prospect, as was Liz (although she had no memory of having been told in the first place that it was to be fused). Things seemed to be looking up; the operative plans meant that Liz eventually could return home from Mary Free Bed without the necessity of any more surgeries. We texted out and otherwise notified our cadre of prayer supporters this news.

As I was working that week, I was up and down the hill from Butterworth to St. Mary's and back numerous times. Tuesday was spent giving Liz two more units of blood and otherwise getting her ready for surgery. I went home that evening anticipating a better night's sleep and being back at St. Mary's early the next morning for the surgery. Our daughter, Jackie, had gone into labor late that afternoon, and there was a lot of levity being exchanged on our family text thread as we anticipated the pending addition to our little tribe.

Our good spirits suddenly changed when we all received a frightening text from Jackie's husband, Brek:

"Please pray right now!!"

Despite our anxious queries, no further texts from Brek were forthcoming. Something catastrophic was happening, and we had no idea what it was; all we could do was pray, nonspecifically, for God's favor on Jackie and that little boy. The family thread quieted down immediately, and the few texts that were posted were curt and sober. Most simply said "Praying!"

It was stunning how fast things could change.

CHAPTER **11**

Liz's surgery was scheduled for early afternoon, so I was able to go to work the morning of Wednesday, February 3, my grandson Isaiah's birthday. By then we had all heard the grim news, catastrophic indeed. During Jackie's labor, a physician had come in to break her water to facilitate the birth. Unfortunately, Jackie had a previously undetected condition with excessive amniotic fluid in the uterus, called polyhydramnios. One of the main complications associated with this condition is prolapse (pushing out) of the umbilical cord when the mother's water breaks, which is exactly what happened in Jackie's case. As her water was broken, the umbilical cord and a hand had prolapsed out of the uterus, turning a routine delivery into a panicked emergency.

It was at that time, just before midnight, that Brek had sent out his abrupt text to our family. Jackie had been taken for an emergent C-section, as the blood flow to the baby was compromised by the prolapsed cord. It took only about 15 to 20 minutes from the time the water broke to the time Isaiah was delivered by C-section, but the physicians attending Jackie had told Brek that Isaiah had almost certainly experienced a critical degree of anoxia (lack of oxygen to the brain) during that time.

Isaiah was rushed to the Neonatal Intensive Care Unit (NICU), where he was placed into a medically induced coma and had his body temperature cooled to reduce his metabolism and minimize the extent of the anticipated brain injury. He would remain so for a week before they would gradually warm and wake him to determine the severity of his injuries.

In the wee hours of the morning, I had already started to text out a desperate request for prayers from my personal group of close prayer warriors. I felt guilty for adding a new burden to their efforts on behalf of my family, and I apologized in that text if I was wearing them out. I had been reluctant to reach out to them yet again, but my grandson's life was at stake, so I had warily gone ahead with the request. To a person I was told that this was certainly no imposition, while a few even indignantly called me out for suggesting that a request for prayer could ever be perceived as a burden. I loved those brothers and sisters so much right then.

There were not many updates forthcoming on little Isaiah, as, at this juncture, only time would tell. I was in room 836 in time to travel with Liz to the preoperative area at just around noon. Dr. Sandman told us again that it would be a lengthy procedure, maybe around 3½ to 4 hours. I spent the next 5½ hours in the St. Mary's surgical waiting room working on my computer and being much in prayer for my wife and her surgeon, as well as for my grandson.

When he was finally done, Dr. Sandman told me he had pieced and plated her ankle back together to preserve function. Liz's right ulna (wrist) had not been fixed at Butterworth because it had been determined to be stable but had recently become displaced, so Dr. Sandman had also plated that wrist fracture. I imagined him in the operating room tediously piecing my wife's shattered ankle back together, piece by piece. I thought this was nothing short of heroic.

The next few days were a blur of running up and down the hill between work and St. Mary's to see my wife while also running over to the Butterworth NICU to visit little Isaiah. He was so beautiful slumbering away in that cold coma; it was hard to imagine that there was anything wrong with him. Numerous tests were coming back with favorable results, but these were always accompanied by a guarded prognosis. He had suffered anoxia for up to twenty minutes, so we could hardly expect there wasn't going to be significant brain damage. Liz, as expected from the extensive nature of her operation, was experiencing a considerable amount of pain in her ankle. And she asked a lot of questions about her new grandson.

Saturday, February 6, was wake-up day for little Isaiah, so the NICU staff began to wean him off his sedation through the night for a 5:00 a.m. MRI scan of his brain. After favorable results from the MRI scan were reported, Isaiah was allowed to remain off the sedation, with a wait-and-see period of watching for wakefulness. Jackie was holding her papoose-wrapped newborn later that afternoon when his lids quivered and slowly opened, allowing mom to see her baby's eyes for the first time.

Throughout Saturday that was pretty much the only response Isaiah showed, which was not altogether unexpected. The physicians had told Brek and Jackie that it would take a while for the sedation medication to be cleared from Isaiah's body and that, along with the cooling and the birth trauma with significant anoxia, it might be some time before he achieved complete wakefulness. As Jackie told me later, "I held him, and he just passed out on my chest."

Unfortunately, he did not progress as quickly as was hoped, and his somnolence became a matter of great concern as the days rolled by without much improvement in Isaiah's alertness level. Thankfully, an MRI scan on that afternoon showed no worrisome findings, a result that was greatly celebrated after a morning of intense prayers.

I spent early Sunday morning, February 7, racing through my rounds at the Spectrum hospitals before stopping by to say hi to Liz on my way to church to lead the adult Sunday school class. I was very tired in church that morning, and my mind was prone to wander. Liz's heart rate had been ever-so-slightly elevated, and her affect had seemed just a bit off when I had seen her. Something had been different that morning, but as I had been in her room for only a few minutes I had chalked it up to pain meds and fatigue. I tried to put myself at ease, but I was uneasy.

I arrived back to room 836 just after noon and shared lunch with her. I was encouraged that she had been advanced to a surgical soft diet again, but she was not taking much of anything that day. I ate most of her lunch and then settled back into a rocker-recliner to wait for the Super Bowl to start. Denver was playing Carolina, and being a San Francisco 49ers fan, I didn't have much rooting interest. Still, as always, I was anticipating the novel advertisements that are rolled out each year for the Super Bowl telecast.

I never really got comfortable in that chair, however, because it was becoming steadily clearer that the mental changes of which I had first seen a hint that morning were gradually worsening. While Liz had been readily conversant when I had arrived for lunch, she was progressively more lethargic and less interactive. Whereas we had been carrying on a conversation around noon, by 4:00 p.m. she was replying only in short sentences and slurring some of her words.

I was alarmed enough to call for her nurse, who checked Liz's vital signs. Her heart rate was now up into the 130s, and her blood pressure had also begun to rise. I told the nurse I felt that Liz was getting septic, but she assured me that this wasn't likely since her temperature was normal. I knew that developing a fever isn't necessarily part of the septic picture, but once again I didn't want to be "that" family member, so I did not press my concerns.

By 5:00 p.m. Liz could no longer carry on even a semblance of a conversation, and I had begun a running debate with the staff over my insistence that something was dreadfully wrong. Her heart rate had risen into the 150s and her blood pressure to the 190s/90s, so despite the lack of a fever it was becoming clear that something ominous was happening. The internal medical service tends to be lightly staffed on Sundays, and it took a while to get a physician's assistant (PA) to come and evaluate Liz. She expressed some concern but was not as alarmed as I was after having witnessed the dramatic mental change throughout the day. The PA ordered some blood cultures and told me she would consult with her attending physician, who was busy elsewhere in the hospital.

My son Tom showed up around 6:00 p.m. in his nursing scrubs to share dinner with his mom before heading across the hospital to start his 7:00 p.m. shift on Hauenstein 3. All thoughts of dinner were instantly forgotten as he saw the shape his mom was in. He was immediately alarmed as I tried to explain what had been going on throughout the day. Tom was blunt with Liz's nurse.

"I would not accept this patient on my floor, and our acuity is higher than yours is." He asked to have the floor charge nurse present and began to press the same argument with her. The nurses were busy with other floor duties, and it was approaching the time for the change of shift, so they were in and out of the room. By now Liz was no longer verbally responsive, and to me she appeared to be dying. Between texting out a multitude of urgent prayer requests, I was ringing the bedside call button and pleading to have an attending physician immediately come to see my wife.

I was grateful that my kids were picking up the burden of soliciting further prayer because we needed a lot of it now. I needed to focus on my task at hand, even as my cellphone consistently binged with assurances of "Praying now" from numerous contacts. Liz's nurse came in to hang a bag of intravenous Lopressor, a medication ordered by the PA to lower Liz's blood pressure. While the pressure was high, I felt some reservation about using Lopressor because, if this was indeed sepsis, it was very likely that Liz's blood pressure would drop precipitously into a shock range, at which time the Lopressor would prove to be counterproductive. I questioned the nurse but again didn't press my point.

By now I was terrified that this was becoming a moment in which I could lose my wife, who seemed to be trying to die in front of my eyes. At some point Tom called a "rap," a rapid response that is answered in most hospitals by a critical care trained individual who comes immediately to make a rapid assessment of a critical situation and determine what level of treatment acuity is needed. Tom told me that anyone, even a family member, can call a rap, so he did just that at that critical juncture. An experienced nurse from the ICU (Hauenstein 2) arrived almost immediately, just ahead of the hospitalist physician.

While the doctor felt that Liz's care could still be handled on 8 Main, I was relieved that the rap nurse disagreed. I suspect the 8 Main nurses were relieved as well. The rap nurse arranged for transport of Liz to the ICU via a stop in Radiology for a CAT scan of her head, chest, and abdomen. Stopping there to do these tests made me nervous, but the Radiology staff had them done in about twenty minutes. I think it helped to again have Randy talk to the hospitalist by phone and convey his concerns and recommendations. By now Tom had belatedly headed over to his shift, after his nursing colleagues had insisted he stay with his mom until the situation was under control. Small wonder he liked working with the staff on that floor.

While Liz received a head CAT scan because of her rapid mental status change, the hospitalist also wanted to get a chest CAT scan to rule out a pulmonary embolism (blood clot to the lungs). I persuaded the hospitalist to forego that test, as it would require giving Liz intravenous dye to make it an accurate study. I was worried about the negative effects the dye might have on her already tenuous kidney function, and I felt it was unlikely that a pulmonary embolism was the source of her condition, which looked classically like septic (infectious) shock.

The transfer proved to be beneficial in another way, as the ICU is directly below Tom's floor, so he was able to visit often on his work breaks while his mother was there. Further, Liz was admitted to room 216, a corner room at the northwest end of the unit, adjacent to a stairwell that allowed Tom to easily run down for a visit and allowed me closer access to the parking lot. Tim joined me in ICU that evening to offer moral support, and Emily asked if she should come as well, but I assured her that Liz was stable at that time. It was great to have a loving, supportive family at times like these.

Liz was cared for that night in the ICU by physicians from the hospitalist staff rather than the by critical care intensivists, who had not yet been consulted on her care. She was started on some IV fluids and began to look better around midnight. Her heart rate and blood pressure had improved, and I felt comfortable going home for the night. I would stop by in the morning on my way to work.

Little did I know that this was to be Liz's "golden hour."

To be honest, I've long hated the use of the words "golden hour" because they are almost always followed by a medical disaster, quite often including patient death. Recall that the use of those words several weeks earlier at Butterworth Hospital had been a harbinger of Liz's abdominal catastrophe and the resultant guerrilla surgery that had nearly taken her life.

When I returned to room 216 early the next morning, there was a flurry of activity, as Liz's heart rate was back in the 150s and her blood pressure now much lower. A hospitalist physician present in the room told me that Liz's morning chest X-ray looked "congested," a term used when the heart is unable to pump blood efficiently enough, causing fluid to back up into the lungs. He had ordered several doses of Lasix, a diuretic that reduces chest congestion by causing the patient to urinate more.

While Liz was having trouble breathing and was clearly short of breath, I had major misgivings about giving Lasix to a patient whose blood pressures were not much higher than shock values, but again I kept my counsel to myself. By the time I arrived, one dose of Lasix had already been given and a second was being prepared. After the hospitalist left, I asked why critical care was not seeing my wife if she was in ICU and obviously critically ill.

"They haven't been consulted yet," a nurse told me.

When I asked how a consult could be obtained, I was told that I could ask for one myself, which I promptly did.

Within minutes Dr. Matt Dikin entered the busy room, asking questions in a staccato fashion to get an understanding of an obviously complex situation as quickly as possible. One of the first questions he asked was to a nurse who was about to administer an IV medication.

"What's that you're giving?"

"Lasix," she answered.

"Hold that!" he ordered before he continued his litany of questions.

I was very relieved to have him there at that moment and liked him and his clinical approach almost immediately. The working diagnosis quickly changed from congestive heart failure to septic shock, as Liz's blood pressure began to drop precipitously. I scribbled a hasty note at that moment: "Mom's MAP 39—she is dying."

Unfortunately, that mean arterial pressure of 39, already well below the number guaranteeing vital organ perfusion, was the high-water mark while I was in the room, as it continued to slide lower from that point.

I moved about as if in a dream, watching like a disengaged bystander the ever more crowded commotion—indeed panic—in that room. Nurses and techs raced around the room, bumping into each other as the nurses prepared the medications for infusion that were being ordered in rapid-fire fashion by Dr. Dikin and his team, while several techs set up the equipment for him to emergently place a central venous catheter.

Liz had only one small peripheral intravenous catheter, which presented not only a lack of necessary access for all of the medications currently being ordered but also could not accommodate the large volume of fluids that needed to be given to check her dropping blood pressure. Complicating this problem was the fact that the body compensates for shock by drastically cutting down blood flow to the extremities, meaning that the venous return from a peripheral (arm) IV, as well as any medications given by that route, is significantly delayed.

There was one critical question now: Could the ICU team get a central venous catheter placed swiftly enough to allow resuscitation from the rapidly progressive shock before catastrophic failure of vital organs—or even death—ensued?

As the equipment for the central venous catheter was being set up, Liz was quickly hooked back up to a ventilator, a simple procedure since she still had a tracheostomy from her stay at Butterworth—just a matter of attaching the ventilator to that existing tracheostomy. IV sedation is quite often given for ventilated patients, especially when first placing them on the ventilator as a measure of comfort. Liz's blood pressure was now almost immeasurable, so there was no way the staff could safely give any type of sedation without pushing her into irreversible shock and cardiac arrest. This didn't matter much, as she had lapsed into unconsciousness well before this point.

Trying to stay out of the way, I pressed myself against a wall, praying desperately as I texted my kids, pleading for them to pray now.

"Your mother is dying," I wrote them.

As the equipment was set up, a nurse shoved into my hands a treatment consent form for me to sign for the central venous catheter procedure. The staff was setting up to place the catheter in her right femoral vein, generally the last choice to place a central line due to increased risk of infection but now the correct choice in this panicked situation, as it afforded the simplest and most direct approach. Saving life trumped risk of infection.

In a daze I was gently but firmly led out of the room. I was nauseated and could feel myself shaking uncontrollably. A care manager was by my side, having apparently guided me out of the room. She was very kind but focused with her following questions:

> If—when—Liz arrested, considering her known liver disease, how aggressive did I want the team to be?
>
> Did I want them to do CPR?
>
> Did I want them to shock her heart?
>
> If she had a cardiac arrest, how long would I want her to be kept on the ventilator?
>
> Had I thought about changing her care to just keeping her comfortable?

At the time those were very difficult questions to hear, but the care manager was very kind and just doing her job.

"Everything for now—I need to talk to my family," I told her.

As I spoke, I realized for the first time that I had been crying.

How long have I been like this?

I figured that my tears had probably arrived right when I had started texting our children, anticipating their grief in losing their mom after her having survived such an ordeal already.

The care manager led me to a small area just past the door to room 216, a foyer that included an entry to that back stairwell. She stayed for a few moments until I not very convincingly assured her through sobs that I was okay.

There in that foyer, on the far north side of the hospital, was a padded bench for family members to sit and wait. Behind the bench was a wall of giant picture windows looking north up the hill to Spectrum Butterworth Hospital, which looked deceptively close. While it was more than a mile away, Butterworth Hospital appeared to be only a few blocks from Saint Mary's from that vantage point. I gazed up the hill at Butterworth and realized I could easily see the west building, which housed the Neonatal Intensive Care Unit where my new grandson lay in a somnolent state despite now being two days off sedation. Behind me the Saint Mary's Critical Care team worked desperately to save my wife's life.

For all I know, she's already dead.

As I stared up out the windows to the Spectrum Health Neonatal ICU, I let out a long sigh. *For all I know, he's already gone, too.*

Standing alone in that foyer caught between two crises, I don't think I had ever felt more forlorn in my life. My phone exploded with calls and texts, but I ignored them for a few emotional moments as I cried out to God.

"It's too much . . . it's just too much. Please don't make me go through this anymore."

I was reminded of another prayer by another, but divine, sufferer many years earlier. Prayers uttered in anguish are not very eloquent but are certainly more passionate. My prayer focused on the "two sleepers," as I called these two family members, and as such they became linked in my daily prayers for some time. All I could muster was to ask God to spare their lives for another day. Today was more than 48 hours past the designated wake-up day for Isaiah. What would his doctors find? It was very unlikely he had escaped his birth trauma unscathed. How severe would the damage be? Time would tell.

I turned to my phone and began the busy task of returning texts and phone calls, texting my go-to list of prayer partners to beg for their help yet again. "Praying . . . praying . . . praying . . . praying," came back the answers in rapid sequence. Though my emotional state interfered with rational thought, I found great relief in the faithfulness of this mighty band of prayer warriors. The prayers of the righteous are indeed powerful; our family needed them now more than ever, as we rested in the prayers of the saints.

One of my first calls was to Jamie, who said he was on his way back to Grand Rapids from his home in Virginia. Having just missed a lot of time from his work as an ophthalmologist in January during the original crisis, he felt reticent to ask for time off again less than a month later. Jamie had just joined the practice a few months earlier, so he was not yet a partner in the group but an employee. He worried about the perception of his taking advantage of the group.

The partners in the practice were having none of that, however, and told Jamie to go take care of his mom immediately. He was eager to see her; as he noted, "She hadn't woken up in January until I had left." Jamie was also looking forward to meeting his new nephew. When he arrived later that evening, I took a picture of him leaning over his mom's bedside, his hand tenderly upon her forehead.

"The prodigal son returns," I wrote when messaging the photo to our family.

Younger bro Tim responded, "Don't let him fool you, Dad! He's leaving again ☺."

Tim had left his school immediately when he was notified of the serious downturn in his mother's health and was soon with me at her bedside. After I had waited in the foyer for a half hour or so, Dr. Dikin came out to tell me that the procedure had gone well and that the nurses had already started running large volumes of fluid through that central line, along with norepinephrine, a potent blood-pressure-raising medication—standard treatments for septic shock. In addition, Liz was started on a combination of broad-spectrum IV antibiotics since, at this point in time, the staff didn't know what organism was causing the infection and shock or where it had come from; the blood cultures from the night before were still not showing any bacterial growth.

As Tim joined me at his mother's side, we could see that her pressure was not yet responding well to the treatment, although the steady decline in her pressure numbers seemed to have been checked. That still left open the question of the aggressiveness of the treatment we wanted to pursue if Liz were to deteriorate further.

For Timmy the Tenderheart, as we had called him as a child, it was an easy decision—if his mom was alive, he wanted to pursue all available measures. The physician side of my own existence always crowded in on every care decision for my wife. My tendency was to concur with Tim at this moment, but I, yet again, did not want to be "that family member" whom the clinical staff sees as unreasonably clinging to desperate measures in a hopeless situation.

We agreed at this juncture to call Dr. Randy Baker for his input. As I have noted previously, Randy had at one time been Spectrum Health's director of critical care and would be well versed with regard to the situation in which we now found ourselves. I was terrified to make that call because I dreaded the answer Randy might give us.

I dialed Randy's cell, and he immediately answered, patiently listened to my report, and began to ask pertinent questions. After a brief silence, Randy offered the opinion I was awaiting, as though it were a Supreme Court decision.

"Jim, I know it looks bad, but I don't think we're at that point yet."

My first thought was that I loved that Randy took ownership of the situation by using the word "we" instead of "you."

"There's a lot going on here, and we don't have a good idea of what the cause of this shock is yet," Randy said. "We need to find the answer to that and treat it appropriately. In the meantime, I think it's reasonable to pull out all stops to resuscitate her until we do know. I think we have to make this goals-of-care decision separately from the liver issue; we don't know how bad the liver disease is or what her prognosis is from that, so that shouldn't factor into any decision we make right now on DNR or comfort care. Like I said, we're not there yet; we have some fight left in us."

My relief was palpable, and I thanked Randy profusely before hanging up. Even though my wife wasn't getting better, the decision to continue to be fully aggressive, even if things were to deteriorate, was a huge load off my mind.

As I have noted, Monday is the one day of the week when my own practice has three clinicians scheduled; from that standpoint it was a favorable day for me to skip work and stay by my wife's side. I was with Tim throughout that day, and Jamie joined us at bedside in the early afternoon when the outcome was still in doubt. Jamie had made an extraordinary effort to be there, hoping to see his mother one more time before she died.

Many assurances of prayers poured in that day. As the morning hours segued into afternoon, Liz began to rally ever so slowly. Her mean arterial pressure, which had stubbornly hung around 35 all morning and past noon, began to inch northward, finally breaching the magic number of 65 by mid-afternoon as the fluids and medications did their job. It was a relief to know that her blood pressure was now at a level that could reasonably sustain adequate perfusion of her vital organs. She was finally out of severe shock after the better part of ten hours; I could only guess what toll her plunge might have been taken on her brain; her GI tract; and, most probably, her kidneys.

At 4:00 p.m. I felt comfortable leaving Jamie and Tim in their mom's room to run up the hill to Spectrum Butterworth to see my grandson. I held that precious little bundle for the first time on the fifth day of his life but was unable to appreciate much more than an eye opening from him. But for me, on that day, that was enough. While I held him, I uttered a prayer for the two sleepers before handing him back to his mother and returning to my wife's side.

While both sleepers remained critically ill, Grandma Liz was in the more dire straits . . . although there remained much about which to be concerned with the little guy. Liz was now on "triple pressors," three different pressure-raising medications. While these were successfully keeping her mean arterial pressure above 60, it was not an ideal situation. Furthermore, her ventilatory support numbers had climbed through the day, indicating progressive respiratory failure, likely from congestion in her lungs as the physicians poured into her the large amounts of IV fluid necessary to keep her blood pressure up.

On top of that, her abdomen began to gradually expand as those same fluids—unable to pass through her damaged liver—began to leak out into her abdomen as ascites, fluid that builds up around internal abdominal organs. The increasing ascites in turn was interfering with the normal downward motion of the diaphragm, further compromising her lung function. We knew that her liver was struggling to keep up with the increased blood flow caused by the fluids as the now weeks-long slow bleeding from her ileostomy began to pick up.

This increased intestinal bleeding resulted in a steady decline in her serum hemoglobin levels, to the point that she was unable to adequately carry oxygen in her blood, and eventually necessitated blood transfusions. The transfusions created still more congestion in her lungs, leading to higher ventilatory support. All of this amounted to an unsustainable vicious cycle that had to be broken for Liz to survive. Unfortunately, at this tenuous juncture all the physicians could do was react to each new crisis in turn, even though each reaction aggravated another part of Liz's care.

To say that she was holding her own that afternoon would have been an overstatement, but she was holding her own by that evening. Our family had even injected a little levity into the situation, as "someone" had included on her whiteboard as one of her written goals, "Pick my favorite child"—directly above where Tom's contact information was recorded. Next to this was an addendum reading, "Brek (in-laws are better)." At least we could still maintain our humor. I felt comfortable enough with her status to go home late that night with Jamie, while Tim again took an overnight shift at bedside.

On the baby front on Monday, Jackie had informed us that morning that Isaiah was slowly waking up and would likely be discharged Wednesday, February 10. Unfortunately, the little guy wouldn't wake up for his 5:00 feeding, so that date got pushed back for at least a day. Tom thought that this was because Isaiah was so cute those nurses didn't want to let him go yet. The more cynical Brek had another idea: "They seem a bit slow right now, so maybe they need the $7,500/night to continue a bit longer."

One of the neat sidelights of that hospitalization was that Lauren, the daughter of my nurse practitioner Annette, was a staff nurse in that NICU unit where Isaiah was hospitalized and spent some time taking care of my grandson. We all got to know Lauren better through that hospitalization, which was fun since she is a sweetheart of a girl and, because her mother and Liz are first cousins, is actually kin to us all (including Isaiah).

That evening a neurology development pediatrician stopped by to do a comprehensive assessment on Isaiah. She told Jackie and Brek that everything looked normal but that they would have to follow his neurologic status for a long time—for years, not months.

Before I went to bed that Monday night, I scribbled another cryptic note:

"Mom rallies. Jamie flies in again. Mom stabilizes in the afternoon. Isaiah waking up; shuttle diplomacy."

Little did I know that this was the last note I would write for a long time, as hope of Liz's survival faded and, at least temporarily, destroyed my dedication to documenting her story.

CHAPTER 12

"I don't want to fight anymore. I just want to die."

Liz mouthed these words to me shortly after I arrived in her room the next morning. I could clearly see that she was not doing well. When Tamara texted to ask how her mom-to-be was doing, I was honest.

"Super anxious. Very sad. Seeing bugs. Very upset that we didn't get here until after 9:00."

Emily, the medical social worker coming out to see her, reminded us that Liz had not tolerated the antianxiety medication Seroquel in the past; we asked the staff to avoid it and try Ativan instead. Even though I thought Liz's statement was the product of a depressive episode and might not reflect her true feelings, I shared it with my kids. Tim quickly responded.

"Let's focus on just the next healing step," Tim wrote. "Randy warned us on day 1 that we would take steps forward and backward in this marathon. We are in the midst of a big fallback and need to be encouraged and ready to take our next steps forward—together with Mom. Let's all commit to lifting up a prayer at noon for Mom to have improvement in her thinking and in her blood pressure. Tell her we're all going to pray at noon for her as a family."

This brought tears to my eyes, as did the responses.

"So sad to hear; I'll be praying," Tamara replied.

"I prayed for Mom," Tim stated.

Jamie, bedside: "We prayed with her out loud, too."

"Me too," Halle put in.

Tamara responded with. "Me three. Always am."

By early afternoon, I was able to give a favorable report: "She's calming down. She wants to get better and be home with kids and grandkids—same goal as before."

I was so relieved that I was not going through this alone.

That evening Randy Baker asked me if he could meet with our entire family the next afternoon. We had all been texting him and calling him separately, to the point that he was hearing concerns and opinions from different people. I assumed that he wanted to get us all at the same place as in terms of Mom's care. We had to send a flurry of texts back and forth to determine a time, as Randy wanted the entire family present.

I was very worried that we were wearing Randy out or that he was being overwhelmed by our sheer numbers. Maybe he wanted to have us pick a single family representative to deal with him. My anxiety level was escalating. To make matters worse, we'd experienced a rare negative exchange with a nurse that evening . . . but this also had the effect of making us realize what an overall blessing our nurses had been.

"A nurse should never say, 'It'll be a while; I have other patients to take care of,'" I texted to the family group chat.

The incident had not been a major issue but just a request to see whether Liz could get privileges to try the sorbet she was persistently asking for. It was not very satisfying for any of us to hear the nurse's response: "Well, you know she's getting everything she needs through her feeding tube."

Tom noted that this nurse likely had *an*other patient, not "others," as they're usually assigned not more than two on the ICU. I don't know what stressors that nurse had going on that evening, but I do know that nursing, and particularly intensive care nursing, can be a very difficult job.

"Must not be Melanie tonight," Tim added, highlighting another gracious professional who was to become one of our hero nurses. But Tim was concerned enough that he elected to come down to stay at his mom's bedside yet again that night.

The next day, Wednesday, February 10, crawled by slowly as we all looked forward to the scheduled 4:15 p.m. meeting with Randy. Jamie came to sit by his mom's side as Tim left in the morning to go to work. Jamie was very impressed with how lucid Liz was that morning and with her ability, finally off the ventilator, to communicate with the fenestrated (speaking) tracheostomy valve in place. She was telling Jamie about how her new grandson was born the day she was dying (not exactly, but close) and how she couldn't wait to see him. She indeed had something to live for again; Brek texted that Liz had been praying for Isaiah out loud the previous afternoon.

It was heartwarming for me to read these texts while I was rounding on my patients up the hill at Butterworth Hospital. Tom, off that day, came down to St. Mary's at lunch to allow Jamie a chance to grab something to eat with me outside the hospital. I have no doubt it was part of the plot to make sure Dad was eating meals. Unfortunately, it didn't seem that Liz's lot was to continue to experience incremental gains and to steadily get well.

"She's taken a negative turn," Jamie texted that afternoon. "Getting a stat CXR (chest x-ray) and the doctor is coming. Heart rate fast. Blood pressure up. Lots of pain. Pray for her. as she is really suffering."

The concern and frustration began to ramp up in Jamie's texts as his mom got placed back on a ventilator.

"Not good. Super tachy (rapid heart rate), ventilated, febrile. Think she needs some fluid but can't get them to do it. At least got the Critical Care PA to stop the Lasix ordered by the hospitalist. Wish we were on 4 Heart. At least the ICU attending would be here for a crashing patient." Then, a few minutes later, "He's here."

Meanwhile, back at Butterworth, I was in a panic, trying to rapidly tie up loose ends so I could go and attend to my wife. Calls for prayers were going out again in urgent fashion that day, and the saints were again raising up their prayers for Liz's welfare. Once more we received numerous replies that our brothers and sisters were lifting us up.

Tom texted to make sure that, if the staff were to do a CAT scan on his mom, they would get the right PAAUW CT scan, as he'd had a chest scan that morning. It was then that we found out that Tom had an aortic aneurysm to go with his previously diagnosed abnormal aortic valve. At that moment the negative news seemed to me to be piling on. But by the time I got to her bedside, Liz was at least stabilizing in response to large volumes of IV fluids and multiple pressors. I felt comfortable leaving her long enough to go to our family meeting with Dr. Randy Baker.

As we all made our way into the family conference room on the ICU, I was nervous, worried that we had frustrated Randy and worn him out. I couldn't have been more wrong. Randy started out with a summary of where Liz had been and where she was at that point in time. Within the first sentence something sparked an intense sentiment in me, and I burst out with an uncontrollable sob. Everyone in the room cast a perplexed look at me, and I didn't blame them. I was surprised as well and felt embarrassed.

"Sorry," I said.

I was still sniffling when Randy reassured me: "That's alright; we all know you've been through a lot."

Indeed, I had been, and I was again more emotionally labile than I thought. It turned out that Randy was not there to "take us to the woodshed" over each of us pestering him with our individual concerns but to warn us that we needed to be very careful with Liz regarding opioid use, both in the hospital and when she was better and able to go home. Randy reminded us that, at the very beginning of this odyssey, he had told us not to think in terms of days or weeks but in the range of six to twelve months. He encouraged all of us to call him at any time with individual concerns and assured us that he would try to answer as best he could. In a few minutes he had given us reassurance that our wife and mom was going to get better and that he was open to each one of us at any time. I loved Randy right then; he was such a stalwart for our family.

We were all comforted at the end of a difficult and stressful day. Beyond this, we had the assurance that we had an extra pair of highly trained eyes comprehensively watching over Liz each day. By this time the Critical Care Service had come to accept and even value our special, trusting relationship with Randy. They got into the habit of consulting him first with important decisions, in part, I think, to be able to tell us, "We already checked this out with Dr. Baker, and he agrees."

Late that evening I sat in a chair at Liz's bedside, holding her hand and mindlessly watching the various tracings and numbers on her in-room monitor. I thought I detected a small squeeze of Liz's hand in mine and turned to see her with her eyes open, able to turn her head, though barely perceptibly, toward me. As I looked intently into her eyes, I thought I saw her mouth the words, "Let me go."

"Let you go?" I asked.

Am I holding her hand too tightly?

"Let me go," she mouthed again.

"Let you go?" I repeated, a realization dawning on me. "Let you go . . . to heaven?"

She nodded her head ever so slightly, again mouthing those three words.

I paused to choose my words carefully before continuing. "I'm *not* going to let you go to heaven just yet. It's not time for that. We've got a home. We live there together. I'm going to take you back there when this is all over."

I squeezed her hand and stared into her eyes. She returned my gaze for a moment before closing her eyes and quietly shaking her head "No."

Liz was convinced she would never see that home again, and I had doubts, too. As the bitter reality washed over me, I wept.

CHAPTER **13**

The next morning Liz had stabilized to the point that the Critical Care docs were working on getting her back off the ventilator. An infectious disease doctor told Tim at bedside that morning that fluid taken from Liz's abdomen had grown a common bacterium, E. coli, which was the apparent source of the septic episode and shock that Liz had experienced the previous day. She was responding to antibiotics and large amounts of IV fluid, but the volume of the latter was compromising her respiratory status. She was indeed very fragile and prone to going into shock. Randy, who had nicknamed Liz "the tigress of fragility," was heavily involved in the care plan that day. In the end he recommended that Liz stay on the ventilator that night to allow her to be safely sedated and kept calm.

Tim noted that afternoon that his mom was "lightly" awake and responsive, nodding in answer to questions and opening her eyes at times. Tim spoke highly of Liz's nurse Kory, who was "unbelievably nice and responsive." She reminded Tim of Joleen from Butterworth, which was high praise indeed. By the time I arrived at around 6:00 that evening, Liz was sedated, though still quite anxious. She was asking persistently for ice chips but was not allowed these, as she was still hooked up to a ventilator; nor did she get her wish to have the restraints taken off her wrists; these, I think, though necessary, increased her anxiety. Tim brought his twins down for a visit, which always picked up Grandma Liz.

After that, the Critical Care service encouraged me to go home, as they had some evening plans for Liz, which included an abdominal ultrasound and the possibility of a procedure involving tapping fluid from her abdomen (paracentesis). The large volumes of IV fluid given the previous day had, because of her advanced liver disease, created a massive amount of ascites (fluid) in her abdomen, and this was now interfering with the flexibility of the diaphragm, compromising her breathing and the possibility of getting Liz off the ventilator. I was reluctant to go home under those circumstances, but Tim assured me she would be alright and that the morrow would bring improvement.

Jackie concurred. "Go home and rest."

Before I left, I was told that "Dr. O" was going to do the tap. This was confusing to me.

"I asked if she was from IR (interventional radiology), and they said no," I texted to the kids that night. "Critical Care and the Emergency Department. It seems odd that a Critical Care doc is doing the tap. It's like Dr. House doing a brain biopsy."

The tap was not without risk of complication, and I was nervous.

"Why don't you go home?" Tim suggested again. "I'll come down and spend some time with Mom in the morning."

I appreciated this but expressed my concern that all the time he was spending with his mom might create resentment at his work. Tim reassured me that, as a principal, he had always excused staff for family concerns and would be failing as a leader if he didn't follow that practice in his own situation.

I hope your school board agrees, I thought.

In the end, I stayed well past midnight, until the procedure was completed, and had another short night of rest. I was beginning to believe myself when I told my kids that eating and sleeping are more discretionary than we think they are.

Friday, February 12, started out well, with Tim reporting that his mom was listening to soothing music and was the most relaxed he had seen her. Tamara texted her encouragement, and I was delighted to see the involvement she maintained in her family-to-be. It was a calm afternoon, topped off when Jackie sent a picture of a wide-awake Isaiah with a feeding tube in his nose and a hint of a smile on his face. The accompanying text read, "This guy just took his whole feed . . . He's kind of a big deal in the NICU." Of course, Jackie's siblings took that literally, since Isaiah was, in reality, four times as big as his neighbor in the next isolette.

When I arrived back on H2, I found that one of our new "nurse heroes," Kory, was taking care of Liz that day. In the course of our conversation, I learned that this impressive lady was a champion speed skater in her other life. Kory had broken several national age records in the sport the previous year and had been named Michigan Female Athlete of the Year in 2015. It was amazing to me in talking to our nurses at various times how accomplished so many of them were in several fascinating outside interests, while we family members saw them exclusively as expert caregivers.

Kory and I discovered that we had a mutual bond in that our family had also participated in a competitive winter sport, luging, although not on the level she had achieved in skating. Years ago, as a Californian transplant to Michigan, I had begun to realize that I would have to develop some outdoor winter interests to make an otherwise long, cold season something I could look forward to. In addition to taking my grade school children skiing regularly, I stumbled onto the sport of luging, which I found out was available "right in our back yard," so to speak.

A Christian friend of ours, Sue Boklaga, was responsible for oversight of some juvenile offenders from a youth compound in nearby Muskegon, Michigan, the home of the Winter Sports Complex. This was comprised of a skating rink, a cross-country ski course, and one of only three luge tracks in the United States at that time. Sue brought her "kids," and I brought mine to try the sport of luging, and soon the lot of them were participating in a Tuesday evening youth league.

A year later Sue and I were officially coaches and enjoying a truly exciting and entertaining winter sport. I participated in luging with varying numbers of my kids from 1991 until Mark, my youngest, quit to play school basketball in 2007. As far as sports competition goes, participation in this sport was one of the highlights of my life, and it changed the perspective of winter for all of us. Instead of dreading our bitter winters, we looked forward to the coldest evenings, when we could count on hard ice and a fast track.

That involvement took us to the Lake Placid Olympic luge track in upstate New York during two different winters, where my kids and I got to participate on a larger and faster version of our own track. It also led to some fame—and infamy—for our family when we visited the Olympic Sports Complex one year during the time of the Winter Olympics. Because the United States Olympic team was away from the complex for the winter games at that time, our little Muskegon group was allowed to bunk in the Olympic Training Center for our four-day stay. This brought immediate benefits, as the Training Center table was set each day with a plethora of delicious food: prime rib or salmon tonight? Which of these gourmet desserts?

I bunked in a very nice room with two coaches from another club, along with a number of youth lugers scattered in the rooms around us, including three of my own kids and eight juvenile offenders of similar ages with whom we had traveled from Muskegon. Unfortunately for the coaches, the cafeteria was open for virtually all hours of the day and late into the evening. In our fatherly wisdom, we coaches thought it wise to establish a rule that no youths be allowed off the floor without first coming to get a coach to go with them. After a steady string of knocks on our door that first night and trips accompanying wide-eyed boys for a late-night foray to the cafeteria, the policy was changed, allowing the boys to go down on their own in groups.

The culmination of our stay came on our last night in the Training Center, when the Olympic luge team returned home from the Olympics earlier than expected but bearing some of the first ever medals won by US lugers—silver and bronze in the double's competition. Several of us coaches were lounging in the lobby at that time, and when we realized the import of the moment we made a quick executive decision to abolish curfew for the night and called the youth lugers down. I'm not sure who was more excited, the thundering horde of starry-eyed teenagers or the medaled Olympians who now unexpectedly stood as heroes in the eyes of that adoring young crowd around them. They graciously let the young lugers try on their medals and patiently stood for a seemingly endless number of photos with those kids. It was a truly heartwarming moment for a father.

The fame? Olympic fever was burning hot (cold?) that year, so the local TV station had asked Sue Boklaga and me if they could send along a sportscaster and television crew to feature stories about our daily adventures on the track, as well as some nightly interviews with our young protégés. My kids gained significant, if fleeting, fame in the Grand Rapids area as Olympic Complex lugers, and my colleagues at work learned another side of me that for the most part had been unknown.

The infamy? My kids and I spent the next three or four weeks patiently answering the same question over and over: no, they were not juvenile delinquents. (I should have seen that coming.) As I mentioned, winter sports participation was a nice bond between Kory and our family; she had gone out to Muskegon just two weeks earlier for her own first experience with luging.

———————

That Friday afternoon I pulled up Liz's recent labs on her patient portal and was dismayed to see a drop in her hemoglobin of more than a full point over the past day and a significantly elevated white blood cell count. Scarier still was a prothrombin time (PT, a measure of the clotting ability of the blood) that likely reflected poor liver function. Most alarming, though, was evidence that her kidneys were not functioning well. Her blood urea nitrogen and creatinine levels were elevated, and I found out from Kory that Liz had produced almost no urine all day long.

After further investigation, I discovered that the amount of abdominal fluid removed the previous night had been 6½ liters, which seemed exorbitant to me. *No wonder she has blood pressure and kidney issues today.*

When I texted Randy this news, he insisted that I had it wrong—that it was likely only 650 milliliters, not 6500 milliliters (we found later that it was indeed 6500 milliliters). I had a feeling there was going to be a price to pay for this and that Liz would be the one to pay it.

Tim challenged me, "Is Mom calm and stable? Stop looking at the portal for now! Let's trust Randy's critical care experience." I appreciated Tim's effort to calm his dad's fears.

"She's pretty calm," I said. "She does open her eyes at times. Responds occasionally to questions. Once in a while mouths 'Help!' Sorry about the portal stuff; doctors are all about numbers."

I paused, then couldn't resist saying, "Wonder what their cutoff is for blood transfusion. Got to be approaching it."

Jamie had flown home to Virginia that morning; already I was missing his steady clinical approach and dry humor. In the background a radio was playing a song, "What if your blessings come through raindrops." Quite appropriate.

Mark happened to come home that afternoon from his student rental house to spend the weekend with me. We were chatting that evening in our living room about his plans to go to medical school, something he had focused on for many years. Indeed, to this day I have a drawing Mark had made as a first grader, not much more than a stick figure dressed in some doctor paraphernalia under the words, "When I grow up I'm going to be . . . a doctor."

Mark had worked hard in college to maintain the requisite high grade point average and had also studied thoroughly and scored quite well on the Medical College Admission Test. He had been to a number of medical school interviews and was now waiting hopefully to hear good news of admission, certainly not a given in a very competitive process. He had already been declined for receiving an interview at one or two schools, so we didn't take for granted that he was going to be accepted to medical school somewhere. In fact, we were talking about alternative plans when, at that very moment, his phone rang with an East Lansing number noted on the caller ID.

"I think this is Michigan State!" he announced excitedly but with a tinge of anxiety in his voice.

From the smile on his face and his silent fist pumping, I knew he was hearing the good news we had been hoping for. Neither of us could contain our excitement as he hung up that call to say, "I've been accepted at State!" There followed a scene of pandemonium, of two grown men jumping around, hugging, and laughing like children at a birthday party. I don't know how many high fives we gave each other or how many times we reflected, "I can't believe it . . . Can you believe it?!"

One of the two Michigan State Medical School campuses was right across Michigan Avenue from the Spectrum Butterworth campus, meaning that Mark and his soon-to-be bride would be able to stay home in Grand Rapids for the next four years. This was very favorable news for the young couple and for their parents as well. As we settled down finally, it occurred to me how sad it was that Mark's mother was not there to share in this good news, a thought that came to me often regarding family events during that long ordeal. Mark was able to tell his mother directly the next day, but how much of the message she understood we couldn't know for sure.

CHAPTER 14

"We're going to turn off her Propofol," the nurse told me when I arrived the following morning. *No more sedation.*

I nodded and sighed, anticipating a restless day with lots of anxiety. And lots of pleading for "help."

As Liz slumbered away through the morning, I checked my phone and noticed the date. February 13 was something of an anniversary for Liz and me, in that it marked the anniversary of the first date we'd had when we were classmates at Calvin College. Maybe that wasn't a big deal, but I was happy for any cause to celebrate. Our fortieth wedding anniversary was still more than three months away, and I was fearful we weren't going to see that one together.

I thought back to the time when I had arrived at Calvin College (now University) as an 18-year-old student. Like many incoming freshmen, I was an emotionally immature undergraduate seeking entertainment and attention . . . and hopefully a girlfriend. Alice Cooper's "Eighteen," a ballad about the transition of youth into adulthood, hit the airwaves that year, aptly describing my own state.

"I'm a boy and I'm a man. I'm eighteen and I like it!"

The freshman talent show was by then a longstanding Calvin tradition held annually on the small island in the middle of what was known as the Seminary Pond. It was open to any intrepid freshmen students willing to display their personal talent. My close friend Bob Van Noord and I realized that this offered a great opportunity to pursue a bit of notoriety, if not fame. I had grown up with Bob in California, and he currently lived in Noordewier Hall with me. The fact that we had no notable abilities worthy of display was not going to prevent us from this pursuit.

First, we found two ordinary kitchen brooms that we cut to size to fit into some borrowed guitar cases. Inspired by the long-playing Everly Brothers, we signed up for the show as the "Noordewier Brothers." After practicing for an hour or so, we were ready for our date with fame.

That evening, after we had walked out on the boardwalk to the island to face our audience, I remember being unable to see anything except a wall of bright light in front of us. Intimidating, but the show had to go on. We played our hearts out, guitar-style, on those sawn-off brooms, the microphone nicely picking up the catchy rhythm we had arranged that afternoon (or so we thought). We were enthusiastically received, as I recall, but it took several months to live down that stunt.

The following afternoon, as I was lounging with a few friends on the front steps of our dorm, hoping to chat up girls coming back from class to our sister dorm, Vander Werp Hall, three young ladies who were passing by stopped.

"Hey, you're one of the Noordewier Brothers!" one of them called out.

Suddenly the anonymity of the night before vanished. Individual faces were no longer concealed behind a wall of light. Now in the company of these girls, I felt awkward. No—I felt embarrassed. But there was no denying the fact that I was indeed one of those Noordewier Brothers, and I wondered about the significance of their giggling when I admitted to that. As we made our introductions, I was particularly impressed with a tall, attractive blond.

"I'm Liz Werner."

Maybe this was not the world's best introduction to a girl. But it got worse.

"Are you guys the 'Official Noordewier Welcoming Committee'?" Liz asked us.

My heart sank, and I'm sure my face turned several shades of red. I found myself speechless, only offering up a very weak smile.

Two days earlier, Bob Van Noord and I had swiped the Vander Werp Hall phone directory from the shared front desk for the two dorms. We had proceeded to call every girl in Vander Werp Hall listed as a freshman and, identifying ourselves as the said "Welcoming Committee," had helpfully offered ourselves for any advice or assistance we could provide. We were very well received, for the most part, which might not have been the case if those female students had known that we were just freshmen like themselves. We hadn't really thought out what the consequences might be when we were identified by those same girls as fellow newbies—as was now the case.

I sensed a bit of outrage in these girls, perhaps mixed with some admiration of our intrepid effort. I think that Liz, in particular, appreciated our creativity. She and I soon became close friends. I had found out early on that she still had a high school boyfriend of several years, which to me was an unassailable barrier to a relationship beyond that.

At that time the Calvin dining halls had a dinner arrangement called "family style," requiring all students to eat together at the same time each evening. Moreover, at dinnertime, each eight-person table had to have a mix of men and women, which usually resulted in a combination of students from the paired men's and women's dormitories. Sharing a mutual group of friends, Liz and I ended up sitting together at the same table most evenings, which strengthened the growing bond between us.

More than dinnertime conversations, I believe that what really cemented our relationship were the near-nightly games of Rook, a card game popular at that time. These were most often held in the basement of the women's dorm and necessitated two-person partnerships engaged in brisk competition. Within a few weeks Liz and I had formed a nightly Rook team that, in my memory, was one of the winningest partnerships that first semester.

Thinking back to those early days of Liz and me being a nightly Rook team brought a smile to my lips in the hospital room. Liz often tells people that she and I grew close by "cheating at Rook" together. By way of explanation—and defense—I must note that the card deck we used was well worn, making it possible to identify many of the cards from the back side. I'm not sure any other teams recognized—or made use of—this advantage to the extent we did. I don't feel it was cheating as much as taking full advantage of the resources provided to us.

Through the first semester of that freshman year, Liz and I became very close friends short of romantic interest, much like a relationship you might encounter on a sitcom like *Boy Meets World*. This changed, however, over the first month after I had returned from spending the Christmas/New Year holidays with my family in California. I made plans to come back from those holidays early, for reasons I no longer recall. I had arranged to stay at the home of the family of Liz's best friend and dormmate, Marcia, until the dorms reopened a few days later. Abashedly, I'll have to admit that my attraction to Marcia, who was unencumbered by a boyfriend at that time, might have had something to do with my early return.

On the eve of my return, I received a call from a very sick-sounding Marcia, who informed me that she was quite ill with a cough and respiratory infection but had arranged for me to stay with Liz's family instead. I was conflicted about this new plan, as I had always respected Liz's relationship with her boyfriend. But I really had no alternative at that point, so to Liz's house I went. While there, I became very fond of her family, including the start of a special close friendship with her dad—unbeknownst to me, my future father-in-law.

It was somewhat of an awkward stay, as I think Liz and I both started to sense that our "best friend relationship" might be evolving into something more than that. Liz had a date with said boyfriend on one of those nights, and I spent an enjoyable evening with her parents and younger sisters. (Ironically, her next younger sister, Jean, took me on something of a date a week later to a high school basketball game.)

Back in the dorms, Liz began to let me know there were some differences developing in her relationship with her boyfriend. She told me much later that my growing friendship with her had not affected her fraying relationship with her boyfriend, but more that the fraying enhanced our own growing attachment. I hope that's true because I had met her boyfriend a few times and thought he was a good guy. While I obviously benefitted from their breakup, I would not want to have been the cause of it.

On February 12 Liz called to tell me that she had broken up with her boyfriend that evening because of something that had been to her "the last straw" (which I don't feel at liberty to identify). She was extremely upset, and I spent some time consoling her, mostly just listening. I wondered what this might mean for us, but I obviously was not going to explore it that night.

The following night, the evening before Valentine's Day, Liz and I were in the basement of the women's dorm with a group of friends when Liz started motioning with her head that she wanted to go somewhere. I was too naïve (she says "ignorant") to fathom what her intentions were, but when she eventually excused herself, I waited for a few discreet moments before following her up to the dorm lobby. There she told me to go to my room. where she would meet me in a few minutes, it being a Sunday night when there were visiting hours for the usually restricted dorm. (I don't know why we felt we had to keep our relationship covert, but we tried to do so for several weeks after that.) I walked up to my room and sat on my bed waiting for Liz to join me, unsure of what to expect next.

After months of being close friends with no romance, I wasn't sure what Liz's intentions actually were—as happens so often when "the guy is the last to know." Liz slipped through the door just a few minutes after me and came over to sit next to me on the bed. I was uncertain of her expectations of me at that moment, but I remember to this day thinking I had never fully realized until that instance how beautiful she was to me. The awkward pause lasted for only a few moments.

"I'm tired of being good," I finally said, leaning over to embrace her and give her a kiss.

What followed was an evening of talking about what our relationship was and would be, along with a few kisses, as many as we dared with the door ajar per dorm visitation rules. I clearly remember what Liz told me: "I tend to stick with a guy; I think I'm going to marry you."

While this frank statement might have scared many other young men, I thought she was right . . . and, after all, why *wouldn't* you want to marry your best friend?

To our children who have always wondered what our first date was like, I'm sorry to disappoint you. My only defense is to say that, in the history of first dates, I doubt there were many that were more loving than this one. The love we shared that night continued to grow throughout our dating years in college; throughout our married years after that; and, indeed, even now these many years later. On every anniversary card I've given to Liz, I've written the words, "More than yesterday, less than tomorrow."

I think—I hope—that's the way of most Christian marriages.

So many tomorrows later, I quietly sat beside Liz's bedside, holding her hand and wishing I could be back on that first date. She slumbered away through the morning and afternoon as the effects of the discontinued sedation lingered in her consciousness, rendering futile the efforts to wean her from the ventilator that day.

The next morning, Valentine's Day, while I was going through my usual Sunday routine of finishing my rounds early in the morning in time to go to church and lead my adult Sunday school class, Randy stopped by to see Liz and texted out a very encouraging note: "Liz looks great. All numbers look good. They are working on weaning."

By 5:00 that afternoon, though, she had developed a fever once again, a recurring afternoon pattern, and was receiving Tylenol and extra pain medications while having blood cultures drawn once again. This was discouraging, and when Tim asked me how to encourage people to pray specifically that night, I suggested, "I guess getting rid of the fevers and hopefully making some progress getting off the ventilator. Most importantly, improved responsiveness."

I should have known that Tim had something up his sleeve.

After a visit from Laura and our granddaughter Kathryn, during which Liz, in her somnolent state, didn't give so much as an acknowledgment of their presence, it was Mark and Tamara's turn that evening, along with Brek. Arriving at 7:00 p.m., they didn't have much better luck until just after Brek left at 9:00 p.m., when Mark relayed the news: "Mom just gave Dad a kiss and kissed his hand, too! It was really nice to see."

This turned out to be one of the most remarkable answers to pray since the accident, not so much in the scope of response but in the proximity of God's answer to a major outpouring of prayer. Right away Tim replied, "WOW!! Tyler just prayed for this a minute ago and texted me."

Tyler is the son of Dave and Camille Van Dyk, who had brought the now famous food basket that had followed Liz from room to room since the first days at Butterworth. Jamie followed up with another comment.

"Just had my community group praying. They were all emotional about the story."

"Really cool," I texted everyone. "I've been sitting here since 12:30, and now it's so worth it."

One of the neatest texts of all was from Brek: "Shoot, I left just in time to miss out on the Valentine's Day PDA" (public display of affection, for the uninitiated), "but I can't say I haven't been praying. I take life for granted too often, so it's amazing how adversity can ultimately strengthen our personal relationships with God."

I had to admit that there were obvious spiritual benefits from all that we were going through for those who were praying with and for us.

One of the most amazing demonstrations of God's love and faithfulness throughout all of this came when I opened my emails the following day to find numerous pictures of family and friends from the previous evening. They were all wearing baseball-style "rally caps" in response to Tim's 5:00 p.m. mass request for virtually everyone we knew to rally in prayer for his mother to wake up and acknowledge his dad's presence at her bedside on that Valentine's Day.

Most precious of all was the photo from Tim's friend Amy Gordon, with her teenage son Will wearing a crazy cap and giving a "thumbs up"; this touching picture of the young boy with Down's Syndrome was especially endearing to Tim and Laura, who have their own two special needs boys with autism. It showed that anyone can come to the throne of God in prayer and be heard. All of those smiling pictures of our loved ones wearing caps sideways, backward, and inside out were a testimony to the faithfulness of God's people lifting us up in prayer—and to God's even more faithful answer.

February 14 was one of those good days that helped carry us through our long ordeal. There had been ups and downs, with plenty of downs, but this day had definitely been an up. And it ended with the promise of another tomorrow.

CHAPTER 15

We became a family bound together by texts and prayers. And prayers and texts.

February 15

"I'm going home tomorrow" the caption read below a picture of Isaiah with a smirk on his face.

"Sweet news that one of 'the sleepers' is finally going home," I replied.

After discovering that Liz's critical labs were stable for a third day in a row and that her blood protein levels were rising (a very good thing), I arrived later to find Liz up in a chair, off the ventilator, and on a trach mask, undergoing physical therapy. Her Fentanyl IV drip had been turned off, which was reassuring to see, considering Randy's concern about opioid use. I was delighted to send out a text.

"Mom woke up suddenly and started mouthing words. She's not happy, but she's all there. She got put back on the ventilator for the night to let her rest. She's agitated and saying she has pain and got some meds for that. So, she's not happy, but I am."

Later that night Tim texted, "Mom mouthed 'amen' when I prayed over her tonight!!" He posted an image of a sunset with the words, "I'm not afraid of tomorrow because I know God is already there." Those words were in my thoughts as I went to bed that night, alone . . . but not really.

February 16

The day began with a picture of a sleeping Isaiah in a car seat over the words, "We busted out of baby jail!"

Despite the excitement and congratulatory family responses, the day consisted of sleepiness and minimal interaction on Liz's part. It was a scary day for me because of Liz's continued poor urine production, carrying through a trend from the previous Friday. Although her blood "kidney numbers" had remained stubbornly elevated, our critical care doc was encouraging. He told me that the poor kidney function was likely ATN, acute tubular necrosis, the result of shock (low blood pressure) on the kidneys. In Liz's case, the doctor felt that the shock had been from the E. coli septic episode she had sustained the previous week and was likely compounded by a blood pressure drop from the aggressive paracentesis (removal of abdominal fluid) the following day.

"The large majority of these episodes resolve on their own as the kidney rebuilds its damaged tubules," he tried to assure me. "I don't think dialysis is going to be necessary."

His use of the "d" word frightened me; I had to admit that the thought had been lurking in the back of my mind, but now it was out in the open. I had been reluctant to think or talk about it because that would be an admission of one more of Liz's vital organs going down, widening her already frightening constellation of multiple system organ failure (MSOF), an entity whereby each new organ insult significantly increases the likelihood of the death of the patient.

At the same time, a check of Liz's blood gases showed that her CO2 (carbon dioxide) concentration was on the high side of normal, a manifestation of respiratory failure. These were discouraging events to text out—two major organ systems down on the same day, although this was not technically the case. The organs had likely been down for a while, and we were just now identifying the nature of those insults. Despite my fatigue, I lay awake in bed that night for some time, worrying about the day's findings and pleading with God to even yet spare the life of the bride whom I was missing so desperately that night.

February 17

"Now I know why she's so restful (aka, noninteractive)," I texted first thing that morning. "They drew arterial blood gases and found her pCO2 was 60 and pH 7.25. So not breathing well and being put back on the ventilator now. Very disappointing after having been off since yesterday morning. Also told her blood sugars have been high. Sneaking suspicion she's getting septic again."

Elevated CO2 (carbon dioxide) levels cause a syndrome known as carbon dioxide narcosis, usually seen in patients with COPD who are being given supplemental oxygen to breathe. It is usually manifested by somnolence and coma. While this is not technically what Liz had at this point, the effects of the elevated CO2 were similar: severe somnolence caused by poor respiratory ability, which in turn compromised her breathing effort even further.

"Does Randy know?" Jamie texted.

"Don't think so," I replied. "They're getting Dikin involved. He's good. No fevers today, and white count under 10,000 yet."

After being mechanically ventilated for an hour or so, Liz began to open her eyes a bit but otherwise remained unresponsive. Dr. Dikin addressed my anxiety by telling me that this situation happens in the face of multiple physical insults such as Liz had experienced, making it harder to keep a patient permanently off the ventilator. He surmised that the 36 hours she had been off the ventilator had been just too long for her at this point. He noted that it had taken only an hour or so of being on the ventilator to "blow off" the extra CO_2, so there were likely other factors than just CO_2 level that were contributing to Liz's somnolence.

Tim came down that evening after his kids were in bed and again stayed at his mom's bedside overnight, until he had to head to work early the next morning. This allowed me to spend a much-needed evening at home to catch up on a lot of "homework" about which I had been procrastinating.

February 18

"I had to give a phone consent for another belly tap at 9:00 this morning."

Though I didn't enjoy having to give my kids updates like this at the start of each day, I was thankful we had the means by which to communicate regularly and effectively. I had been reluctant to move forward with this measure for Liz because I knew there would again be a price to pay, and the kidneys were the organs that would most likely pay that price. Dr. Dikin was aware of this risk, but he felt that the need to reduce the pressure of the fluid-laden abdomen on the diaphragms to allow the lungs to work better was paramount. Every physician is aware that often the treatment of one medical problem will have unintended but anticipated complications with regard to other body functions. I let my kids know why: "It was to relieve pressure on her breathing so they can get and keep her off the vent. Pray that it goes well with no complications."

After tapping off another 6½ liters of fluid from Liz's abdomen, her CO_2 improved modestly to 58, still quite a bit above the normal value of 40, but the ICU staff was able to get Liz off the ventilator again by 11:00 a.m. Once again, the physician side of me began to think the worst and communicate that via a text.

"I have no idea how to explain the CO_2 and pH. It's what you see in a smoker with bad emphysema. This is very concerning. Where did it come from? Is it fixable? I'm waiting to talk to one of the docs."

Randy called me that morning and explained that the respiratory failure was related to Liz's extremely debilitated state and that she should be kept off the ventilator for shorter periods of time each day, while allowing her time on the ventilator at night to rest. While he was still optimistic, Randy did mention the possibility of having to move her to a ventilator-dependent rehabilitation unit to get Liz permanently off the ventilator, although he hoped that wouldn't be necessary. Little did I know that it would take several months to get to the bottom of this ongoing respiratory issue.

By evening Liz's mental status had improved a bit more. When Tim's five-year-old twins came to visit their Grandma Liz, she was able to respond, if ever so slightly. There was a tender moment when Nolan, the little guy with nonverbal autism, spontaneously approached his grandma and gave her a kiss. Whether Liz was aware of that kiss or not, we didn't know, but there were more than a few moist eyes among family and staff that evening.

February 19

"They took her off the ventilator again."

The back and forth of ventilator status made us all leery of getting too excited over this progression any longer. Instead, we were dealing with a thorny issue that almost all families of longer-stay hospitalized patients eventually must address: placement. After consultation with the Critical Care team, I looked to my family for support.

"Critical Care (Lindsey, PA) is presenting the option of going to the Long-Term Acute Care (LTAC) floor. It's here in the hospital on 5 Main, but it is its own independent facility. They say it would be similar to here but with more rehab potential. All the same docs. I presume the downside is there's no Critical Care there. I spoke today with Dr. Iskander, Spectrum's Critical Care director. He told me he's had several patients like Mom also go to Mary Free Bed, even with ventilators.

"Mom is currently on a T-piece, not a ventilator. Not sure she'd need a ventilator again. I asked Lindsey to check into the Free Bed possibility as well. I'd like to hear your opinion on this. Someone is coming to talk to me this afternoon about these options. Since it's Friday, this may not happen until Monday. Thanks. Would love to have someone listen with me this afternoon and maybe go tour LTAC with me. At this point, I'd prefer Mary Free Bed, but I'm trying to remain open."

Jamie thought that both options sounded reasonable but wanted to go with whatever Randy thought; I let him know that I had copied my text to him.

Jackie had some concerns that the staff at Free Bed might not be able to handle all her mom's needs at this point, but Laura wanted to know definitively that Liz could eventually be transferred to Mary Free Bed if we opted for LTAC now.

Lindsey had assured me that that this outcome was possible and that she didn't anticipate a very long stay at LTAC before the transition could be made to Mary Free Bed.

Laura at this point agreed that she didn't feel Liz was ready for Mary Free Bed yet.

Jamie, always the wordsmith, asked all of us a question: "Anyone else think there's a contradiction in a 'short time in the long-term acute care?' Short, long, acute."

I had to laugh at that comment.

"When you're six weeks to the day (actually to the minute right now) into it, you realize that all those terms are relative," I replied.

Jamie noted, though, that his mom was exactly the type of patient who would have been sent to LTAC when he was a resident in training (attending ophthalmologists not usually being much involved in inpatient care).

When the decision was finally made, I texted, "Case Manager (Sandy) was just by. She says they won't take a ventilator patient at Mary Free Bed, so that's out." (This policy was to change later that year, but too late for us.) "She said LTAC is considered a separate hospital, but you keep all the same docs (definitely not true of Spectrum's LTAC over in the old Kent Community Hospital—I declined that option). She is going to make the referral. It won't happen until early next week."

I wasn't the only one who had misgivings about this decision.

"Is she stable enough for LTAC?" Jackie asked. "She just had that CO2 issue yesterday and a blood pressure scare last week."

I tried to reassure my kids (and maybe myself a little bit as well) after visiting the unit. "I think so. I just toured the unit with their liaison, Nicole. It's very nice, and they have ventilator capability. Nicole says their respiratory therapists are very experienced and do a lot of work with decannulating." This meant getting people off the vent and their tracheal tubes out.

"Nicole says they make all the recommendations to the pulmonary doctors. Also, we'd still have the Mary Free Bed therapists up there, and they have a gym. We can go look at it again any time."

I think that my reassuring text started to alleviate the remaining fears my kids had. Laura commented, "Sounds like that might be a good option for Mom. I'm guessing Tim would love to take a look this weekend." All of this was predicated on Liz maintaining a stable clinical progression—which, of course, had not been the case so far.

That evening turned out to be no exception, as I had to text out a heart-rending message:

"I hate to be a downer. Her kidneys are punking out now. Her legs are massive. She had another hypotensive episode tonight and is back on norepinephrine" (a blood pressure-raising med). "I don't think she's going to make it. I think her body is giving up. I've texted Randy; maybe he has an idea. She looks steadily worse to me."

Tim the Tenderheart was soon down at his mom's bedside and finally convinced me a little after midnight to go home to bed, since I had to work the next morning. A short while later Tim texted the family.

"I'm sleeping at the hospital tonight. Pray that Mom's blood pressure goes back up and that we see healing tonight. Pray that Dad is able to get some rest tonight. Mark will be sleeping over there. Love you, Dad—you and Mom are both amazing."

I wept that night until I finally fell asleep.

February 20

After Jamie sent out an early status request, Tim gave a quick reply.

"Mom's urine output remains low. She is calm and alert. Just spoke with the critical care doc a bit ago. Current plan: they are giving albumin (fluid with proteins). The hope is that this will fill in the blood vessels to improve her pressure (she's currently dehydrated because fluid keeps going out into the skin/open areas instead of staying in the blood). Once they get the albumin in, they will use

Lasix (a diuretic) to try to pull the new fluid into her bloodstream and through her kidneys."

This was a layman's description of a frightening constellation that anyone with critical care experience must deal with at some time. Tim assured us that, "Randy is monitoring and available if anything changes and if a fragile decision is needed at all throughout the day." I could only assume that Tim's "fragile decision" meant the ultimate decision when it came time to move Liz to "comfort care."

As I had a short patient list that weekend, I was able to get down to Liz's room early those two days and join Tim in a grim bedside vigil, watching for any positive sign of a potential turnaround.

February 21

On Sunday evening, after a hopeful day following several days of seeing virtually zero urine production, I sent out my last text.

"There's urine in the tube tonight!! Not a lot, but some. This is an answer to prayer. Tell everyone who's praying and ask them to please continue."

Obviously, the kidneys had taken another hit with the recent massive abdominal tap, but we were still hopeful at this point that they could be salvaged. Unfortunately, that hope was predicated on the current treatment, which consisted of pouring intravenous albumin and fluid back into her depleted vascular system, much of which would be leaking back into the abdominal compartment from which fluid had just been drained, again compromising the downward movement of the diaphragms and the related respiratory status.

The cycle continued. But at least Liz was still alive at the end of a long and frightful week.

CHAPTER 16

"Star-crossed owls' love story is like Nicholas Sparks novel."

The headline in the February 22, 2016, *Grand Rapids Press* caught mye eye that Monday morning. The article reported the story of Katherine, a Great Horned owl being kept at the Blandford Nature Center, a nature preserve less than a mile from our home on the West side of the city. The center was caring for this regal bird because of a broken wing that couldn't be rehabilitated. While Katherine the Great lived alone in her pen at the center, she had not been forgotten by her mate, who remained in the wild.

"She can hear his hoots as he watches her from a nearby tree and catches a glimpse of him as he swoops over her fenced enclosure," the article stated. "He occasionally leaves her gifts of rodents to dine on."

True love.

"These star-crossed birds are Great Horned owls, which usually mate for life." But Katelyn Nettler, the education program associate for Blandford, explained that they were destined to be apart for life because of the injury and federal law.

"It's kind of like the Nicholas Sparks novel for owls," Katelyn mused.

Since Katherine the Great's wing could not be rehabilitated, she would never be strong enough to fly to catch food or to escape a predator, so releasing her would be a death sentence. As federal law mandates, only injured animals can live at Blandford, so Katherine's mate could not join her. Further, since mating permits from the U.S. Department of Wildlife and Fish were given out only for rare species, even if the male owl were to be injured and placed in the nature center, he could still not join her in the same cage. Destined to live apart for life, this loyal male owl had been faithfully attending his mate through the mesh of the cage since her injury in 1991, already 25 years.

This amazing story resonated with me as I came back day after day to my injured wife's bedside. I had actually observed that noble male bird several times sitting in a dead snag of a tree as I daily made my way past the intersection where Elmridge Road dead-ended into Blandford Nature Center property. Now I knew why. Although my own experience at this point had encompassed only a little over six weeks, I felt that it echoed that of this poor owl. While the story made me feel lonely, especially at night, I also found it strangely comforting. I shared this with my family, who appreciated the similarities to our own situation. They shared the article with other relatives and friends, and soon my bedside vigil became known as the owl watch. For months, as I kissed my wife goodnight each evening, I would mutter the following words:

"Owls mate for life."

Maybe it was just a silly saying, but for us it expressed how we felt about our situation.

The name Paauw, like many in West Michigan, is Dutch; it translates to "peacock" in English. It had apparently been a noble name in the 17th century; one of our early ancestors had owned much of the southern part of the New York/New Jersey area, including Staten Island. While certainly wishing that Staten Island had remained in the ancestral holdings, our family did not manifest much in the way of nobility, but we did embrace the meaning of our name. Peacock doormats, ceramics, and knick knacks dotted our homes, and I suspect a few of our daughters-in-law grew weary of the peacock brand into which they had married. Now, however, owl-adorned paraphernalia began to pop up, first on get-well cards and then in more substantial items, continuing in our home to this day. We may be peacocks by name, but we are owls at heart.

As far as Liz's course that Monday, I sent out an early morning text plea: "We need to be much in prayer today for better kidney function. Mom's kidneys are putting out about 15 ml/hour today." Sixty milliliters per hour is considered the lowest end of normal kidney function.

"She has a massive amount of extra fluid in her body and needs to be putting out ten times that amount or more. The extra fluid is the biggest concern today. Also, her doctors are planning to tap off fluid around her right lung today. Pray that this goes well and without complications, getting off a beneficial amount of fluid."

"Dialysis?" Jamie asked.

Dr. Goushaw, a nephrologist, had indeed been consulted that day to address Liz's fading kidney function. He turned out to be one of the most gracious and reassuring clinicians I had ever met. After hearing his report, I let my kids know the following news:

"The kidney doc just came by; one of the kindest physicians I've met. For the medical people he says this is acute tubular necrosis (ATN); the kidneys are heavily shocked. He sees no indication for hemodialysis (HD) at this time. Her electrolytes are good. She has no acidosis that would harm the lungs and necessitate HD. He says ATN almost always improves, 75% of the time completely and most of the rest of the time partially. If recovery is delayed, HD may become necessary, but he likens the situation to a cast for a broken bone—when the bone is healed, the cast comes off. He says that when the kidneys start to work again in a situation like this, they can't concentrate the urine very well, so the patient loses a large volume of water, which would be a good thing for Mom. This doc was so kind and encouraging; I think God sent him to me in a time of great need."

My kids were also much encouraged by this report. Jamie gave me a great suggestion to send a note of thanks to Dr. Goushaw and his supervisor. "I've always appreciated when patient or family has taken time to do that," Jamie pointed out.

Unfortunately, in the press and the urgency of that week, I neglected to do that, and it eventually became impossible to do anyway, as Dr. Goushaw became ill himself and had to leave his practice. I can only hope that he might someday read this story. If you do, Dr. Goushaw, thank you so much for the kindness you showed in the middle of that very dark time. You were a godsend to us.

Later that day Liz had a liter of fluid removed from around the right lung. We were told that it would take a day or so for the lung to expand into that newly opened space but that we might need to repeat the procedure at a future date.

Unfortunately, by the next day her kidney function was worse.

"Mom's kidneys are still pretty shocked," I texted to everybody. "After a lengthy talk with the kidney doc, we decided to proceed with hemodialysis (HD). This is a temporary measure to clear blood toxins until the kidneys start working better again. Dr. Goushaw reassures me that they will, but sometimes this takes several weeks. The kidneys must literally regrow cells to repair themselves.

"The main risk of HD is having to place a new central venous catheter, which adds a risk of infection. Benefits of HD are that it protects the lungs from acid buildup and other toxins, protects the heart from being stressed by fluid overload, and improves mental function and a feeling of well-being. When the kidneys begin to work better, the HD can be stopped."

Dr. Goushaw explained this in a calm fashion and noted that, at this point, the benefits of HD clearly outweighed the risks. He said we would be using "gentle" HD, a term that had a calming effect at the start of yet another scary medical intervention.

A break in my updates came while I witnessed a heartwarming exchange of messages among our children as they looked out for their Grandma Marie, Liz's mother, who had begun to show some signs of dementia. Out of four sisters, Liz was the only "in-town" daughter, so she had been the designated family member who took primary responsibility for caring for Marie. Her sister Sue was now trying to pick up the slack, but living across the state in Ann Arbor made this difficult.

"Has anyone been taking care of Grandma?" Mark initially asked.

Tom, who lived closest to Grandma Marie, had gone over to her independent living apartment the previous weekend to assist her on a matter with which she needed help. Mark pledged to call Grandma Marie later that day to remind her that she could call him with any issues she needed help with. I didn't have more than an observatory role in that conversation that day, but I was very proud of those grandkids.

A dialysis catheter was placed the next afternoon. Tom stopped by to see his mother on his way up to his 7:00 p.m. nursing shift on Hauenstein 3 (H3), the neurology floor directly above ICU. He reported that dialysis was now running and that the dialysis nurse was planning to remove two liters of fluid that evening. I had been invited over to Tim and Laura's house for dinner that evening (part of the ongoing conspiracy to make sure Dad was eating right, I suspect). Everybody was pleased to hear that the HD was going smoothly.

Matters finally came to a head regarding Liz's mental status. A Neurology consultant readied a comprehensive work-up to determine why she was not waking up despite the discontinuation of sedating medications. We had been through this once before, more than a month earlier at Butterworth Hospital when I had finally prevailed on the critical care staff to order a head CT scan. As you may recall, that test turned out to be normal, and she began to wake up a day or so after the scan. Thus, I knew that there was precedence for Liz to wake up slowly from sedation; still, as her lethargy dragged on, our concerns heightened.

On Tuesday she was starting a 24-hour electroencephalogram (EEG) and video, looking for seizure activity that might possibly be identified as the cause of her somnolence. This study involves a video recording of the patient for 24 hours, while an EEG is simultaneously performed to see if there is any seizure-like physical activity that corresponds to wave-form evidence of seizure activity on the EEG tracing. When that study was reviewed the next afternoon, some seizure-like waves were identified on the EEG tracing, but no corresponding physical activity suggestive of a seizure. Nonetheless, Liz was started on an antiseizure medication that was to be continued for the next six months.

Unfortunately, this also meant that Liz's antidepressant medication had to be discontinued, as it is known to lower the brain's threshold for having a seizure. This was a very serious matter, as depression had become a big issue for Liz, dating back to her stay at Butterworth Hospital. We would address this again in the future. A head CT scan done that same day showed no evidence of cerebral hemorrhage (brain bleed) or lack of blood flow characteristic of a stroke. This was again a great relief to me, as these clinical entities are known to occur after episodes of septic shock.

Since it had been noted that Liz had not been moving her legs for the past week, a cervical spine (neck) MRI was done at the same time, especially since she had undergone several previous cervical spine surgeries. Much later, Liz was to tell me that, throughout her time in intensive care, she had often thought she had become quadriplegic, as she was unable to move her limbs from her debilitated state. The fear of spinal injury had not been as great a concern for me, but it was still comforting to hear that her spinal cord was fine. Maybe even more so because yet another issue had popped up over the previous few days—a twitching of Liz's mouth that appeared to manifest seizure-like activity.

Tom gave us the update, and his timing was good since his "favorite doc in the hospital, Dr. Farooq, the neurologist" was on Mom's case. When Dr. Farooq came to talk to the family, he gave Tom a hug. The doctor didn't believe the phenomenon to be seizure activity because the mouth movements didn't correspond with any EEG "spikes." This was good news indeed—one less organ (brain) to worry about, although Liz did continue to have similar twitching issues even through the end of the year.

The following day brought yet another crisis, as Liz spiked a fever again, and numerous bacterial and fungal cultures were taken from various parts of her body.

"Mom is critically ill again tonight," I texted to my kids and prayer partners. "She developed a fever in the 38s today and a rapid heart rate. Randy Baker noted that her antibiotics were stopped yesterday, so he's going to make sure they get restarted today. Pray for her to be relieved of this fever and whatever infection she might have that's causing it."

Since the source of the fever was not yet identified, Dr. Andrew Jameson, Liz's Infectious Disease doctor, felt obligated to restart broad-spectrum antibiotics—a "shotgun" technique to find coverage for whatever was causing the fever until a more specific treatment could be determined. Infectious disease doctors are not fond of this approach, but sometimes it's necessary.

Tom stopped to see his mom at the end of his overnight nursing shift.

"Mom had some bouts with high heart rates, 125, temps of 101.1, and blood pressures in the 160s most of the night. The temps are finally coming down, and she opened her eyes and looked at me twice and even squeezed my hand once."

Grateful for the update, I thanked Tom and said I was praying for a better day today. Not long afterward I sent out a lengthy text to our family and prayer partners, since I continued to formulate comprehensive text messages that I could copy and forward to them.

"Mom opens her eyes to my voice and looks toward me. She doesn't squeeze my hand but is spontaneously moving her right arm frequently this morning. She hasn't had Tylenol since 4:00 a.m., but her temp is down to 99. They're just giving her an antifungal antibiotic, which I'm guessing Randy Baker had them start last night (he said he would stop by between cases to see me this morning). She looks better overall than last night. I'm hoping and praying that this may be the beginning of a mighty act by God in answer to hundreds (maybe more) of prayers by his people. Thank you so much for your faithfulness in prayer for our wife, mom, and grandmother."

While staying with me overnight at the hospital, Tim texted out the prayer that had become known as "Liz's Psalm," Psalm 30:

> I will exalt you, LORD,
> for you lifted me out of the depths
> and did not let my enemies gloat over me.

LORD my God, I called to you for help,
and you healed me.
You, LORD, brought me up from the realm of the dead;
you spared me from going down to the pit.

Sing the praises of the LORD,
you his faithful people;
praise his holy name.
For his anger lasts only a moment,
but his favor lasts a lifetime;
weeping may stay for the night,
but rejoicing comes in the morning.

When I felt secure, I said "I will never be shaken."
LORD, when you favored me,
you made my royal mountain stand firm;
but when you hid your face I was dismayed.

To you, LORD, I called;
to the Lord I cried for mercy.
"What is gained if I am silenced,
if I go down to the pit?
Will the dust praise you?
Will it proclaim your faithfulness?
Hear, LORD, and be merciful to me;
LORD, be my help."

You turned my wailing into dancing;
you removed my sackcloth and clothed me with joy,
that my heart may sing your praises and not be silent.
LORD my God, I will praise you forever."

As individuals and family, we prayed this prayerful psalm often during our long ordeal, and it always brought us great comfort.

Meanwhile, I updated everybody on the Grandma Marie front: "I just called Grandma Marie back after she left a message yesterday. She's a mess, super-anxious. She's definitely feeling isolated. We're going to have to come up with a plan for reintegrating her back into more family activities, especially with Tom and Em leaving for a week."

They were preparing to leave for a weeklong excursion to Mexico. Jackie responded that she had just spoken with Aunt Sue's daughter, Amy, who assured Jackie that their family and Maria, another of Liz's sisters, were calling Marie daily.

"She's just mad because they're leaving out a lot of details about Liz."

This was a necessity because we had learned that full disclosure to Marie unnecessarily ramped up her already debilitating anxiety.

While Liz's blood cultures remained negative on Wednesday, she still had high fevers and so was scheduled for an abdominal and pelvic CT scan at 3:30 the next morning, on Thursday, February 25. These proved to be negative as well, but Liz's physicians felt there was an infection somewhere that hadn't yet been identified; apparently it was responding to the antibiotics, as her fever subsided that day. Unfortunately, Liz's dialysis "vas cath" was not working adequately because of kinking and stretching and would have to be changed before she could undergo the dialysis.

"She needs the dialysis because her urine output is expected to remain low for several weeks," I texted to my kids.

This was wishful thinking, as we were to find out.

"On the bright side, she opens her eyes and clearly returns my kiss but is not more interactive than that."

Did she know who I was? Was the kiss even intentional? I couldn't say for sure, but my nightly prayer was filled with gratitude and praise.

Although I doubt she heard, this was actually the first night I whispered these four words to my wife: "Owls mate for life."

CHAPTER 17

The issue of disagreements between hospital staff and family members has been around for as long as hospitals themselves, but when some of the family members happen to be in the medical field themselves, these disagreements can take on a nuanced form. That Friday, a major, ongoing issue began to percolate more vigorously after I had sent a text to the family:

"Critical Care just came by and reviewed all. Dr. O is talking about discontinuing all the antibiotics except the caspofungin (antifungal) and moving her to the long-term acute care hospital (LTACH). Maybe it's time, but I'm nervous about that because she gets really sick in a hurry."

It became immediately clear that this plan was not met favorably by our kids, especially those involved in the medical field.

"I don't think that's a good idea, since we don't know for sure which antibiotic is working," Dr. Jamie offered. "I'd rather keep her on them for a while. If they need to stop them, I'd stop them one at a time and have her monitored in ICU while they do it. See what Randy says."

Nurse Jackie responded, "Isn't it too soon for LTACH? Shouldn't she be stable for a few days first?"

"They seem so eager to get her off their service and their floor," I answered.

"That's what I was thinking," she agreed. "It's like they don't know how to take care of her, so they just want her off the floor."

I expressed my concerns that her critical care doctors were underestimating her fragility. Also, as LTACH still used paper, as opposed to electronic, charting, Randy would have very limited ability to follow Liz's progress. He might have access to her lab work and test results, but certainly not any clinical notes. I felt as though moving Liz to LTACH would effectually "blind" our go-to guy.

The text thread moved into a discussion of how long we thought Liz would need to stay in the ICU before we would be comfortable moving her to LTACH.

"I think she should at least have 4–5 good days in a row first," Jackie suggested.

"I told Tim a week," I replied. "At this point she's had one day."

Jamie texted back, "At least a week. Or I'd consider Spectrum again."

"Well, I was thinking a week," Jackie wrote. "But seeing as how they want her gone right away, I thought I'd lower my expectations to 4 days."

Tim pointed out that they wouldn't move her yet that day ("Dad won't sign if they ask him to"), and we agreed to check with Randy before entertaining any further discussion of LTACH.

Meanwhile Liz remained, at least in my mind, critically ill. A text I sent out that day summed up her condition: on a ventilator, on hemodialysis, with an active undiagnosed infection and a SIRS (systemic immune response syndrome) two days ago, recent blood transfusions, and undiagnosed altered mental status. Further, that afternoon I had noted that Liz had "some kind of respiratory problem

. . . She was agitated so they gave her Dilaudid, but she still has a rapid heart rate and elevated blood pressure. They had to put her oxygen up to 100%, but it's back down to 60%."

That afternoon Liz had a different type of dialysis catheter placed to eliminate the problem with kinking. I noted that her Fi02 (ventilator-provided oxygen percent) had been turned up to 100% again during the procedure but had been tapered back down to 50%—her baseline being 40%. In general, the Fi02 can serve as a mark of respiratory function; the higher the Fi02 needed to oxygenate the blood, the worse the lung function is. Although they were "getting some watery, blood-tinged secretions when suctioning" after the procedure, I followed the advice of my kids and left to go home for a while to rest.

Leaving the hospital, I wondered if my reluctance to allow Liz's transfer to LTACH was reasonable. I began to run through her condition in my mind. As I was entering nearby Interstate-131, Dr. O called me to report that Liz's post-procedure chest X-ray showed opacification (whitening) of her left upper lobe. Dr. O thought it was a mucus plug and said she was going to do another procedure called a bronchoscopy, placing a scope down the airway into the lung to visualize what was happening and to possibly suck out excess mucus that had plugged her upper lobe. I asked if I should come right back, but she said no.

"Makes me nervous, though," I texted when I arrived home. If I had any doubt about it being too early to move her to LTACH yet, it was dispelled by this latest turn of events.

Before I went to bed that night, I texted my prayer warriors and our kids: "Rough day for Liz. She developed respiratory difficulties when they were working on a weaning protocol and had to be put back on full support at 100% oxygen (she started the day on 40%).

Her dialysis catheter wouldn't work, so the ICU doc changed it over a guidewire. The follow-up chest X-ray revealed that the left upper lobe was opacified (shady), indicating a mucus plug that needed to be cleared. She had to have an emergent bronchoscopy to remove the plug. After that procedure an attempt was made to start dialysis through the new catheter, which wouldn't work. Another procedure was done to get the catheter unplugged, but that also failed. No dialysis tonight, and they'll have to place another new catheter in a different location tomorrow. This girl needs a break. Very discouraging day."

The numerous responses of prayer and support from our friends and family put me in a much better state of mind, especially this text from Jamie: "What a long day. Sounds like the girl isn't the only one who needs a break. Still praying hard. My kids pray every night for Grandma in the hospital."

Despite the rough day, I slept well, resting in the prayers of the saints.

Prayers may not always be answered in the way we desire or expect; sometimes they can be answered after an extended period, while at other times improvement can materialize overnight. Either way can be amazing. February 27 was one of the latter. After our family had solicited the specific intervention of numerous prayer partners the previous evening, I was able to text my kids that Saturday morning:

"Mom is awake and answering questions appropriately. She kisses me and tells me she loves me. And of course, the inevitable 'I need help!' She was awake most of the night, but what do you expect after two weeks asleep? She may end up sleeping much of today, but it still might be a good day to come see her."

Jackie excitedly replied that maybe it would be a good day indeed to bring baby Isaiah up to meet his grandmother for the first time.

Interventional Radiology (IR) came up that morning to change her dialysis catheter yet again, placing a longer (but still temporary) catheter. They noted that, if Liz were to need dialysis for more than a week, she would have to go down to IR to have a more permanent "tunneled" dialysis catheter placed. I hoped this would not be the case and anticipated that it wouldn't—again markedly underestimating the sequelae of septic shock.

Dr. Dikin, Liz's Critical Care doctor that day, came by to explain to me that Liz had a left lower lobe pneumonia—of which I had previously been unaware; this had been the cause of the previous day's mucus plugging and the resultant bronchoscopy. They were treating the pneumonia, but it would make it much more difficult to wean Liz off the ventilator.

By that afternoon I was happily able to text out to family and friends a beautiful picture of Liz kissing her new baby grandson as I held him up to her. The emotion through return texts was palpable, as we rejoiced in God's faithful answer, allowing Grandma to meet the grandson she had been so eagerly anticipating before her accident— on his 24th day of life. Three weeks earlier it had been uncertain either of them would make it to that meeting.

Another positive arrived. After dialysis had removed 7½ pounds of water, Liz was able to "wean" on the pressure-support mode of the ventilator for more than ten hours that day; to that point she had not made it to five hours on any given day. On the following day, Sunday, Tim came by to file and cut his mom's toenails, which had begun to look terrible. Tim's kind act reminded me of someone else who had humbled himself to tend to the feet of those he loved.

By Monday Tim was able to text out a picture of a smiling Liz with the message: "Mom is feeling VERY sassy today! Smiling, teasing nurse Kory, and looking good." Of course, "good" is a relative term; the bar was set low for Liz, given her starting point.

We weren't the only ones who thought that Liz was looking better. A Critical Care physician's assistant informed me that afternoon that plans were being made to transfer Mom to the Long-Term Acute Care Hospital (LTACH) inside St. Mary's Hospital the next day. I expressed my concern that Liz still had a fever of 101.3 and historically had gotten quite sick rapidly with infections.

I also told her that I didn't have a lot of confidence in the hospitalists who would be caring for her there because they would not be very readily available if something were to happen at that facility, and their clinical acumen to date regarding sepsis had not inspired my confidence. Lindsey pointed out that we could call for the rapid response nurse ("call a rap") if something were to happen, but I reminded her that Liz's family members might not be there around the clock. I was concerned that, if Liz were to become septic some night, there might not be an appropriate urgent response.

While these words unfortunately proved to be prophetic, Lindsey responded that she had spoken with Liz's Infectious Disease doctor. Although he would be redoing cultures that evening, the doctor felt comfortable allowing Liz to be moved to LTACH the next day. Critical Care also didn't think the thoracentesis (tapping fluid off the lung) that Randy Baker had suggested was necessary.

"Barring an episode tonight, Crit Care will sign off tomorrow and transfer us to LTACH," I texted. "I'm nervous for Mom. She's 100.3 degrees, so something is not right."

My kids agreed. Jackie texted that she was "not OK" with LTACH, arguing that her mom needed more attention than LTACH patients typically receive. She suggested that we transfer Liz back to Spectrum Butterworth if the Critical Care team was so eager to divest themselves of her care. Jackie questioned what Randy's opinion was on the matter of transfer and if he could still be involved with Liz's care if she were transferred to LTACH.

Tim had anticipated these questions and had spoken with Randy, only to learn that Randy did not have treating privileges at LTACH and would have to secure these privileges to stay involved. He learned as well that all medical records at LTACH were still paper based, meaning that one would have to physically go to the floor Liz was on to review her treatment records. Jamie objected to having his mother transferred while she was still having fevers despite being on antibiotics. All our kids had deep concerns about the plan to stop antibiotics at the time of transfer.

At Randy's suggestion, Tim and I had a face-to-face meeting with Dr. Dikin (critical care attending) the next day to express our concerns. To our relief, Dr. Dikin agreed that, given her persistent fever, Liz was not yet ready to transfer to LTACH. He was going to go on a "fishing expedition" to track down the source of Liz's persistent fevers, which he thought were most likely related to a process in Liz's lungs or to her injured and repaired left foot. He directed his workup in that direction.

We were all grateful for this change in the direction of care. A small relief was better than none.

CHAPTER 18

It doesn't take our family much impetus to engage in a text thread of merciless teasing. On March 1 an unseasonably robust snowstorm visiting Grand Rapids prompted our good-natured mockery. Even though the storm didn't live up to the National Weather Service's billing of a severe winter storm, Jenison Christian School had closed for the day, in large part because Jenison Public Schools, with whom they shared some buses, had closed first. Although Tim didn't have much choice in terms of keeping Jenison Christian open once the public schools had made their move, our family text thread lit up with endless taunting.

I have to admit—I was the one who started the brouhaha by taking the opportunity to slander two districts with one stone.

"You wimp, Tim. I see you're closed. You're worse than Lynchburg."

Lynchburg, Virginia, home to Jamie's family, had gained great notoriety within our family after having exhibited a regular pattern of school closings for relatively extended periods of time at even the hint of bad weather. Jamie, who relished the reputation his area had for "soft" school closings, objected not to my caricature of Lynchburg's wimpiness but to my suggestion that JCS might be worse.

"No fair," Jamie said. "No one is worse than Lynchburg. If they stay closed all week, then maybe."

"We haven't had school in a week," Tim confessed. "Two days of break, two days of snow, plus a weekend."

Even Jamie had to agree now. "Wimp," he accused, adding, "We are at 10 days if you count 2-hour delay days. And we have only had about 1.5 inches of snow."

Laura jumped into the fray to defend JCS.

"That's wimpy. Today's snow came out of nowhere. Absolutely no snow at 4 a.m. and crazy everywhere by 5 a.m."

I closed the conversation with an expression of my frustration with the city: "Thank you, Grand Rapids, for not plowing the streets today. Good thinking to save you resources for later. It's only March."

The lighthearted texting brought some solace during this season. *It's nice when the family thread can be full of carefree banter instead of having to focus on unfavorable medical news.*

There was plenty of the latter to come that day. Lindsey, the Critical Care PA, informed me that LTACH had had a dialysis bed open up and that they did not want to miss the opportunity to move my kids' mother to that bed. Dr. Igwatu of Infectious Disease no longer thought Liz's fevers were a symptom of infection, but he was going to check her urine culture one more time and would continue to follow her at LTACH.

Good luck getting enough urine, I couldn't help thinking.

I told Lyndsey that I had great concern over this plan because Liz had had fever and tachycardia (rapid heart rate) throughout the previous day, signs that had historically signaled sepsis for her. Lindsey countered that Critical Care was going to restart Liz's betablocker that day to control her rapid heart rate. A betablocker is a medicine that slows the electrical conduction in the heart and is used either to

reduce elevated blood pressure or to slow rapid heart rate. I pointed
out to Lindsey that the use of betablockade in Liz to date had been for
the former, not the use she now intended.

The Critical Care team was hoping to make the move with our
family blessing and agreed to readdress the matter with us later in the
afternoon. I think we would have been more agreeable to having Liz
move to a step-down floor within St. Mary's Hospital, but this option
was not being offered.

Meanwhile, the Paauw "blogosphere" lit up with opposition to
the plan. Jamie voted to get a cardiologist involved for the tachycardia
(rapid heart rate), which we thought was most probably the result
of Liz's persistent fever, in which case a betablocker would not be
indicated. Jackie pointed out that the decision should not rest
foremost on bed availability but on her mom's condition. Tim agreed.
When he was with Liz during her dialysis run that day, he noted her
temperature to again be 100.3. She was more awake than she had
been recently but continued to perseverate on the word "help."

The afternoon texting brought more levity into our lives. After
Tim shared his recent discovery that his family had a raccoon living
in their fireplace chimney, all his siblings offered advice on how to get
rid of it. Of course, some meant to be helpful, though others were
facetious.

"Stick your head up there to make sure it's really a raccoon,"
Brek suggested; he then offered that he, Mark, and Tim "might want
to put on hockey pads, baseball gloves, etc., and chase it around with
hockey sticks, all while screaming like little girls."

Laura jumped on this offer, welcoming all for beer and coon-
chasing, which Jamie insisted should be videotaped. Tim brought up
the inevitable comparison of that visual with the John Candy scene
of chasing a bat in a cottage from the movie *The Great Outdoors*. He

notified his realtor brother-in-law, "Brek, we may need a different home. This one has coons."

Jamie remembered chasing a bat with a tennis racket as a kid in a cottage in the Upper Peninsula.

"Anyone else old enough to remember Dad smacking it out of midair?"

"Legendary," Tim agreed.

"Urban legend, that is," I countered, but Tim knew better. Tim texted us a Facebook post that eventually turned out to be one of the most "liked" and shared he had posted: a picture of his grinning mother with the caption: "I just told my mom that Laura and I have a raccoon living in our fireplace that we can hear and whose paw we have actually seen. I explained that I have to get it out tonight . . . Her reaction seen in this photo. Thanks for your moral support, Mom."

It was good to splice in a little levity, but we soon got back to the business at hand.

When I came in to see Liz later that afternoon, I was quite concerned that her abdomen was notably more swollen with a new erythematous (reddened) area around the lower aspect of her surgical wound. Her temperature was 101.4. Given the appearance of her belly, I was beginning to suspect that the focus on lungs, urine, or ankle as the source of Liz's fever might have been misdirected.

Jamie questioned whether dialysis might be able to remove some of that abdominal fluid (ascites), but Liz had just finished a dialysis run that had removed three liters of fluid a few hours earlier. I thought we needed to have Randy examine her abdomen since he had participated in that final surgery. After Tim arranged for Randy to see Liz the next morning, I was relieved to hear that. Liz's hands looked great, but her feet were markedly edematous (swollen) in the face of a very large amount of ascites and poor wound healing.

I stayed until 11:00 that evening, but when I returned at 7:00 the next morning I sensed that Liz was feeling lonely. I texted out a call to see if anyone could come down, which resulted in an early afternoon visit by Tim, another in the midafternoon by Mark and Tamara, and still another by Laura later that evening. It was great having such a close-knit and supportive family.

Randy saw Liz the next morning and was concerned about a wound infection and possible peritonitis (infected abdominal fluid). He recommended expanding the spectrum of Liz's antibiotics, while talk of transferring Liz to LTACH subsided for the time being.

Later that evening I texted a picture of myself sitting beside a sleeping and ventilated Liz and titled it "Date night." It reminded me again of why we were "owls." Judging from the responses, the picture was a source of encouragement for many of our prayer partners when Tim posted it on his Facebook account.

Something of note happened that evening during our "date" that was to have ramifications much later. While I was holding Liz's hand—which remained unresponsive to my touch—I spoke to her about memories I thought would be meaningful for her. We had been on a cruise with my mother, my siblings, and their spouses just a few months before Liz's accident. This was only the second time we had taken one. Liz loved everything about a cruise—the activities, the food, the excursions—while I was not enamored of the experience, liking best the "days at sea" when I could curl up in an overstuffed chair in the library and read a book as the ocean slid by. We were hardly off that ship before she began to pester me about going on another cruise with just the two of us, or perhaps with our kids and grandkids.

Even though I had grown up in California, I had never been a beach-and-sun type of guy, much preferring a backpack trip or a day hike in a mountain wilderness. As I sat there holding that seemingly lifeless hand, prattling on about fond memories with no apparent response from Liz, I grew discouraged. But in a moment of inspiration an idea struck me, and I leaned forward close to her ear to softly tell her about it: "When you get better from all of this and come home, I'm going to take you on a cruise—promise."

Did I detect the slightest upturn of the corners of her mouth, the softest squeeze of her hand? I couldn't be sure, but at that point I would have promised her a rocket trip to the moon if it would have made her happy.

Liz gradually started to improve on the new antibiotics, and by Friday, March 4, talk of a potential move to LTACH began to circulate once again. As Liz's temperature had begun to normalize, I came to feel more comfortable with the move. It was the next step toward getting her back to Mary Free Bed, which had all along been our real goal, since we recognized that that event would signal the likelihood Liz might finally make it home. Dr. Bourboneau, her Critical Care doc that day, talked to me about trialing Liz off her ventilator with a trach cuff, an oxygen mask that would fit over her tracheostomy, for lengthening periods of time to allow weaning from her ventilator.

The issues that had now come to the forefront for Liz were anxiety and depression. I was lobbying to restart the antidepressive medication that had been held because of increased seizure risk, arguing that her depression was real, while seizure risk was theoretical. I emphasized the need to encourage more visitation, and Tim immediately stepped up to organize visits by himself and his siblings in a more scheduled way.

I would be remiss in failing to mention the faithful visits by our pastor, Rev. Dykstra, and other members of our church, as well as a steady stream of cards from numerous prayer partners, family, various churches, the seminary, and others. A special cohort of friends regularly came and sat with Liz in the afternoons, and especially when she had dialysis, which she particularly disliked. Sue Host, a longtime neighbor; Sue Elenbaas, a friend from her Healing-the-Children days; Jane Elzinga, another longtime neighbor and friend; her close personal friend Meridel Gracias; and a few others shared this noble duty.

In addition, Meridel and her husband, Dr. Vince Gracias (also a longtime friend of mine), took members of our family to dinner near the hospital a few times just to give us a break from the wearing routine. Over the long course of Liz's hospitalization, Mark and I enjoyed the hospitality of several of our church friends, the Bonts, Kuperuses, and Masts, who refused to take "no" for an answer and hosted us to some delicious meals (and some homebrewed beer, in the case of the latter.) Our other children experienced similar blessings within their own church.

The family of God is awesome, and I am certain we could not have endured all that we did without their lifting us up daily.

On Sunday, March 6, the doctors were confident enough to try Liz off her ventilator on the trach cuff. Although she did well by her "numbers," she felt uncomfortably short of breath during that episode. We chalked this up to her extreme anxiety, which certainly was playing a role in every aspect of her care, although we were to find out later that there was more to this than just the anxiety. Dr. Dikin decided to restart Liz's antidepressive medication that day, since the anxiety that was overwhelming her at that time was certainly more significant than a remote risk of seizures.

Despite her anxiety, I was able to text my kids that their mom had been off the ventilator for ten hours already and that her oxygen level had maintained around 100%. In fact, Liz had done so well that the critical care team decided to leave her on the trach cuff overnight, as long as she tolerated it. Unfortunately, I also had to admit that she had been dealing with massive anxiety and had been calling "Help!"

continuously throughout the day. Liz's physicians had tried small doses of Haldol, with minimal success.

I implored my children and our praying friends to include the matter of Liz's crippling anxiety before our faithful God—and, as always, prayers for return of kidney function. I had to admit to our kids that their mom was only "somewhat with it" and barely answered questions between pleas for help. Laura noted that, when she had left the room at 4:00 that afternoon, the incessant "Help, help" was being interrupted by "Lord, have mercy!" This was very hard for me to hear. Tim exhorted our family that "We need to step up our visits to encourage her."

As I sat by Liz's bed that night listening to those pitiful cries for help, I knew that Tim was right—but we were all getting exhausted.

There not being much conversation with Liz that afternoon, I pondered the fact that the Calvin College spring break was scheduled to begin at the end of the week, but now that break promised to be an uneventful affair for our family. At the beginning of the school year, I had arranged to have this spring break week off from work, as Mark and I had made plans to drive down to Florida with Tamara to spend time in Grandma Marie's condo on Marco Island. We had also made plans with my brother Don and his wife, Winnie, on the Space Coast of Florida to spend a day with them before heading back up north. The events of January 8 had threatened these plans, and, as Liz's hospitalization dragged on, we had reluctantly canceled our trip.

On this Sunday, March 6, my sister Joan called from California. "Jim, you're going to Florida this week."

"You know that's not possible. Liz is super anxious and being moved to a new place; she's going to need someone at bedside for the next week or two, so we can't go."

Joan surprised me with her response: "Mom and I are coming to Grand Rapids this coming Saturday; we're staying for a week so you guys can go to Florida. We'll take care of Liz."

The idea was instantly intriguing to me, but I felt guilty about even considering it.

"I can't do it, Joan. I think my place is here with her. I'd love to go, but I probably need to stay here with her." Joan was not having any of that. "Jim, you've been in the hospital continuously for two months; you're going to burn yourself out. Mom and I are capable of this, and you need to have a break. We don't know how much longer this is going to go on."

Fully desirous of going but not completely comfortable with the plan, I polled my kids that afternoon and found that they were unanimously in support of the idea. Several pledged to step up their visits the following week to convince me to go. Finally, I accepted the offer, pending Liz's approval, and quickly made plans with Mark to rent a car and leave the coming Friday with Tamara for the trek to Marco Island.

Given Liz's mental status that day, I waited until the next morning when she had a brighter moment before approaching her with the plan. To say that Liz had always gotten along well with my mother would be an understatement; they have always had quite a strong mother-daughter relationship. Her bond with Joan is also tight, and they have really enjoyed each other's company over the years. Hence, it didn't surprise me that, not only did Liz immediately approve of the idea, but she strongly endorsed it. I texted our kids soon after this.

"FYI, Grandma Edna and Joan are flying out Saturday for a week to take care of Mom so I can go with Mark and Tam to Florida. Really cool. They love me."

It took only a few hours before I began to reconsider. "Wow. I'm having a lot of anxiety about leaving Mom for a week," I texted the kids.

Jamie reassured me: "You need to go. Mom will do great. Are you driving? Virginia might be on the way!"

"I hope she's better mentally by then. She's so anxious and afraid. I feel so sorry for her."

"You need to go," Laura quickly seconded. "A change of pace will do you good."

Tim went so far as to look up one-way flights home from Fort Myers, saying that, in case of emergency, he could get me home on any given day by 6:00 p.m.

"If that is acceptable, go without worry. If not, stay. We will support you regardless."

I was still not completely convinced.

"I'm not overly concerned about an emergency, although you can't predict. Just worried she'll miss me and be super anxious."

Tim reassured me, "I'm not sure she can tell time accurately right now anyway, and she'll have Laura/me/gramma&Joan guaranteed."

This helped ease my anxiety a lot, but we had other issues to deal with.

Just before noon on Monday, March 7, I was notified that Liz would be transferring to LTACH between 2:00 and 3:00, so I put out a call for someone to help me with the transfer, only to find that everyone had job and school responsibilities. As it turned out, no help was needed. Although LTACH was not the destination I would have chosen for her to go, it was nonetheless good to finally have Liz back out of intensive care exactly a month after she first was admitted there in such dire condition. When she had first been transferred into the critical care unit back on February 7, we had no idea that it would be a month before she made it back out . . . but, given her condition at that time, we also had no assurance she would make it out alive at all.

My report the next morning, on March 7, was more encouraging: "Mom is much calmer and more rational this morning. The nurse gave her the 'as-needed' drugs last night and says she had a good night. She talked to me rationally a bit this morning and then fell back asleep. Not a single 'Help' so far!"

This date was a milestone for us, as it marked exactly two months since Liz had been in the accident. We had never expected anything like the ordeal we had been through, but here she was, out of critical care and just a step away from returning to Mary Free Bed, always our penultimate goal. Liz's nurse took a picture of me next to Liz up in a stretcher chair on a trach mask, with just a hint of a Mona Lisa smile on her face. I texted the picture out on our family thread with the following caption: "Afternoon chair date—best date I ever had."

I understand that this picture was posted on Facebook by several of my kids and drew hundreds of comments, reassuring us of the continuing prayers of the saints.

This day was also the beginning of a remarkable prayer campaign. I was excited to text about Liz, who was still on dialysis three days a week: "BTW, Mom got straight cath'ed of 150 mls of urine, I think late last night. She now has a Foley in, and there's a small amount of urine in the bag, maybe 100 mls. Is this significant? I don't know clinically, but it's a major encouragement to me. It's the current biggest prayer issue. Maybe Tim can organize a day of prayer for Mom's kidney function to return."

Tim texted back that he was on it and, as always, did things in a big way. By day's end I was able to report some encouraging but also discouraging news to my kids and our prayer team.

"Mom had a good day. More restful than the past few weeks although some anxiety—but nothing at all like even two days ago. She sat on the side of the bed with the therapists and even was up in the chair for an hour. There is definitely some urine in the catheter, although not much. It is urgent that her kidneys work sooner rather than later. A new nephrologist, Dr. Banga, came in last night and thought the previous doc's label of End Stage Renal Disease was premature.

"That was the first time I heard that diagnosis for Liz. ESRD basically means your kidneys are no longer functional and you'll need dialysis for life, or until a kidney transplant. He went on to give me the statistics: 50% chance of eventual recovery of kidney function at two weeks after injury, 25% chance of recovery at 4 weeks, and only 10% chance at 6 weeks. Mom passed 2 weeks last Friday, so it's extremely important that recovery happens soon.

"Almost everything else is gradually moving forward, so this is the greatest area of concern for Mom. As you have probably seen, Tim is organizing a special day of prayer tomorrow through social media, specifically to focus on recovery of kidney function. God has been overwhelmingly merciful to Mom through nine long weeks. He will continue to bless Mom's recovery, as always working through the prayers of the saints. Please join in special prayers tomorrow for recovery of kidney function."

Once again, I remembered that sometimes God answers prayers overnight and sometimes much further down the road but that, either way, his timing is always perfect.

Later that night Jackie texted out several heartwarming pictures of Grandma Liz actually holding her new grandchild, Isaiah, for the first time. Lying in bed with her trach mask on, Liz was too weak to make an attempt to hold little Zay on her own, so I had to curl her arm onto her chest and then hold the little guy in that arm. Zay threw his arm over Liz's face, and she kissed that tiny arm, her first kiss while holding her youngest grandchild, and quite a memorable one. The final picture showed Liz cheek-to-cheek with Zay, the first real smile I had seen on her face in a long time. The text "had an emotional visit with Mom tonight" accompanied the pictures, which appeared soon on a number of Facebook posts.

We were finally starting to hit some favorable milestones.

CHAPTER 19

Throughout her first week at LTACH, Liz made slow but steady progress in physical conditioning. She was extremely deconditioned after her latest month in ICU so was not able to engage in much more than repetitive attempts to move her arms and legs in bed. At least once a day Liz was moved from her bed to a chair, an activity she detested and that invariably led to a series of calls, "Help, help!"

We had a large group of Christian family and friends specifically praying for kidney recovery, but there was not much by which to be encouraged that week on the kidney front. Liz still had an indwelling Foley catheter, upon which I became fixed whenever I was visiting her at her bedside. I would watch the little trickle of yellow in the curl of the tubing at the side of her bed and imagine that it was getting bigger as I stared at it. I would try to battle the urge to gaze at it and force myself to focus on something else around the room, but that tube would soon draw my eyes back like an irresistible visual magnet. Sometimes I would give in to my OCD tendencies and lift the catheter tubing up to drain those drops into the bag hanging down from her bed railing, only to be disappointed as they disappeared into nothingness in that bag.

On March 8 I texted the following: "Mom's got respiratory junkiness tonight (that's technical Jamie—an ophthalmologist wouldn't understand). I had them suction her, but she's still breathing fast. Also, I just emptied some urine into the bag that had collected in the dependent part of the tubing. Not a lot but definitely something."

By the end of the day shift, the accumulated volume was nearly immeasurable; no more than 20 milliliters most days. As Liz remained on hemodialysis in her room three times weekly, I began to notice how much this took out of her. While at the beginning of a run she might be reasonably interactive with me, by its completion she would be quite sleepy and virtually nonresponsive to my efforts at conversation. I learned to bring my laptop computer on those days so that I could accomplish some work when she slipped into that somnolent state. I understand that everyone reacts to dialysis differently, but I hated to see Liz like that and dreaded to even think about a lifetime of those three-days-a-week experiences.

At some point during that week the staff noticed that Liz's gastric feeding tube (G-tube) was leaking a fair amount. This issue was in my wheelhouse, so I looked at the site. The tube was sliding out much too far, almost certainly from a rupture of the balloon on the internal part of the tube that was designed to keep it in place. This was not altogether unexpected after two months of the tube having been in place. I texted Randy to let him know, as he had been the surgeon who had placed that tube back in January.

Randy was doing several surgeries that day at St. Mary's, so he grabbed a replacement tube and brought it over to the LTACH unit, where the two of us replaced the old one. It took us some time to get the previous tube out, since the balloon was only partially decompressed, and we could not drain the remaining water from it. We finally managed to remove that tube, the new one easily sliding into place. This didn't seem to be a noteworthy event, but, as we found out, it was to lead to significant future ramifications.

All that week during Liz's lucid moments, I expressed feelings of misgiving about my leaving her for the week, but she vigorously insisted that I go and spend time with the kids.

"I had my best visit yet this morning," I texted everybody. "I talked to her again about taking Mark and Tam to Florida for spring break, and she was encouraging of it. I told her I was having a lot of anxiety over it, but she said, 'You'll have fun.' She was fine with my mom and sister Joan coming to take care of her that week."

In that same text I mentioned running into a Mary Free Bed representative who had agreed to have one of their rehab physicians come over to LTACH to evaluate Liz for timing of the transfer back there.

"I feel God working through all of this in a mighty way."

Right up until the day before we left, I was still not completely at ease with the concept of leaving Liz, but a number of friends and several pastors encouraged me to follow through. I gave one more report the night before we left: "I just found out that Mom got her trach changed today. They apparently put a speaking valve in. After lying quietly for 40 minutes she suddenly yelled out, 'Help.' I nearly jumped out of my chair."

Jamie commented that the speaking valve was "a mixed blessing. It makes you remember that she's there, but I'm sure it's much more exhausting." To which Tim responded, ". . . he says from Virginia." Jamie replied, "I can hear it from here."

In the end Mark, Tamara, and I loaded up a rented Dodge Journey and pulled out Friday afternoon, March 11, after saying goodbye to Liz. Mark and Tamara had taken Grandma Marie to dinner the previous night, at which time "Grandma made sure to bring along the updated list of Sunset House North rules and regulations so she could read them to us as we ate." Marie's condo was notorious in our family for some truly draconian rules, as expressed by Tom: "You don't need to know them all. Just the summary or golden rule: no having fun."

As agreed, Tim stayed with his mother that afternoon so she wouldn't feel abandoned by being left alone immediately after we left, with my mom and Joan not arriving from California until early Saturday afternoon. They went immediately from the airport to LTACH to spend time with Liz, reporting to me that she was doing fine at about the time we three travelers were pulling into Grandma Marie's condo in Marco Island.

Unfortunately, Liz's moments of lucidity waned over that next week, for reasons that became clearer after I had returned to Grand Rapids. Not only did she not remember our numerous earlier conversations wherein she had encouraged me to go to Florida, but to this day she does not recall any such discussions. She related to me later that she spent the week of my absence upset that I had left her, and in her confusion (hopefully) was demanding to see a divorce lawyer—confirmed by Joan.

I'm still trying to fully convince Liz to this day that those conversations about the Florida trip did occur, although she remains skeptical. But Liz also doesn't remember Joan being at her bedside that week, even though Joan sat patiently with her sister-in-law for eight hours daily for most of that week, a fact documented by both Joan and our family. My mother spent several hours visiting Liz most days that week as well. So, if it sounds like I'm throwing myself on the mercy of the court of public opinion, . . . well, I am.

Joan filled me in several times each day by text (mostly) and by phone. For the most part Liz was at least stable, if not making small gains, but her LTACH admission continued to be complicated by extended episodes of confusion and anxiety, indeed more the norm than the exception. Joan was frank in telling me that Liz was often disoriented to the point of having to be placed in wrist restraints, which Liz despised with a passion and which resulted in a lot of bedrail shaking. Liz also spent much of the day calling for "help," even with Joan sitting at her side. Her respiratory status did manifest steady if slow improvement, and she was able to remain off the ventilator for most of that week.

One major negative was the pressure ulcer Liz continued to experience over her tailbone, now already two months in duration; of all the places she suffered pain—and there were a number—this was consistently the worst. Further, it impacted her ability to participate in therapy and made sitting in a chair extremely uncomfortable for her. The nursing staff had been dressing it with Mepilex daily, but, unfortunately, a pressure wound forms quickly but takes months to heal.

Of anything Liz suffered from in her long hospital course, because of its persistence this was the worst. While I am generally loathe to criticize fellow clinicians, all was not well with the care given Liz those two weeks.

Before I left, I had experienced difficulty in getting staff to respond in a timely manner. I suppose this might in part have been perception, having come from a high acuity unit, where a nurse is assigned to only two patients, to a lower acuity unit where a nurse may have up to five patients. But I sensed what I would call a lack of timeliness on the part of many of the staff at LTACH. While there were some exceptional nurses on that unit, I felt that these were not the norm.

Jackie, herself a nurse, at several visits had difficulty getting a nurse to respond in a suitable fashion at all, and specifically in getting her mother up into a chair. Although Liz was supposed to be up in a chair a minimum of twice daily, Jackie noted during several evening visits that she had been left in bed all day. While Liz's resistance to being placed in a chair may have made it easy for staff to leave her in bed, it was disappointing to find that, while we had been promised that Liz was moving to a unit where she would get more therapy, she was getting less.

Moreover, her "PRN" meds (those given by patient request, as opposed to on a schedule) were often given more than an hour after having been requested. When a patient's two main complaints are pain and anxiety, I would expect those meds to be given in a much timelier fashion.

Joan recounted that, during much of the time she had watched over Liz, she had felt as though she had to badger the aides to get Liz up into a chair and the nurses to bring pain and antianxiety meds in an expeditious fashion. Joan related that it had been a difficult week watching Liz suffer crippling anxiety and pain because the nurses "had other patients." I was very grieved to hear that this was happening to the lady who was more and more becoming my hero.

I was very encouraged throughout that week away, however, to receive texts from our family verifying that they were taking their increased visitation responsibilities seriously.

Jackie: "The Steinbrecher's and I are going around 1:30."

Tim: "Great! K and I are going this morning." (The former text led to a beautiful picture of Liz looking sweetly down on a peaceful Isaiah snuggled up against her side.)

"Her leg is healing!"

"Mom got her haircut today."

"I'm here during dialysis tonight."

"OK; I saw her last night."

And this telling note from Tom indicating that Liz's mental status was a concern: "She sneakily whispered after looking around the room for the nurse, 'Where's your car? Quick, let's go.'"

Laura concurred, "She's been saying that all week; 'Take me home in your car. I've got to get out of here.'"

Liz's continued confusion was disconcerting, often coupled with hallucinations involving escaping from that unit.

Offsetting all of that was the electrifying report from Joan on the evening of Thursday, March 17, that Liz had suddenly produced 1600 milliliters of urine that day, after nearly nothing all week. I excitedly texted out the news to our kids (who in turn passed it along through their social media), as well as to my cohort of other family members and close friends who had expended a lot of energy praying for this moment.

My phone blew up with the responses of praise and thanksgiving for this long-awaited announcement and the likelihood that there was still life in those kidneys after all. Earlier that afternoon Jackie had texted, "The Mary Free Bed coordinator stopped by; she's shooting for transfer to Free Bed this Monday when Dad will be back." This was also indeed a very encouraging report.

During that Florida excursion I made a point of trying to talk to Liz by phone two or three times daily, but these were not always meaningful conversations due to her ongoing confusion. Nonetheless, despite the frequent disconnect, I sensed that she was very excited to speak with me, never openly (at least to me) expressing any resentment over my absence. Indeed, she seemed to be living vicariously through these conversations, asking at times if we had done this one or that one of her favorite Florida activities yet. For our part, Mark, Tam, and I spent the first part of the week relaxing in Marco Island before heading across the state on Wednesday afternoon to have dinner and spend the evening with my brother Don and his wife, Winnie, in Micco on the Space Coast of Florida.

From there we drove through the night to western Virginia, to Jamie and Halle's home in Lynchburg, where we spent the day enjoying some time with the three grandchildren—Nathaniel, Lexi, and Tori—Liz and I don't get to see as much because of the distance between our homes. We tried to sneak in a few naps because of the previous night's journey, but the kids were so excited to see us—in particular their soon-to-be Aunt Tamara—that that wasn't happening much.

We left for Grand Rapids the next morning, Friday, March 18, the same day my mom and sister were saying goodbye to Liz and heading back to California. They had come to Grand Rapids for six days, and I had not seen them even once, but I was tremendously grateful to them for their caretaking service, which had allowed me to have that week of rest. I had gained back a pound or two of weight and felt much better rested than I had in some time despite the lengthy travel arrangements. During that week I had tried to send out even more texts than normal, recruiting many saints to lift up prayers for my wife in my absence, foremost for improved kidney function.

We travelers spent considerable time talking about getting back to school and work; about the upcoming wedding; and, most of all, about the miraculous recovery to date of our wife and mother—for Tamara, mother-to-be. I mentioned that Liz's and my own fortieth wedding anniversary was barely a month away. Secretly I was gaining confidence that Liz and I might actually celebrate that day together.

CHAPTER 20

Mark, Tamara, and I pulled into the Saint Mary's parking lot at 8:00 p.m. on Friday, March 18, and made our way to the LTACH unit, the three of us having decided to make a quick stop to see Liz before wearily heading home after a few long days on the road. There was no nurse at that moment in the dimly lit room, and Liz was apparently sound asleep. I was reluctant to awaken her but knew she would be excited to see us, so I shook her gently. She turned out to be very difficult to arouse and was strangely subdued in her reaction to seeing us. Further, she was still obviously quite deconditioned, not able to make much effort at returning our embraces.

Looking at her, I noticed that her eyes seemed more sunken and her face more drawn than I had remembered. Part of this may have been from my not having seen her for a week, but, frankly, she looked awful to me, and I was fearful for her wellbeing. Worse, my eyes were drawn to her monitor, where I could see that her heart rate was in the 130s range.

I immediately walked around the unit until I found her nurse, who was playing on his cell phone in the break room. Responding to my request for assistance, he followed me into Liz's room and busied himself with checking her pulse-oximetry monitor. When I asked him how long Liz's heart rate had been elevated, the nurse responded, "Since before my shift."

"Well, what's her blood pressure?" I asked.

"Last time I checked it was 90 over 40," he answered.

My mind quickly did the math.

A mean arterial pressure of 57. Too low to be consistently perfusing her kidneys. Liz was obviously in shock.

I did a quick survey of her IV pole; her tube feeding pump was running at 50 milliliters per hour, and there were no IV fluids infusing.

"Well, what are you doing about it?" I asked the nurse.

"We're following it," he said.

I was stunned. "She's in shock. She needs to be getting fluids."

"We don't have any orders for an IV," he informed me.

I was very upset now; every hospital unit has stated protocols for rapid treatment of shock because of the severe consequences when it's left untreated.

"She's in shock; your floor has a shock protocol, and this is not it," I stated. "Her kidneys just started working yesterday after a month; she needs fluids now."

The nurse agreed to contact the on-call (St. Mary's) internal medicine physician's assistant to pass my comments up the line. In the meantime, Mark left to drop Tamara at her house and head home himself. Tim came down at around 9:30 p.m., after his kids were in bed, as was common practice for him. I was in the process of trying to convince the on-call PA who had just arrived that Liz needed fluids— and lots of them—to preserve her newly recovering kidney function. I was relieved to have Tim join me in the fight because he had seen his mother in shock (pathologically low blood pressure) enough times to recognize it and fear its consequences.

Tim weighed in passionately as we tried to convince the PA that her fear that fluid resuscitation would do more harm than good was not warranted in Liz's current clinical condition. She finally conceded to run a fluid "bolus" to see how Liz responded, giving an order to the nurse and leaving the floor to resume her "regular" assignment in St. Mary's Hospital. While Tim and I were relieved to have the order given, our frustration mounted as we alternatively watched the minutes ticking by and the monitor bearing witness to the ongoing shock Liz was experiencing. As with a lot of treatment in that unit, the time between when the order was given and when it was enacted seemed inordinate.

The situation turned ominous when Tim and I started to notice Liz's heart rate momentarily dipping into the range of 30–40/minute. These episodes happened so quickly that at first I wasn't sure I was actually seeing them, but as I stared persistently at the monitor and as they became more frequent, I realized they were real, not artifacts. Tim asked me what those heart rate decelerations represented, but as my experience did not extend to an explanation for what we were seeing, I had to admit that I didn't know (although I would soon learn). A half-liter bag of intravenous fluid was finally hung at midnight at a rate of 500 milliliters per hour—not very robust, but at least something.

As the fluid ran in, Tim—my partner in OCD—and I compulsively watched the monitor reflecting Liz's vital signs as the heart rate began to inch back down and the blood pressure up. When the fluid ran out an hour later, I called out for the nurse. When my patience ran out with waiting, I finally circled around the unit to again find our nurse in the break room toying with his phone. After being notified that the IV bag was empty, he jumped up and followed me back to Liz's room. Tim and I began to forcefully lobby for more fluid, as it had become apparent that the nurse had no intention of hanging a second bag.

"The PA gave me an order for only this one bag," he explained.

"You gave at best what would be a half fluid bolus, and Liz is starting to respond to it. She needs more—this is critical."

The nurse finally agreed to call the PA back, only to find that she had left the hospital at midnight. We insisted on seeing a physician but were told that she was busy in the St. Mary's emergency department seeing patients who were "more critical" and that she would get here when she could. If she was indeed seeing other patients in the ED, Tim and I doubted their needs were more critical at that point than Liz's concerns.

We sat at her bedside hopelessly watching her pressure drop again and her heart rate rise while the nurse studiously avoided us. Her urinary catheter—which had been producing a modest but regular amount of urine earlier in the evening—gradually slowed down and finally trickled to a stop altogether at about 2:00 a.m. I can't describe how both heartbreaking and infuriating this was to us.

Tim and I spoke glumly of the disappointment our prayer partners were going to experience after the excitement of the report of the previous day's urine output. Our eyes kept getting drawn back to the IV pole, empty of any fluid now except for the remaining pump for Liz's continuous tube feeding, the number reading 50 milliliters/hour, a far cry from what she needed at this time. But, as dismayed as we were at Liz's clinical situation, it was about to get worse.

At 3:00 a.m. the embarrassed-looking nurse came in, walked over to the IV pole, and turned off the feeding pump, Liz's last source of fluid.

"The doc was told there had been a concern earlier today that the feeding tube was displaced and wants us to turn off the feed until we get an X-ray to verify its position. She's wondering if that's what's causing her sepsis."

Tim and I were incredulous. I examined the feeding tube, which slid easily in and back out until it stopped when the internal balloon cinched up against the stomach wall, as it was supposed to. I objected strenuously. First off, it seemed very unlikely that there was a problem with that tube. And if the physician knew that Liz was in septic shock, whether from the feeding tube or something else, why didn't she come to see the patient?

"What type of X-ray is going to be taken?" I asked.

The answer given made me even more upset. It was to be a plain abdominal film (KUB), which would not delineate the position of the tube. I insisted that they order that the X-ray be taken with contrast (liquid dye) infused into the tube. This was especially important in that Liz's previous gastric bypass had left her with irregular anatomy, rendering a plain abdominal X-ray useless.

"I'd like to see the nurse supervisor," I said.

When she appeared, she defended the choice of X-ray because it was "protocol" to get a plain abdominal X-ray before anyone could resort to a contrast X-ray. I knew this had to be fabricated.

"I know that's not true. How can you possibly have a protocol that tells you to do the wrong X-ray before you can take the right one?"

The supervisor defended herself. Part of her confrontational attitude probably came from her having been told that Tim and I had been upset for hours and from likely hearing reports of the conflict in Liz's room that night. Tim and I were not backing down, however. After months of hospital dealings, we were finally getting past the fear of being "that patient family" and just focusing on advocating for our family member. The supervisor remained firm, though, and left us alone with Liz, awaiting the "wrong" X-ray.

When the X-ray tech finally came in, she was holding a paper requisition with a perplexed look on her face.

"This says they want to see if the end of the feeding tube is in correct position, but a KUB is not going to show that," she told us.

I just threw up my hands in exasperation and shook my head. The tech took the KUB but was back thirty minutes later to take a re-do with contrast, reporting that a radiologist had "chewed her butt off" for having taken an X-ray she should have known was improper. Tim and I were tempted to ask the tech to please go tell that to the nurse supervisor, but at this point we just wanted to move the process forward.

By 5:00 a.m. Tim and I finally ran out of patience waiting for the X-ray report that would allow the TFs to resume. Liz had now been in shock for hours, receiving no fluid at all for the last two hours, with no medical input since the previous evening. Frustrated beyond endurance, Tim and I finally decided to take matters into our own hands. We began to unplug Liz's bed and make ready to physically move her ourselves. A nurse showed up and asked us what we were doing.

"We're going to take her down to the emergency department to find a doctor."

The nurse supervisor quickly came into the room to tell us that we couldn't do that, but Tim wasn't intimidated.

"I'm sorry it's come to this, but you can't stop us."

She disappeared, but as we were rolling Liz and her bed out the door she came running back to tell us that the doctor was on her way up. Tim and I agreed to wait five minutes; the physician was there in three.

I hurriedly told the young St. Mary's physician, who was obviously harried, what the clinical situation was and that Liz had been in untreated shock for the better part of a day. The physician was very apologetic, saying that she was stretched too thin, although she realized that this was not an appropriate excuse for Liz's lack of treatment. She ordered a fluid bolus immediately and began the workup to find the source of Liz's sepsis. As she turned to go, she leaned close to us to quietly speak: "Don't tell anyone I said this: get your family member out of here now. We come here only because our St. Mary's contract says we have to."

With that sobering thought, she was gone.

We took those words to heart. When the regular hospitalist team came to round on Liz later that morning, Tim and I lobbied hard to have Liz transferred back to St. Mary's, either to ICU or to a "step-down" unit. We, of course, never mentioned our conversation with the night-call doc. The daytime hospitalist, one whom I had encountered earlier in Liz's admission and whom I respected, entertained our fervent request for a few minutes but finally decided against it.

"We can take care of what's going on with her here at LTACH."

Tim challenged him. "At what point would you agree that she's too sick not to go back to ICU?"

The physician paused for a moment before answering: "If we have to place her back on a ventilator, I would agree to move her back to intensive care."

By now it was after 11:00 a.m., and Tim and I were beyond weary. Knowing that Jackie would be by to see her mother that afternoon, we hugged Liz and each other, said our goodbyes, and headed home for some much-needed rest. At that point Liz was just starting to be responsive, as the IV fluids slowly caught up with her septic picture. On the way home I was devastated to reflect on the price Liz was going to pay for that long night.

Liz awakened enough as the day went on to participate in a Facetime call Jackie set up that afternoon with Liz's sister Sue, a visit that perked up Liz quite a bit. That turned out to be short lived, however, as the next day she could not be aroused and slumbered the day away. Tim shared a posted prayer request for us to send to our praying friends:

"Please pray for our mom's kidneys. They showed signs of function over the last few days and now have dropped again. Pray that the function will return immediately—every day that passes increases her chances of permanent failure. Also pray that she might be a candidate for transfer to Mary Free Bed tomorrow—we are all eager for this to happen."

Unfortunately, Monday brought a new crisis that changed our focus for Liz from Mary Free Bed to survival, as the mysterious heart decelerations that had begun on Friday evening took center stage.

Tim was at LTACH early when the transport staff moved Liz to a gurney to take her to the radiology department. A small amount of feeding solution had leaked around the insertion site of the feeding tube on Saturday, mainly because the internal balloon securing it was under-filled with water and the outer bolster meant to secure it to the skin was loose. I had readvanced it myself, refilled the balloon, and tightened the outer bolster to better secure it in place, after which it had worked fine. The leak, however, had been reported at the nursing shift change, and an order came through to shut off the tube feeds until the tube could be changed by Interventional Radiology.

IR wouldn't do the tube change until Monday, so Liz was left without any nutrition for the time being. I disagreed with this plan, as the feeding tube was relatively new and was working fine, but I was a family member, not her physician. (Turning off the feeding was not an innocuous thing to do. Liz received a large amount of insulin each evening with the assumption that her tube feeds would be infused around the clock. If the tube feeds were stopped, the insulin already "on board" could precipitously lower her blood sugar.)

As Liz was moved to the gurney Monday morning, her heart rate immediately dropped to 30 per minute, recovering back to 96 per minute as the staff quickly moved her back to her own bed.

Unfortunately, her blood pressure did not recover with the move back, and she was now back in shock. Rather than heading to work, Tim, who had spent the night again, stayed at his mom's bedside as several physicians tried to figure out the source of the shock.

"Pray," Tim texted our family. "They are moving up dialysis in the hope of removing some fluid. I am trying to wake her up—she's been sleeping for 24 hours."

Shortly following, Tim texted, "They want to put her on a vent."

I was at work at Butterworth Hospital when Tim took the unusual step of phoning me to ask for help. As I hung up, I immediately went to work contacting Randy before heading down the hill to LTACH. Jamie brought up what all of us were thinking, that maybe they should transfer her back to the ICU. Laura admitted that the thought had crossed her mind, too, questioning LTACH's ability to provide the level of care Liz now needed.

"They promised Dad they'd put her in ICU if she went back on the vent," Jackie reminded Tim, who was already on board with those sentiments.

When the hospitalist caring for Liz that day approached Tim with the decision to place Liz back on a ventilator, Tim pointedly reminded him of his statement two days earlier about allowing an ICU transfer in that eventually. By now there were three physicians in his mother's room, including a pulmonologist who insisted that it would be safe to leave Liz in LTACH on a ventilator.

Recalling the Friday night episode when we couldn't get a physician to come to Liz's room when she was in shock, Tim was having none of that. He refused to consent to a ventilator for Liz, taking a stand for what he felt to be right for his mom. This was a bold commitment by Tim, who always called himself "the nonmedical child"; he later told me that he was overwhelmed by the medical team confronting him but felt his stand might be critical for his mom.

"If you don't let us hook your mother back up to the ventilator, she's going to die," the pulmonologist told Tim.

"I'll be very sorry if that happens," Tim responded. "But you told me that if she needed the ventilator she would be moved back to ICU. We have not had good experiences here, and I don't think it's safe for her here anymore."

After finally reaching Randy between two surgical cases at St. Mary's, I hurriedly explained what was going on in Liz's LTACH room and that Tim was trying to stand firm with the medical team.

"I'm on my way," Randy said, hanging up and rushing over to 5 Main, where LTACH was located.

Tim was relieved when Randy, still in his surgical scrubs, strode into the room and asked to see Liz's bedside chart. After glancing quickly through the chart, he handed it back to the hospitalist.

"This is not primary respiratory failure," Randy said. "She's in shock with a metabolic acidosis. She needs to be transferred to the ICU right away. I have a case to get to."

With that he turned and hurried off to the operating room. Relenting, the hospitalist finally agreed to have Liz moved to the ICU. She was quickly placed on the ventilator and transferred back to Hauenstein 2, room 204, where pressors and rapid fluid infusions were added to treat her shock.

Tim texted and posted an update to our prayer partners: "Our mom had complications this morning when being moved for a procedure. She is stabilizing, but we are worried about her mental status, kidneys, and overall health. Pray for her blood gases to normalize and her mental status to improve (currently tracking with her eyes but not awake yet). We will be heading back to ICU today instead of to Mary Free Bed until this is resolved. Thank you for surrounding us in prayer. We feel it and need it. God is good, and we know He is present in the midst of another storm."

Shortly after Liz arrived on H2, Randy Baker came by with a PA
to exchange Liz's feeding tube over a guidewire with a new tube. Liz
was then taken down to radiology to have a CAT scan of her abdomen,
looking for the infectious source of the sepsis that had now made her
critically ill once again. While in the radiology suite, her heart rate had
dropped to 30 per minute again, and she was given an intravenous
medication, atropine, which had brought it back to a normal rate.

As the afternoon wore into evening, I texted a gloomy update to
our family and others that reflected my feeling that Liz had missed her
opportunity to make it to Mary Free Bed and was now likely to die.

"A pretty devastating day, and Mom is now in need of forceful
prayers. After having a septic episode from an unknown source over
the weekend, her respiratory status and kidney function (which had
shown remarkable signs of recovery Friday) have both declined. Her
kidney numbers have climbed, and urine output dropped off. She
was placed back on a ventilator and is back in ICU instead of Mary
Free Bed Rehab, as we had hoped for and expected today. Her mental
status is worrisome in that she is minimally responsive. Her labs
indicate that this current episode is more of a metabolic disorder than
a respiratory one. Pray that the doctors will figure out what it is and
be able to correct it and that her kidney function can yet be restored."

I also expressed to my kids that I was concerned that Liz's mental
status might be reflecting a brain injury from having had her blood
sugar drop too low after her tube feeds were held.

The previous day on LTACH a blood sugar of 40 was noted at
one point, necessitating intravenous glucose. It was entirely possible
that the blood sugar had been even lower than that at some point
in time. That evening the staff placed Liz on a form of continuous
hemodialysis because her blood pressure was too low for her to tolerate
the usual intermittent hemodialysis.

The one bright spot for me was being surrounded by Christian staff. Our nurse that evening was Wendy, a Christian lady I had gotten to know well in her previous position working in the Butterworth ICU. The Critical Care doctor was one I hadn't met before, but she endeared herself to me immediately when she asked if she could pray with me. My son Jamie makes prayer with his patients part of his regular practice, and being on the receiving end of this support was very comforting.

Later that evening, while I was chatting with Wendy as she worked over Liz, I saw her face go white, and I could see her staring at the monitor behind me.

"I need help in here!" she yelled out the door.

Turning my head as the monitor began to alarm, I was stunned to see a "flat-line" where Liz's heart rate had been. Wendy quickly grabbed some atropine out of a med drawer and had it pushed in through Liz's IV in less than a minute. As ten staff members rushed in, I saw the heart rhythm start to pick up on the monitor, first 30 per minute and eventually back over 100 per minute.

Relief soon washed over me—relief that we were out of LTACH and in a unit where the nurse was present at the bedside and knew immediately what to do in that circumstance. And relief that Tim had stood firm like a lone soldier in the gap. I believe he had saved his mother's life.

Later on, a cardiologist told us that Liz had what was called sick sinus syndrome, an entity not primary to the heart but seen in the presence of some other systemic illness, such as sepsis, and characterized by variable and alternating aberrant cardiac rhythms. It could still be lethal, as we had witnessed, if not treated correctly.

A silly thing, I know, but when Liz had moved to LTACH I was pleased to switch from parking in the ramp to parking in a surface lot in front of the main hospital. While these were side-by-side, the surface lot was a step closer to Mary Free Bed, and that move had brought me comfort, as if where I parked my car made some difference.

That night, as I once again trudged through the skywalk to the ramp, I found myself despondent. As I looked south out of the skywalk window, Mary Free Bed seemed to be a mile away. *It might as well be a thousand miles away for all the good it'll do.*

I had serious doubts that Liz would ever make it back there.

That night I reflected on the events of the day, how we had been hopeful that morning for a transfer to Mary Free Bed, only to have Liz once again critically ill in the ICU by the end of the day. I was experienced enough to realize that each critical episode significantly lessened her likelihood of survival.

Despite the serious set-back, on the next morning, March 22, our family was exchanging texts about their relief on being out of LTACH.

"Very thankful she's out of LTACH and back in ICU."

"And now we know not to send her back."

"Agreed!"

I summed up the planned course of attack that morning: "Mom is on minimal vent support; she responds when pressed but is very sleepy yet. Her night nurse told me her heart rate dropped whenever they laid her flat or turned her to her left side. Turning her shifts her weight, putting pressure on her great vessels and affecting the amount of blood flow into and out of her heart. Cardiology is scheduled to see her today.

"Because of a few air bubbles seen on her abdominal CT scan—a potential sign of infection—Randy has ordered a diagnostic belly tap to see if her abdominal fluid is infected from a possible feeding tube leak two days ago. IR is going to do this at 2:30, and any fluid being removed will be replaced with albumin (protein)."

When the tap was done, we were told that the fluid looked infected and maybe represented the reason for the fevers, the shock, and the low heart rate. Liz was awake and mouthing words, and everyone was encouraged. Jackie asked if Liz was still on CVVHD (continuous hemodialysis)—she was. Tim ("I'm the non-medical one") clearly disapproved of our medical abbreviations.

"Is she still on pqrstuvwxyz?" he texted.

"Continuous dialysis," Jackie replied with an exasperated emoji. "Is that better for you?"

Jamie was not going to miss a chance to disparage his little brother.

"Dialysis has to do with kidneys, Tim. Those are organs in your body that eliminate bad products from the body through a liquid substance called urine. Continuous means it's all the time."

Apparently Tim was not amused. "Phew. Glad we consulted the ophthalmology guy, right, Mark?"

Not being in medical school yet, Mark deferred: "I haven't got my short coat yet, so I don't know."

They all agreed that their mom was getting better when she brightened up and started yelling for "Help."

On Wednesday, March 23, I sent out a favorable report.

"Mom had a very good night. She was anxious so they gave her Fentanyl twice, and she slept all night. She had one episode of heart rate drop to the 40s with suctioning. She's sleepy but arousable and responsive. They're going to put her on vent pressure support and see how long she can make it. The report on the abdominal fluid so far is positive only for white blood cells, which indicate likely infection. Hopefully we will have another day of forward progress. Also, this afternoon I found out where I stood in the pecking order: Mom: 'I need Jane (Elzinga)'—Me: 'She's coming tonight.' Mom: 'What time?' Me: '6:30.' Mom: 'Sooner.' Me: 'I'm here now . . . Is she better than me?' Mom: 'Yes.'

My evening text was a little grimmer: "Mom is hanging in there but very anxious and frustrated. They're trying to wean her off her ventilator, but she made it only two hours in the weaning mode (pressure support) this morning before her heart rate went up and she had to go back on assist control (full support).

"The critical care PA just told me that her abdominal fluid from yesterday's tap is growing enterococcus, a type of bacteria normally from the bowel. It'll be difficult to treat; it showed up even though she was already on antibiotics that should have covered it when she got sick last Friday. There have been no spontaneous drops in heart rate today, although I just saw her drop from 110 to 65 with tracheal suctioning. She's so fragile right now. Please continue to guard her with your prayers."

I texted the same message to dozens of prayer partners that evening, and, despite the unfavorable events of the day, I went to bed with a sense of calm that night that had been lacking the night before.

Prayers were being answered the following morning as Liz was once again placed on the weaning mode of the ventilator. She had no fever, and her blood pressure remained stable. The latter was important because stable blood pressure was a prerequisite for getting Liz off the continuous dialysis to the preferred three-times-weekly schedule she had been on before. The nephrologist even offered encouragement that return of kidney function was still a possibility. As I noted on the family text, the biggest problem of the day was "terrible anxiety."

Jackie suggested that the heart rate drops might simply be from a vaso-vagal response (stimulating the vagus nerve in the chest) with tracheal suctioning. Tim reminded us all that this was the term we had used when Tom had fainted in the heat as a kid and fallen into the roadside dirt (now mud) next to the car while relieving himself in a desert near Marfa, Texas, on a family road trip to Mexico.

Tim remembered that one of his own shoes had fallen out of the car at "that little desert escapade" and that he had gone to Mexico with only one shoe. We had stopped at a "no shoes, no shirt, no service" restaurant, so Tim had hobbled in with one shoe on, leaning on Jamie's shoulder to feign a sprained ankle so we would be served.

"Why didn't we stop at Walmart and get you another shoe instead of having you act like you had a sprained ankle?" Jackie asked.

"You know the rules in the Paauw family," I had to remind everybody. "You lose your shoes, you have to go without."

Even Liz, now awake, had to smile at that exchange. It was good to be able to jest on occasion amid dark times.

My afternoon text introduced a thorny topic that would take center stage for a few weeks.

"Mom's mad at me. Not sure why; she just says I lied to her. I just had an hour-long talk with Sandy, a care manager. As I anticipated, we developed a problem when Mom's continuous dialysis went down, immediately making her LTACH eligible . . . They don't want to leave Liz in ICU just because she's on a ventilator, and the only alternative is this or another LTACH. I said I have three kids who would refuse that adamantly. I mentioned the possibility of going to Spectrum (they call this an EMTALA transfer). Sandy said that would be a very difficult move to accomplish unless we could come up with something Spectrum has that St. Mary's doesn't. She thought maybe Randy might come up with some sort of GI reason to do it."

Jackie immediately weighed in. "NO LTACH . . . I REFUSE!!! SUCH HORRENDOUS CARE!!! It wasn't just last weekend but the whole time she was there. Oh, and Dad ripped them a good one so they especially won't like us."

I pointed out that Sandy understood our feelings and, being a St. Mary's person, was not trying to defend LTACH. I also pointed out that it was Tim, not me, who had ripped LTACH a new one. Tom agreed.

"No LTACH; here's something that Spectrum has that Saint's doesn't—doctors who come see patients when needed."

Although this wasn't true, I had to laugh at that; I was pretty sure Sandy wasn't going to be down with that. Jackie suggested moving her mother to Spectrum ICU and then transferring to progressive 6 South when she got off the ventilator because "Spectrum treats Dad like royalty." Although this seemed like hyperbole, there was an element of truth in her statement, and I entertained serious thoughts about Jackie's proposal. Jackie went on a rant about all the ways in which LTACH had mistreated her mom, finishing with, "I could write a book, but I'll stop." Actually, she just had.

I proposed that several of the kids join me in a meeting with Sandy about the matter. Jackie immediately volunteered because "this will not happen; it's negligent care." I cautioned my kids not to lump St. Mary's in with LTACH, since they were technically two separate entities. I relayed to our kids that when the care manager asked me if we'd had a nursing problem or a physician problem, "I told them both. It's not all the nurses, either. Tosha and Jeff were great. It only takes a few lazy ones to hurt the patient's recovery."

Another serious issue we were dealing with as a family was Liz's worsening anxiety, which initiated one of the most comprehensive text discussions our family engaged in. Almost every family member weighed in at some point. It started when I expressed a realization that "We are probably enabling Mom's anxiety and some overly needy behavior . . . She needs some tough love."

Due to her anxiety, Liz especially hated to wake up alone at night. Tim asked if a psych consult might be useful, and Laura mentioned that maybe Psych could give us different approaches or strategies to try with Liz to lessen her anxiety. Emily, a Psych-Med social worker herself, noted that those would probably better come from Social Work or Palliative Care.

The ICU team started a conversation about the consideration of moving Liz toward "comfort care" again—aka, withdrawing aggressive treatment options to allow her to pass away. Tim immediately checked with Randy on this and then texted us: "Randy doesn't think comfort care is the next step—and I agree with him. We are 3 months from a 110-mph accident on Mom. Yelling 'Help!' doesn't constitute dying. She needs better control of sleep and anxiety."

"I guarantee the ICU team thinks she will eventually succumb to all of this," I pointed out. "The odds say they are right. If Mom doesn't want to get better and cooperate, however that happens, she has no chance."

Mark asked whether the staff was doing any therapy with his mom.

"At Spectrum we took Mom on a lap around the unit. It took like four of us to do it, but we did," he recalled. "We also had that PT come in every day and force her to move, even though she could barely hold her head up. Maybe she needs some actual therapy to feel like she's making some progress. If I were stuck in bed all day and no one was moving me, I would start freaking out, too. If a team came to move me and sit me up every day and I was wheeled around, I might feel like I'm actually getting somewhere. We need her to move and feel like she's actually getting better."

It gave us all pause to imagine how we would feel lying in bed for months with little sign of progress.

"She fails the vent weaning not because of physical intolerance but because of her anxiety," I stated, though this would eventually turn out to be wrong. "I'm very certain the next suggestion from Sandy will be 'What have you guys thought about letting her just be comfortable?' Emily, any suggestions on how we make and activate a plan?"

"When caring for Mom, we should encourage her to take personal responsibility, reinforce the progress she has made, and remember that, if we need to stay away from the situation to provide the best care, that is OK," Emily replied.

Halle also had suggestions that we found helpful: "One of the best things is to pick one battle at a time. Everyone will get too stressed out trying to deal with all the issues at once. Maybe setting up some type of schedule in advance of who will come and when would give her something to look forward to. Not trying to impose my views on anyone, but I know you all have to be exhausted. It's been a long time. Praying you figure out what to do."

"That's a great idea, Halle," Laura enthused. "We all need to spend time with her but also need time away."

Tim chimed in, "Scheduling would be my preference—it builds a feeling of consistency."

As I have noted, this was one of the best family meetings we'd had about Liz's care. Who says texting is impersonal? Of course, the magical mood was broken when oldest brother Jamie finally contributed: "Wow. Like 300 messages. Can someone summarize the morning, since I don't read very well?"

Nurse Jackie's mocking comment proved to be the final word for the day: "I'm a doctor, I can't do things for myself . . ."

That afternoon, Mark tried a new approach to his mom's anxiety: ignorance.

"Mom called out 'help' just once, and we ignored it and just kept talking about other stuff. She seems pretty okay right now, actually. She's smiling at my jokes and stuff."

"If she laughs at *Mark's* jokes, call the nurse because something's gotta be wrong," Tom commented.

Mark agreed. "Haha, I pushed the nurse button to let them know she was laughing at horrible jokes."

CHAPTER **21**

The large neon sign with bright green lettering split the darkness of the night. I stared at it through the window in Liz's ICU, tormented by the words "Mary Free Bed Hospital." The building stood in the near distance just beyond a large parking lot. *It might as well be a continent away from us.*

Despite our initial happiness to be back in the ICU, we were each tense over Liz's progress—or lack thereof—now that she was there. We all understood that there were only a few scenarios in terms of how this would play out, short of her somehow miraculously transferring straight back to Mary Free Bed, an outcome that seemed nearly impossible. The probabilities of being transferred back to LTACH or simply not surviving the ICU at all were much higher. This didn't stop us from searching daily for signs of progress that might lessen those probabilities.

Day by day, we observed little progress on most fronts: respiratory, kidney, mental/anxiety. The plan to schedule and rotate family visitors was working well from our standpoint but seemed to be making little, if any, difference in Liz's anxiety. And every evening I stared out that window, longing to be under that green sign.

On Saturday, March 26, Tom stopped in at 6:00 a.m. to visit his mom before his nursing shift one floor above; he came again later to sit for a while during his lunch break. I was in at 7:00 a.m. before my shift at Spectrum and back again in the evening. Jackie stopped by for her turn in the afternoon. That night I summed up the day for everyone.

"Mom was somewhat anxious this morning when I saw her before work and still when I got back this afternoon. However, she has been doing well on the ventilator weaning mode since this morning; her anxiety had prevented her from making it more than an hour or two any day previously this week. I think she's been off at least 6 hours so far today.

"I babied her this afternoon with a foot massage with some expensive lotion I found again in the bottom of a bin in the room. She loved it! Right now we are listening to some piano CDs sent to us by our friend Mary VandeGuchte (yay, North Carolina; praying for Mom!) Mom has been very relaxed and in fact slept for 45 minutes. She's supposed to get dialysis today yet. On that note she had a pathetic amount of urine produced overnight, but her nurse just told me it picked up significantly since this morning. Nothing like last Friday, but at least a little better than yesterday. I feel God answering prayers in this quiet afternoon together. Almost like a date . . . don't we live an exciting life?"

Three days later, on March 29, Jackie came in to give her mom a manicure and noticed an episode of atrial fibrillation with what is known as rapid ventricular response. Later that evening Liz had another, yet different, rapid heart rate: supraventricular tachycardia. This made me worry, since as I regularly told everyone, "Her heart has been the one strong organ." I presumed these incidences were more manifestations of sick sinus syndrome, not a primary issue stemming from the heart, but we seemed to be making very slow progress at best.

The following day Liz went to the operating room to have some hardware surgically removed from her right foot and ankle, a surgery Dr. Sandman said went well. In fact, her main pain afterward was not foot pain but that associated with the ongoing pressure sore by her tailbone.

Remarkably, Liz slept well that night and was in good spirits the next day when Tom, who had worked through the night, reported, "Mom slept well last night. I checked on her twice, and she was asleep both times. She's in great spirits this morning, smiling and chatting with me! Vitals look good. She's bragging to me about her surgery and how the hardware's out now."

Liz had now been back in the ICU for ten days, and this was the first day she wasn't plagued with anxiety. I think I was correct when I noted, "What a difference Zoloft makes when it finally kicks in." Unfortunately, a conversation I had later that day revealed some grim news:

"How much urine has Mom been producing?" Tamara asked me.

I loved it that Tam called her "Mom."

"They took her Foley catheter out, if that gives you an idea," I said.

"I'm not sure. Is that good?"

"Bad," Mark answered. "Means no urine."

"Oh," Tamara replied.

Just before noon the next day, Friday, April 1, I was able to let everybody know that Liz had been off the ventilator and on a t-piece for over an hour. She did have a panic attack at that point, but with much reassurance she hung in there for four hours until her heart rate dropped. Despite being placed back on the ventilator on "pressure support" (the weaning mode), her heart continued to be irritable, with frequent rate drops that necessitated that Liz be placed back on full ventilator support. Although this was discouraging after such a strong performance off the ventilator that day, I told Liz we were all very proud of her and that she was a hero. She didn't open her eyes but did manage a slight smile, telling me that she was proud of herself as well.

Later that day I noticed that, when the nurse changed a VAC (vacuum) dressing on her foot, Liz had significant bleeding from an ulcer on her foot that had been debrided at the last surgery. The nurse called Orthopedics to come address this matter, but Ortho deferred to the Plastic Surgery team. Plastics in turn referred the situation to the Wound service, who had already left the hospital for the day. Liz had received a unit of blood for a hemoglobin level of 6.9 the previous day, but it had still been 6.9 this morning, necessitating another unit of blood. I had wondered where the blood was being lost, and now I knew; someone was going to have to fix this. No wonder that, when I woke her up that day, Liz just smiled and mouthed that she was "pooped."

The storm hit the next morning, April 2, when a new doc came in to tell me Liz couldn't stay there in the ICU but had to go to a long-term acute care hospital (LTACH), either there in St. Mary's or elsewhere. When I objected, she mentioned an LTACH at nearby Metropolitan Hospital. I asked if Sandi, the care manager, was there that day; she was, even though it was a Saturday, and would come to speak with me later.

I was perplexed that the staff was so eager to transfer Liz to an LTACH when she was still on a ventilator and her heart rhythm was all over the place—earlier that morning I had requested Cardiology to come to see her for that reason. They suspected that the arrhythmias were due to the irritation of ventilator weaning, dialysis, and suctioning, but I pointed out that Liz was still having the arrhythmias when she was asleep with no stimulation. I was not pleased with the Critical Care physician's approach.

"We're slowly being boxed in," I texted to everybody. "It would have been nice if this lady had introduced herself and talked to me a bit before confronting me with getting Mom out of her unit. She walked in and said to Lindsey, 'How about LTACH today?' Not cool."

Making it worse, Liz apparently had a large reaccumulation of fluid around her right lung for which an ultrasound was to be done to see whether the fluid was amenable to being tapped off again to help her breathing.

Unfortunately, Liz heard the conversation about being moved soon and became very anxious about it. Tim weighed in after talking to our liaison for the insurance company.

"I just spoke to Kendra. She is calling Dad. She said that this was not the plan and that she talked with Sandi yesterday, who said Mom would likely stay in ICU until Free Bed or go to a Saint Mary's floor in between, if needed."

Indeed, Kendra did call to reassure me that, because of what had happened at LTACH previously and because Liz was covered by straight auto insurance, as opposed to a blend of auto and personal health insurance, the usual rules would not apply. Allstate would cover whatever the docs decided was right. Kendra told me that the plan they had agreed on the evening before was to get Liz off the ventilator while in ICU and then transfer her directly to Mary Free Bed.

Kendra assured me that this new doc had not spoken with anybody about Liz before confronting me. My own blood pressure began to come back down. While I was on the phone with Kendra, Liz's nurse had prayed with her. When I asked her about that, this godly nurse told me that Liz had gotten very anxious, so she had felt Liz needed prayer support. I told her that I loved her for doing that with my wife and made sure my kids knew as well. Such a blessing to have Christian caregivers. I, in turn, forwarded that favor to Tim by texting out a selfie, dressed all in blue for Autism Awareness Day.

As it happened, the chest tap was not scheduled for that day or the next because of weekend scheduling, but a cardiologist did come by to evaluate Liz's arrhythmias. His diagnosis was still sick sinus syndrome from the constant stress on her heart, a diagnosis that was not a major concern and certainly not worth the risk of placing a pacemaker. He assured me that Liz's echocardiogram revealed a very strong heart.

"We always knew she had a big heart," I texted. "Good to know it's as strong as it is big."

~

While our family text thread had been created in January to share up-to-date news about Liz with all our kids and spouses, one of the neat things about it was the banter that occasionally popped up about humorous family events, even in some of the darkest moments. The NCAA basketball championship semifinals were being played that evening, and our son Tom finally looked as though he were going to win his first "plaque."

The extended family on Liz's side had established a bracket-picking tradition in the 1980s, complete with a plaque on which was engraved the name of the winner of each year's contest. As the family had expanded into a new generation, it had become ever more difficult to take that honor, along with the plaque that would hang in the winner's home for the next year, not to mention the exalted title of "Grand Poobah (PB)." Over the years fierce inter-family and even intra-family rivalries had developed. Poor Tom, along with his cousin "Basement Bob," had set a record for futility, going the longest time without winning a plaque. Now Tom appeared to be on the verge, and the rhetoric flowed, including references to an unfortunate auto-correction changing "rooting" to "tooting."

Mark: "I'm tooting for Tom."

Tom: "I will probably only answer to 'PB' soon."

Mark: "If Nova wins this game, do you automatically win?"

Tom: "I automatically won when I turned in my picks" (strong talk for a record loser).

Dad: "It's ova with 'Nova."

Tim: "I'm 'tooting' for Tom. too."

Jackie: "LOL. Is it bad that I was thinking about 'tooting' for Tom, too?"

Tim: "And since I'm 'tooting' for Tom, I'll be happy to call him Poobah for the next year."

Dad: "I rooted for him first. After the second night (see MSU), I started 'tooting' for Tom."

Jackie: "LOL."

Dad (as 'Nova' wins): "Poobah, Poobah, Poobah—let the trash talk begin."

Tom: "Yaaaaaaaaaay!!! PB! I've been working on this since the early 90s!!!"

Tim: "Congrats, Tom!!!!"

Dad: "It's almost a shame. Tom's losing streak was historic."

Jackie: "I'm already bummed we can't tease him next year about it."

Tom: "This is literally one of the greatest achievements of my life!" (hopefully hyperbole in the moment).

Jamie: "Not to worry. Bob is still the most historic. He's the Cubs."

Brek (tournament director this year): "You might want to double-check my math before celebrating too much."

Jamie: "Shouldn't that have been done before now?!"

Dad: "Whoa! That's like Dewey beats Truman!"

Tom (realizing he might have to wait two days yet): "Well, I'm not worried; my team just won by 50."

Tom: "Also, our Easter egg microbrew hunt might be on News 13" (I'm almost embarrassed to admit that he had invented an Easter egg hunt for his buddies in which the wives hid craft beer for their husbands).

Dad: "We should celebrate your poobahship at a microbrew next week." (Yes, we do live in Beer City.)

Tom: "Deal!!!"

Dad: "Wow! You are excited."

And so it went . . .

⁕

On Monday, 1800 milliliters of fluid was tapped off from around Liz's right lung. Unfortunately, her ventilator weaning did not progress that day because her heart rate dropped into the 20s. Her foot continued to bleed heavily, and the Wound service came to investigate it. The good news came from the Infectious Disease doc, who reported that no bacteria had grown from the previous week's abdominal tap. When Tim asked what the biggest prayer need was, I responded, "No arrhythmias, foot wound to stop bleeding. As always, urine production."

Tom visited his mom several times that night and noted that her anxiety about being moved was starting to improve. Liz smiled at him the next morning and sarcastically mouthed, "I'm going home next week, right?"

Throughout that week Liz made slow but incremental progress. Her ventilator weaning efforts continued to be hampered by dropping heart rates. Anytime the weaning efforts coincided with her hemodialysis or physical therapy, her heart rate would almost certainly drop. On Thursday, April 7, Liz traveled to Interventional Radiology (IR) to have her temporary VasCath dialysis catheter changed to a tunneled PermaCath. This was an indication that her docs didn't think kidney recovery was likely, but we made it a matter of continued prayer.

One day as I helped the Wound nurse change Liz's foot VAC dressing, I was surprised at how gruesome the high ankle wound looked. It was larger than I anticipated and had exposed tendons. Plastic Surgery was telling me that they would cover those three foot/ankle wounds the following week with skin grafts and muscle-skin flaps. The care management staff was working to coordinate her eventual transfer to Mary Free Bed, the staff of which was saying that Liz had to be off the vent for four days before they would accept her back. That weekend physical therapy got her up into a chair for the first time since she had been moved back from LTACH.

Liz traveled from IR to CAT scan, where she underwent a chest scan before returning to the ICU. The CT caught me by surprise. Apparently a chest surgeon had been consulted about recurring fluid around Liz's lung. When I asked the ICU physician's assistant about that, she mentioned possible surgery to remove and prevent recurrence of the fluid. She suggested that the surgeon might be thinking of removing the lining of the right lung, which I thought might be a huge stress for Liz in her current deconditioned state. On the other hand, the ventilator weaning efforts had not been going well; every time they put Liz on a weaning ventilator mode she complained of shortness of breath, even when her oxygen levels looked okay.

Early the next morning, Friday, April 8, I met with one of our heroes, Dr. Dikin, the Intensivist, who reviewed Liz's chest CT scan with me. Dr. Dikin pointed out a thick rind of material that basically obliterated most of the airspace on the right side, leaving a small area at the top of that lung as the only part that was still functioning—almost her entire right lung was a "whiteout." Although her left lung was much better, it had also lost airspace at the bottom due to a fluid collection there.

Dr. Dikin noted that the trouble Liz was having being weaned off the ventilator was a factor of operating cumulatively on less than one full lung. He told me that the chest surgeon would like to do a thoracotomy on Monday, April 11, to strip away that rind like an orange peel. As he would likely have to leave two chest tubes in place, I was guessing that this would be a painful experience for Liz. The chest surgeon wanted to meet with me at noon the next day—which was bad timing, since I would be working.

"She likely won't be able to get off the ventilator without it," I texted my kids. "And if she did get off, she would be a pulmonary cripple."

I broke down and wept when I told Liz about it, but this only made me feel worse. *She needs me to be strong.*

The dialysis nurse surprised us right after that since we weren't expecting dialysis that day. Liz adamantly refused dialysis, since she despised it anyway, and the previous day it had been discontinued early when her blood pressure had plummeted, necessitating the additional run this day. It took me 45 minutes to get her to agree to it, after which she was so anxious she wouldn't let me leave for some time. I was very late to work.

As I lay in bed that night, my racing mind would not let me fall asleep. I was all too aware that this day marked exactly three months since Liz's original accident. Randy Baker had told us early on to prepare ourselves for at least six months, likely longer, for full recovery, but now we were halfway there and not perceptibly any closer to that milestone than when Liz had first been admitted to the hospital. In some ways we were further away. As a former pastor of ours used to say, a lot of tears watered my pillow that night.

Our kids wasted no time in rounding up prayer support for the pending surgery. Tim volunteered to be there Saturday at noon to meet with the thoracic surgeon, who turned out to be an old friend of mine from the days when he had worked at Spectrum Health years earlier: Dr. Behrooz Shabahang ("Bruce" to me). It was a very cordial meeting, which Tim summed up in a family text:

"We just met Mom's lung surgeon. He knows Dad well, used to work at Spectrum and has been doing many of these surgeries over the last 26 years—a very nice and cautiously optimistic guy. Said it will take 2–3 hours because he won't finish the surgery until he knows her lungs are open and working again. She should immediately experience better breathing. CT showed only a fraction of the right upper lobe with air. Middle and lower lobes were completely sealed shut. He is confident this is a good idea, and in looking at the CT it is clear (even to me) that this is the right thing to do.

"Mark, he said that if you want to do a month's rotation with him sometime, he would love to have you. He is also an MSU grad. He made my day when he said, 'Your mom is family to me. I will take care of her.' And he gave me a hug. Incision will be 6 inches long above 5th rib from the back to her side. 3 chest tubes will be placed for 6 days to ensure ribs secure to lungs again without any more fluid buildup. He said that it may have no drainage, but he had learned this is the right amount of time from 26 years of doing it. 1 tube for each spot where buildup happens in the lung, since it is complex, not just in one location."

At about that time Jackie asked for prayers for Isaiah as well, as the little guy had a very important medical appointment the next day also, to monitor his development for any significant delays. It was going to be a big day for our family, and prayers were solicited from many quarters.

Surgery on Monday morning, April 11, was delayed for an hour for blood transfusions to correct Liz's low hemoglobin level but then went off at 8:30 a.m. amid a flurry of prayers from around the country. Jamie's community group had spent a long time in prayer the previous night, and we heard confirmation of prayers from Rev.

Corey Dykstra from my church and Rev. John Curry from Tim's. Westminster Seminary California let Tim know the West coast was sending up many prayers, also. After a few hours Liz returned to her room, followed shortly thereafter by an excited Dr. Shabahang. I was also excited as I texted to our kids:

"Dr. Shabahang told me the surgery went great, better than expected. He was able to drain off all the fluid, which was in multiple small compartments. He didn't have to do a decortication because there was no remaining debris after removing the fluid. He asked the anesthetist to give a big ventilation, and all three lobes of the right lung popped fully open. He was quite excited to tell me that. He said there was virtually no scarring on the lung from this process, so should be no residual compromise of lung function. He took off the part of the lining of the lung on the inner surface of the chest. He thinks she will be much improved."

"Praise the Lord!!!!!" Tim texted, speaking for all of us.

Laura noted that she had just listened to the Christian pop song "10,000 Reasons" on the radio, the same song she'd heard the last time Mom had major surgery.

To top off this red-letter day, Jackie, on her way home from an appointment with baby Isaiah to determine if he had any major developmental delays from his traumatic birth, told us that there were no concerns at this time but that Zay would need to be seen until after two years old to monitor language development. I told Jackie I often prayed for her mom and Zay together, "the sleepers" who a month earlier had both been sedated in the ICU at the same time.

Mark commented, "Such exciting news today!!" To which I had to reply, "Yes. Feeling so loved by God and our brothers and sisters today." Texts and Facebook posts were on their way out to let our many faithful prayer partners know the answers those prayers engendered.

Dr. Shabahang returned later that afternoon to report that the chest X-ray showed that Liz's right lung "looks perfect." All three lobes were 100% inflated and looked much better than he had anticipated. Dr. Shabahang entered our pantheon of heroes that day. As for me, I had a lot of thanksgiving to offer that night when I went to bed. Maybe it wouldn't be so long after all before I could bring Liz home to that room.

The next morning, Tuesday, April 12, Jackie visited her mom and reported that she was alert and responding appropriately, although having some pain. Jackie noted that her mom had currently been on pressure support (the weaning mode) for over an hour and was doing great.

The staff was trying to conceal their actions from Liz when they switched modes on the ventilator, as it had become apparent that, when she was aware they were switching, she didn't tolerate it well. Unfortunately, it seemed as though every time we made a step forward, something popped up to check our joy. Liz had had fevers through the night, so another belly tap was scheduled that afternoon in Interventional Radiology. The Infectious Disease (ID) doc was skeptical that the last abdominal culture had truly been negative.

When I left later that afternoon, Liz was doing great on the pressure support mode. I let our kids know that I couldn't imagine her not being on a t-piece within the next 24 hours. I ran into Randy Baker in the parking lot, since my car was parked five spots from his and we were leaving at the same time—meant to be. He had been praying for Liz's surgery the previous day and asked a lot of questions: kidneys, skin, belly, mental function. I felt so blessed to have such a skilled and godly physician overseeing every aspect of Liz's recovery.

After coming back to the hospital a short time later, the ICU PA informed me that Liz's belly tap showed a recurrent infection, so they were restarting antibiotics and consulting Randy again to see if he had any suggestions to finally get rid of it. Tim asked why they didn't just keep his mom on antibiotics, but Dr. Igwatu from ID had told me that he was worried we would eventually select out resistant bacteria by doing that.

One humorous side note from our association with Dr. Shabahang came the next day during our family texts: "I just met Laura Gelderloos; she's a nurse practitioner for Dr. Shabahang," I texted out. (Gelderloos was also our Laura's maiden name.)

"Yup; I see her notes all the time," Tom confirmed.

"The other me," Laura told us. "We had our anatomy grades switched a couple of times back at GRCC. Used to have dentist appointment mix-ups, too. She went to Calvin."

I quickly responded. "She said you both went to Calvin and that you had the same dentist. She's married and going to change her name. So now there won't be any Laura Gelderlooses."

Early the next morning, Wednesday, April 13, Tom texted out a picture of his mom, up in the chair. I was coming down the walkway into the hospital at that very moment so was excited to converse with her. Unfortunately, Liz had been given some pain meds to enable her to move to the chair and was consequently quite sleepy, although she gradually woke up.

Dr. Igwatu arrived to tell me that he was very perplexed about the recurrent abdominal infection; he postulated that there might be a persistent small leak from the bowel. He was anxious to hear Randy's take on the subject. Jackie, who was employed by Randy's group, was actually working with him that morning and was able to tell us that Randy had already seen Liz the previous night. He had ordered a contrast GI X-ray study "from above" through her feeding tube and "from below" through her ileostomy that day, as well as another one through her "pouch" stomach the next day to see if he could identify any leaking bowel.

Liz's nurse later reported that there were no suspicious areas on any of the studies. But Liz was able to tolerate a low ventilator setting all day, as well as the removal of three liters of fluid on dialysis without a blood pressure drop, so progress was being made.

As I lay in bed that evening, I was offering up petitions and prayers of thanksgiving, still not fully sure how this would all end up.

I returned late the next morning to find that Liz had been up in a chair on a trach mask (off the ventilator) for an hour and a half, although she was not very happy. Being up in the chair made her right chest sore, and her blood oxygen saturation was marginal (91%) but steady. It was good to have her up in a chair, in part because we signed some legal forms this day—wills, trusts, and powers-of-attorney.

Liz did great with that, other than that she had to use her left hand, which wasn't pretty. Tim, our only left-hander, was excited to welcome her to that club: "the only right-minded people in the world." Liz was half asleep as it was, and I had to wake her up a few times to finish her name, which turned out not to be much more than the scrawl that our attorney said was acceptable. When I texted word of this to the kids, Emily, the medical social worker and therefore the stickler for rules, had to pretend she wasn't hearing that, texting back a hands-over-ears emoji and the message, "La la la la . . . I'm not listening."

"It's OK, Em," I assured her. "When her hand stopped moving, I just grabbed it and gave her some help. Kinda like a puppet."

This, of course, elicited a grimacing emoji from Em, which prompted me to ask another question. "I've got the wrong glasses, Em; is that a smiley face?"

She was not amused.

Sometime later that day a Mary Free Bed liaison came to evaluate Liz for a potential eventual transfer to that institution. To say that this nurse was underwhelmed would be, well, an understatement. She kept commenting to me on how immensely deconditioned Liz was, and she did not seem hopeful that Liz would qualify for the acute rehab floor at Mary Free Bed on which she had previously been admitted more than two months earlier. A lot had happened to Liz since then, and most of it had been bad—bad as in debilitating.

When the liaison left Liz's room, I immediately set about texting my close friend Kristen Duthler, who held a similar Mary Free Bed liaison position at Spectrum Health. Kristen had facilitated Liz's original transfer to Mary Free Bed back in late January, and when Liz transferred over to St. Mary's a few days later I had extracted a promise from Kristen that she would make sure she would be brought back into Mary Free Bed when the time came.

Neither of us had known in early February that that time would be more than two muscle-wasting months later. Nonetheless, I reached out to remind Kristen of her promise, asking if she could intervene in the process to get my now non-qualifying wife back into the acute rehab floor at Mary Free Bed. As deconditioned as Liz was, I knew that her only likelihood to survive would entail being admitted back into the highest level of rehabilitative care.

This was outside the scope of Kristen's job, as Liz was at St. Mary's rather than Spectrum Health now, but I was not squeamish about calling in a favor in what I saw as a life-or-death decision for Liz. Kristen endeared herself to me for life by immediately reassuring me that she would speak with Dr. Ho and make sure the transfer happened. (Sorry, Dr. Ho; it turns out that Kristen actually does have you wrapped around her finger.)

Results from the fever workup began to trickle in later that day. The final radiology reading of her abdominal studies from the previous day had revealed no areas of concern for a leak, but the tapped abdominal fluid, although negative for bacterial growth, revealed high levels of white cells with low glucose concentration. In view of the continued fevers, it was very likely that Liz had a persistent abdominal infection—with no sign of why it kept coming back.

Despite that, when I arrived on Friday afternoon, April 15, I found Liz off the ventilator for more than 24 hours and tolerating the end of her three-hour dialysis run, albeit with a marginally low blood pressure. Liz had not been having any arrhythmias, so I had asked the nurse to hold her antiarrhythmic metoprolol that morning before her dialysis, as the metoprolol caused lowering of blood pressure.

The nurse assured me that it had been only a small dose and shouldn't affect Liz's blood pressure, but I thought otherwise. I asked the critical care team to write an order holding Liz's metoprolol on the mornings when she was to have dialysis. Her "sick sinus syndrome" seemed to have improved after Liz's chest surgery, so I was not convinced Liz needed the metoprolol any longer anyway.

While our kids wondered when the staff would start to remove the three chest tubes that remained in place, which were a source of considerable discomfort to Liz, there was still too much drainage coming from the tubes. The team didn't want that fluid to build up in her chest again.

When I came in early the next morning, I encountered Wendy, the nurse who had saved Liz's life a few weeks earlier, in the parking lot. Wendy's overnight assignment had been the room next to Liz's, so she had, at my request, kept an eye on Liz for me.

"Her fever came back so she became confused," Wendy told me. "She slept only a few hours. She kept yelling for 'help' and even rattled her bed rails."

This was something we hadn't seen her do for a few months.

Liz was wiped out that morning and hardly acknowledged me at all. Since I spent the afternoon sawing some trees with Tim, I recruited Mark to come and monitor his mother until our close friend Jane Elzinga came to sit with her at 5:00. Jane was among that small group of close Christian friends who came often to sit with Liz through the long afternoon hours, especially during dialysis times, which tended to discourage Liz and almost always wiped her out.

When Tom came by early the next morning, however, he found his mother alert and chatty, asking for a handheld game of some sort to help her regain some hand dexterity. Jamie immediately recommended Candy Crush, apparently with an ulterior motive. Tam and Mark suspected that he was just trying to recruit a "referral" to give him extra lives (apparently that's a thing). Jamie brushed them off with, "I'm playing right now. Stop interrupting. Just beat level 1422." It was one of those days on the family text thread—complete with a wandering discussion of how much Tim looked like Kiefer Sutherland.

As Liz had been off the ventilator for more than three days, the intensive care team signed off on her care. On Sunday, April 17, a hospitalist, Dr. Kim Turke, saw Liz in the morning, starting what was to become a lengthy patient relationship with this skilled and compassionate physician. Emily had had several miscarriages at that point in time, and Dr. Turke's husband had been her physician through those difficult experiences. Emily assured us that they were "a wonderful couple."

That morning a pulmonary physician changed Liz to a fenestrated tracheostomy, one with a valve that allowed her to speak. It was wonderful to hear that squeaky voice after such a long time. We were thrilled when Dr. Turke spoke of Mary Free Bed (thank you, Kristen Duthler!), but she warned us that Liz wouldn't be ready to transfer there until Thursday or Friday. Dr. Turke wrote conditional transfer orders to a regular floor in Saint Mary's, orders that wouldn't be completed unless the ICU needed her bed for someone else. Otherwise, Liz was to stay where she was until the transfer to Mary Free Bed.

Liz still had two chest tubes to be removed, likely the next day when Dr. Shabahang returned from vacation. Dr. Turke also asked Randy to schedule an upper endoscopy the next day as part of the continuing effort to find the source of Liz's recurring abdominal infection. Dr. Igwatu, Infectious Disease, assured me he was going to leave Liz on antibiotics for a long time.

In the meantime, although she was massively deconditioned, things were slowly starting to look up for her recovery.

"Her vital signs have been very stable, and she was taken off the heart monitor today," I texted the kids. "There are no more signs of the rate changes they said were a manifestation of 'sick sinus syndrome' from the stress of everything she's been through. Still scheduled for dialysis three times a week, but who knows? God is fixing Mom one step at a time. I'm starting to get excited over the prospect that she might make it to Mark and Tam's wedding on June 3."

I was present later that afternoon when they decided to catheterize Liz's bladder to see if she was making any urine. I let the kids know to "pray for urine." Liz was so hopeful for positive news on this front that it was heartbreaking for me to see the disappointment registered in her face when the results were known. A sad-faced emoji told our kids the story: "50 mls." But we were determined in continued hope and prayers for return of kidney function, even now after more than two months of none. Still, the bright green "Mary Free Bed Hospital" sign across the parking lot did not seem so far away any longer . . .

The chest tube removal and the endoscopy proceeded uneventfully, and on the evening of Tuesday, April 19, I was moved to text out, not only to our kids but to all our prayer partners, a grateful testimony of God's faithfulness to Liz:

"Since her chest surgery Mom has made steady progress, I think the best she's done over these 3 months. She has been off of the ventilator for more than 5 days and is enjoying using her voice after having her trach replaced with a speaking model 2 days ago. Not sure how this will work out for me, though; she managed to borrow a phone this afternoon and called me at work: 'Where are you?' (Of course, I came right over). She has had no fevers recently, and all tests for a GI leak have been negative. At this time the plan is to move Mom to Mary Free Bed as early as Thursday; several of their staff have contacted me to say how impressed they are with Mom's progress since the chest surgery. Dr. Shabahang also came in today and expressed that he was thrilled with the outcome. We are thanking God for his mercies, which are new every day."

My kids were thrilled.

"Praise God!" Jamie enthused.

"WOW!!!!!!!!!!!!! God is good," Tim elaborated.

"I guess she can get back to her fav pastime and talk on the phone," Jackie commented.

"Second fav pastime; don't forget shopping," Jamie interjected.

On Wednesday the Wound service changed Liz's VAC dressing but had no word on when she might get skin grafting; we had seen the Plastic Surgery resident once or twice but not in a week or so. Later that day Tamara texted out a picture of Liz taking a spoonful of apple sauce from a Speech therapist who was there to test her swallowing abilities—the first food she had taken in two and a half months. Em questioned the status of communication between Mark and Tam when Mark expressed surprise that his fiancée was visiting his mom.

"Tom likes to use the 'find my phone app' to keep track of me," Emily told everybody.

"Yeah, Mark, you should get a 'stalk me' app too; that's a sign of a healthy relationship," Tim remarked.

But it was okay because Em came through with "Don't worry, Tamara, I will show you all the ways to trick that app."

Thursday, April 21, turned out to be that day we had longed for over the past 82 days, by my count—moving day. It seemed surreal to realize that we were going back to Mary Free Bed at long last. Tim left work early to meet me in Liz's ICU room at 3:30 p.m. It took us about a half hour to load up all the other stuff on several carts and to follow Liz on the long trek through hallways and tunnels to Room 3122 in Mary Free Bed.

As we passed through one lengthy ground floor tunnel, we came to a blue line painted across the floor that demarcated St. Mary's Hospital from Mary Free Bed Hospital. Tim and I celebrated like a couple of little kids as we rolled across that boundary. I could see that Liz was happy, too, although not able to show much exuberance in her deconditioned state, with a tracheostomy minimizing her voice. The joy of finally making it back to Mary Free Bed against all human odds brought tears to my eyes, but so did Liz's pathetic effort at celebration, which served to reveal what a shell of her former self she had become in the past three and a half months.

As we turned through the doorway of her new room, we observed a picture of a helmeted kid riding a bike on the wall just outside her room. The inscription over it read, "It isn't like a miracle. It is a miracle." How true that was for us! Tim and I embraced as the St. Mary's staff helped the Free Bed staff settle his mom into her new room.

"We finally made it," he stated quietly.

"Yes," I answered through my tears, "we finally made it."

Indeed, we felt like Pilgrims. And like them, the first order of business after Liz was settled in was to offer up a heartfelt prayer of praise and thanksgiving to the One who had kept Liz safe and brought her back to this place.

Dr. Ho, her rehab doc, came in shortly afterward to do an initial evaluation of his returning patient. It took about thirty seconds for him to turn an apprehensive look toward Tim and me and say incredulously, "She's *really* deconditioned."

Tim nodded in agreement and smiled. "Yep, and we're hoping you're going to fix her."

Liz couldn't do much more than turn her head from side to side, and that only with great effort. At that moment I could see the realization dawn on Dr. Ho that he had been snookered, yet he remained committed.

"Then we'll fix her," Dr. Ho confirmed.

Under my breath I thanked Kristen again for arranging Liz's return to the acute care side of Mary Free Bed. To this day I believe that transition saved Liz's life.

CHAPTER 22

Morning dawned on Friday, April 22, and I was tired. Liz had been very anxious the night before and had begged me to stay overnight, so I had gone home Thursday evening to bring back some work attire for the next morning. Liz was confused and had rung the nurse call button at least every half hour. By early morning she had increased the frequency to every fifteen minutes; she also called me over frequently to bring her ice chips. In my bleary morning state, I was grateful that her nurses were some of the most patient I had ever encountered.

As I was preparing to leave for work, the staff told me that Liz's first scheduled therapy was to be at 11:00 a.m. but that they often added therapy on a patient's first day. I knew that Liz was scheduled for dialysis in the St. Mary's dialysis unit that afternoon, and I anticipated that she would sleep better that night. I went for a quick bike ride after work before joining Liz in the dialysis suite. She was wiped out and kept pleading "Help!" to me. I sat with her in Dialysis for two hours but was unable to carry on a conversation with her so eventually left to catch up on home stuff. I felt bad leaving with thirty minutes to go in the dialysis run, but I decided I'd rather spend my time with her in her room later.

Laura was just arriving to visit Liz as she got back to her room from dialysis. Liz was excited with the news that Laura brought: Liz's sister Sue, daughter Amy, and granddaughter Katie were coming from Ann Arbor the next day to help Liz's mom buy a dress for the upcoming wedding before coming to visit Liz. Her spirits had picked up noticeably by the time I got back that night.

On Saturday morning I texted out a surprising update:

"Dr. Sam Ho, rehab specialist, came by this morning to see Mom. He told us his plan is to get Mom home (!) for a break with a 24-hour aide as soon as she is medically stable, and then bring her back for more intensive therapy (he didn't say if this would be inpatient or outpatient). He thinks that after 15 weeks in the hospital she needs to get home ASAP, as an encouragement to her.

"Because of her anxiety and poor sleep the last two nights, he is also ordering a sitter to be with her at all times when family is not. Mom is very excited about both things. Today she has occupational therapy (up in a chair for her first shower in 106 days), physical therapy, speech therapy, and PT again. They mean business here."

Jamie finally addressed the always hovering elephant in the room: "When can we start looking into liver and/or kidney transplant qualifications/options? Few months of rehab first? Could possibly have living related kidney and liver donor."

"Kidney," I agreed. "Not sure about liver."

It was grim to be waging this long battle and still have end-stage organ disease waiting at the finish line.

On Sunday, April 24, we began to try to track down a few loose ends. When Liz had first come to Mary Free Bed back in January, we had brought a suitcase full of her clothes, including several specially designed items that her sister Jean had made by hand to accommodate her new ileostomy. Jean is a magician with anything regarding knitting or sewing, and she had produced an amazing line of uniquely designed clothes within a short period of time.

Liz had not worn any of the items before urgently transferring back to St. Mary's Hospital in late January. The reader may recall that a representative from Security at Mary Free Bed had stopped by at that time to pick up Liz's suitcase, with a promise to store it for us until we returned to Mary Free Bed. Liz had been asking about that suitcase now for several days, with no results.

Early in the afternoon an embarrassed head of Security had come to apologize that their team had discovered that the suitcase had been given to charity back in late March because they didn't know what had happened to Liz in the meantime. When we asked why they hadn't just asked around, the Security guy said that someone had tried to find us but that no one had apparently thought to look in St. Mary's Hospital. After two months of hearing nothing from us, they had assumed that Liz had died and would not be coming back, so they had donated her things where they thought they might be useful to someone.

Furthermore, they didn't remember where they had donated the suitcase, so we had no option of trying to track it down. We did have to laugh a bit at the visual of a customer bringing back to a Goodwill store somewhere a bunch of defective blouses that each had a velcroed flap on the lower right area in front. Jamie summed up what we were all thinking: "That adds to the legend of her recovery. 'We never had a suitcase that long so we assumed that person didn't make it.' She's the most epic mom ever."

Later that afternoon Tim, who had been trying to track down his mom's cell phone, which had not been seen since the crash, got off the phone with Sprint. The phone had not been used since January 7, the day before the crash. Mysteriously, the police at the scene had somehow been able to find Jackie's cell number to notify the family of

Liz's accident but claimed to have never seen the phone. Another of life's mysteries that was never to be solved.

Late Tuesday evening I sent out a progress report to our kids and prayer partners: "Mom is settling into a routine here at Mary Free Bed. She gets multiple therapies in the morning followed by 3–4 hours of dialysis on Monday, Wednesday, and Friday afternoons. Needless to say, those three days are not her favorite. Tomorrow she has occupational therapy (getting dressed), in-room physical therapy, speech therapy, occupational therapy in the gym, and in-room physical therapy, all before lunch.

"And speaking of lunch, Mom had her first food other than ice chips in about 3 months; chocolate pudding. She didn't care for it—too rich. Guess 3 months of not eating will change your taste perceptions. She still has many moments of depression and anxiety. For now she is assigned a sitter for all times when family is not in the room, and she is grateful for that. She has an orthopedic appointment Thursday; hopefully she'll get weight-bearing privileges. Still not sure when she'll have skin-grafting on her right foot. It's so nice not to have life-threatening issues every other day. I'm thankful to God to be where we are."

That same day Tim finally brought in a new cell phone for Liz; her sitter was going to have to help her use it, but it was a nice development to keep her in touch with her family. Liz did have a room phone, but she often carried her new cell phone with her to out-of-the-room therapy in the hope that a family member would call and give her a reprieve from her workout.

The nature of hospitals is that, as soon as you get admitted, the case management staff starts planning on getting you back out. Despite her being massively deconditioned, the situation was no different for Liz. I stopped by Mary Free Bed early on Wednesday morning, April 27, hurrying to make the usual 8:00 a.m. Wednesday morning Surgery educational meeting at Butterworth.

Liz was in good spirits when I left, and a few moments later, as I hurried across the walkway over Michigan Avenue, I ran into Dr. Sam Ho coming across out of Spectrum's Heart Center. He let me know that X-rays had shown a continued "nonunion" (failure to heal) of Liz's ankle, but he believed it would yet heal with more movement of that ankle as she got into therapy, noting that ambulation was more of a long-term goal for Liz.

Dr. Ho also mentioned that he thought it would be beneficial to get Liz home as soon as possible with a 24-hour aide—this would be possible only because she was covered by straight auto insurance, not the auto-private blended insurance. I had chided Liz at times for her costly propensity to get extended warrantees, the most life insurance, and the highest form of auto insurance, but now that tendency was turning into a real blessing for our family. Dr. Ho's plan would entail Liz's coming in for outpatient Mary Free Bed therapy as a comprehensive and very long-term process.

That same day I encountered Sue Taylor, another Mary Free Bed Intake Coordinator working at Butterworth, and told her what Dr. Ho had suggested. When Sue asked me how I felt about that plan, I expressed concerns about taking Liz out of Mary Free Bed before she had made significant progress toward becoming more independent. Sue was of the opinion that we shouldn't move Liz home until she could be taken care of by a single aide—and probably be weight-bearing. Sue thought this would take a few months. She also noted that, if Liz would have to have skin-grafting surgery on her ankle, she would need to be non-weight bearing for another 12 weeks.

Every Wednesday a multidisciplinary team met to discuss a comprehensive plan for Liz's recovery. Shortly after talking with Sue

Taylor, I was called by Ashley, Liz's Mary Free Bed care manager, about that meeting. Ashley told me that, per Dr. Ho's plan, Liz might be able to go home in four to six weeks, possibly in early June. Ashley seemed taken off guard when I expressed my concerns about that plan, but she promised to make work of reassessing the whole situation.

When I discussed this later with Liz, she told me that she didn't want to go home until she could be a lot more independent. After nearly four months Liz longed to be home, but we were both afraid that a move to outpatient therapy would forfeit the intensity and comprehensiveness of the care she could receive as an inpatient. Our kids weighed in with their agreement to this sentiment.

The next morning I texted out a picture that I had titled, "Mom driving herself to her Ortho appointment," with Liz steering her motorized wheelchair by herself, her nurse rolling her oxygen tank beside her. To see their mom with even that limited modicum of independence was exciting for her kids:

Tim: "What?!?! Is this a hoax?!"

Laura: "Looking good!"

Brek: "She's not biking to her appointment like the kid in the picture? What kind of rehab place is this?!?!"

Jackie: "Watch out, everyone!"

Tim: "Haha. Way to go, Mom!!! I'm sharing this photo!"

Tom: "Wahooo!!!"

Clearly the picture had touched an emotional nerve for these loving kids who had endured months of grim news about their mom and were eager to hear something positive.

Furthermore, I was able to report even more exciting news as a result of that Orthopedic appointment. Dr. Sandman informed me that X-rays of both her wrist and her ankle looked good and that Liz would be allowed to begin full weight bearing, an advance that would greatly enhance her rehabilitation capabilities.

Dr. Sandman noted that Xrays typically lag behind the actual healing so might give the appearance of a nonunion in the face of normal healing. I clarified the plan with Dr. Ho later that afternoon. He wanted to get Liz medically stable, perhaps over four weeks, prior to sending her home for a few days with 24-hour help, and then bring her back for more therapy as an inpatient. Dr. Ho agreed that Liz would need more inpatient therapy after that brief homecoming.

"A day of inpatient therapy is worth a week of outpatient therapy," he noted.

I explained all of this to Liz later that day in dialysis. She seemed satisfied with this plan, if not with ongoing dialysis.

Tom stopped by Dialysis on Saint Mary's 8 Main for a visit before his night shift and helped me wheel his mom back to her room in Mary Free Bed. Unfortunately, after a day marked by good news, I had to text out a distressing request to our kids and prayer partners late that evening:

"Mom needs a lot of prayer now. She had a very hard day and is weeping tonight. She woke up with a nosebleed at 4:00 a.m., and they couldn't get it to stop until after 1:00 p.m. It delayed her dialysis by an hour. They tried to change the VAC dressing on her foot, but it also started to bleed. They couldn't get it to stop either so had to dress it with gauze instead, which they've had to change several times because the bleeding still won't stop.

"As we were watching a movie together, she told her sitter she wanted to pee. That's heartbreaking to me because she wants it so desperately. I told her that everything will be OK. She said she's trying so hard. She said she thought today she just wanted to go to heaven.

"As the staff were going to get her up to the commode, they noticed her ileostomy bag had popped off due to a ton of foamy stuff I had never seen before. They're still trying to get a new bag on because the ostomy just keeps pouring out. She looked over at me and said, 'I just want to go to Glencairin and crawl into my own bed. I know I'll never get there; it just won't work.' Pray for her hard tonight. She's overwhelmed and very depressed."

The next day, Friday, April 29, dawned a little brighter. Tim texted me that Liz had called him that morning (on her new phone!) to say that she'd had a good night's sleep, an answer to prayer already. Tim noted that dialysis days were extremely tough on his mom, which had likely contributed to her down spirits the night before.

Saturday, after a breakfast of thickened orange juice with speech therapy (she liked it!), the physical therapist told me that he was going to get Liz standing on the following Monday, the first time in almost four months. Liz also got to use her new phone to talk to Jamie for his birthday, as well as to two excited four-year old granddaughters who had been praying nightly for her. Dr. Ho came by to reinforce his plan to send Liz home in four weeks for a few days as an encouragement. The kids were relieved to get my text that noon.

"Mom just told me 'I can see a rainbow today; I'm not in it yet but I can see it.' What a difference a day makes. And prayer."

Speaking of prayer, an army of prayer warriors continued to pray for Liz's recovery from what had long since been determined to be End Stage Kidney Disease. Liz almost daily asked the staff to place her on a commode (not a small task) so she could try to urinate, but always was placed sadly back in bed with no results. "I'm trying so hard," she would tell me, as if by sheer effort she could will herself to make urine.

It would break my heart to see her be so expectant each time. After no urine for several months, though, a bolt out of the blue struck.

Early on Saturday morning, May 1, I texted the kids, "Don't know if you've all heard yet, but mom peed 225 ml of urine at 12:30 last night—and no catheter. Best 1:30 a.m. call I ever got. She's super excited."

Our brood was more than thrilled; Tom, who had worked that night, texted, "I celebrated with her at 1:30 a.m.! I had M&Ms and Wheat Thins, and she had ice chips ☺." I was happy to have someone else eating those peanut M&Ms to which I had become addicted. When they asked me how excited their mom was, I related the touching conversation we'd had that morning:

"Were you really excited when you peed?"

"Yes; I was so excited I just wanted to squeeze your hand."

"Were the nurses with you? Were they pretty excited?"

"No. They were out in the hallway."

"So you were all by yourself?"

"I wasn't by myself. I was with God; I was praying."

Liz made slow but steady progress through the next week as we began to look forward to some family milestones that six weeks earlier we could never have dreamed Liz would make. Tamara's graduation from Kendall School of Design was set for Saturday evening, May 7. I went to see her senior project and was not surprised at all when she got a job offer to work at a local house-and-garden store in floral design starting the following Monday. Liz would miss the luncheon to celebrate her mother's birthday at a local restaurant that coming Saturday, but the day after that was Mother's Day, and we planned to bring the party to her.

On the clinical front, Liz was back in Saint Mary's for a thoracentesis on Saturday, May 2, to drain off fluid from around her lung. She tolerated this very well; not much procedurally bothered her anymore. Tom noted how she was doing when he visited her one day.

"She's doing really well right now with speech therapy! But she's talking too much, so the lady can't feed her all the lemonade and orange stuff."

Liz called me early Tuesday morning to brag that she had just peed 300 milliliters of urine in a bedpan "on command." Dr. Randy Baker, visiting her, called this "liquid gold," which, indeed, it was. Liz called Jackie to boast to her as well, telling Jackie that she couldn't wait to "rub it in" to the night nurse who wouldn't let her try to use the bedpan since she knew Liz was in renal failure. Ashley, the case manager, reported after the Wednesday team meeting that Liz was "moving steadily forward on many fronts." Of note, I wrote my first diary progress note that day, May 4, since I had given up doing so on February 8; apparently, I had finally become convinced that Liz might yet survive.

Unfortunately, as so often happened with "the Tigress of Fragility" (Randy's term of endearment for Liz), at about the time she showed steady progress a complication would pop up. A gastroenterologist concerned about the continuing large amount of abdominal fluid—ascites—Liz still had, asked Interventional Radiology (IR) to tap off some of that fluid to begin the process of "burden-reduction" of the ascites. I hurried over to Mary Free Bed to accompany Liz.

As I had before, I argued against having her tube feeds discontinued, a common practice to prevent potential aspiration of tube feed material during a procedure in which sedation is used. Dr. Randy Baker, months earlier, had placed Liz's feeding tube into the "remnant stomach" created by her previous gastric bypass surgery. This remnant stomach was an organ that was completely separated from her esophagus and, as such, offered no possibility of aspiration.

Moreover, Liz, being a diabetic, was given insulin to cover the sugar in the tube feeds. Whenever the tube feeds were stopped, there would be no more sugar entering her body, but any insulin that had been given would still be acting to lower her blood sugar—which is why I did not want to see the feeds turned off. However, I was overruled, and the feedings were held because "that's what we always do."

Later in the waiting room after a tap that produced only 30 milliliters of fluid, I became alarmed when Liz squeezed my hand hard and told me she felt awful.

"I'm dying," she gasped.

The attendant IR nurse told Liz she was fine—her blood pressure and heart rate were okay—and sent us back to her room. On our arriving back at Mary Free Bed, her nurse immediately checked her blood sugar, which was found to be a startling 25. There being no glucose pen available, Liz had her tube feeds restarted and was given glucose tablets to take by mouth, after which her blood sugars slowly recovered. I was more than relieved to see those numbers normalize.

Two days later our hospitalist, Dr. Snyder, informed us that tests on the tapped ascites revealed a high level of white blood cells, indicative of a likely intraabdominal infection. A CAT scan of Liz's abdomen was ordered, so I came over to Mary Free Bed to help a tech bring Liz to the CAT scan area, making sure her tube feeds were not held again.

A large group of extended family members gathered at a riverside restaurant early Saturday afternoon to celebrate Grandma Marie's 87th birthday. Coming from Butterworth, where I was working that day, I brought Annette, my nurse practitioner; being Liz's cousin, Liz's mom was "Aunt Marie" to her.

Just as the food began to arrive at our table, I was called by Dr. Rodgers, the hospitalist working that day, and was alarmed to find out that the CAT scan from the previous day had revealed a very large, 28 x 14 x 14-centimeter intraabdominal abscess. Dr. Rodgers had ordered that Liz be transferred back to Saint Mary's Hospital. After I hung up, I was called almost immediately by Liz's Mary Free Bed nurse to give consent by phone to transfer Liz to 4 Lacks at Saint Mary's. During what had promised to be a nice birthday party, I spent almost the entire time in the lobby on the phone.

By the time I got to 4 Lacks after work, Liz's tube feeds had been discontinued again, and her blood sugar had dropped to 35. With treatment the nurses had gotten it back up to 89 and felt it would be safe to recheck it in two hours. I argued strenuously to have Liz's blood sugar rechecked sooner than that and to have her tube feeds restarted as soon as possible. When Liz's blood sugar was finally rechecked two hours later, with the feeds still not started, it had dropped back down to 50, requiring the staff to give her intravenous dextrose to bring her blood sugar back up. With the IV dextrose running, her blood sugars began to stabilize in the low 100s, so I finally felt comfortable enough to head home.

That following Sunday morning I discovered that Liz's blood sugars had continued to dip throughout the night, so she had been transferred to a floor with a higher acuity (fewer patients per nurse) to allow closer monitoring. Ironically, Liz had ended up on Hauenstein 3, Tom's floor; after nine different rooms, I guess this had been bound to happen. Tom was working the day shift and was able to stop into his mom's room often for a visit.

I texted Randy immediately to see if he could place an order to resume Liz's tube feeds, and he went right to work on it. I had learned to feel blessed to have the medical knowledge to monitor my wife's condition, as well as the medical friends to turn to for help. That day Liz and I recommitted to sharing more regular evening devotions together, starting with the book of Psalms. I couldn't have imagined what a tremendous blessing that was to become for both of us, and the practice continues to this day.

The following morning Liz had an abdominal drain placed, which immediately produced more than a liter of infected fluid; by the time I joined her in Dialysis that afternoon, more than 1500 milliliters of fluid had already been removed through the drain, which had been left in place in her abdomen. The cultures from the abdominal fluid eventually showed rare, slow-growing bacteria not usually involved in infections, as well as yeast. How these had come to infect Liz's abdomen was a mystery. We were met in Dialysis by a Mary Free Bed Intake Coordinator who promised us they were saving her room. We hoped they'd save her clothes this time, too!

Tuesday, May 10, was another eventful day. Liz and I were surprised to find that she was to go back to IR to have another abdominal fluid pocket drained, this one on the left side and more superficial. We didn't receive any advance notice, finding out as the transport staff arrived at Liz's door. She was just finished with physical and occupational therapy so was already exhausted. We were relieved later when the new drain produced only "serosanguinous" (clear yellow) fluid, which eventually proved to be sterile, with no infection present.

Jamie was finding out that his own MRI had shown a devastating constellation of injuries to a knee he had injured simply jumping off a three-foot-high rock with his daughter a few days earlier. Surgery was required, and he was going to be non-weight bearing for six weeks. Dr. Jamie was worried in that he had joined his ophthalmology practice less than a year earlier and now would have to miss significant time at work. Several of Jamie's brothers kindly reassured him that those were very similar injuries to what Steph Curry had experienced the previous year, meaning, in their words, that when Jamie was healed he should be able to score 40 points.

One of the bright moments of that day was when nurse Rachel Catanella, doing "skin audits" to monitor for skin ulcers and infections, came in to check Liz's drains and catheter dressings. Rachel had spent a number of years on 4 Heart (surgical ICU) at Butterworth and had, in fact, trained my daughter, Jackie, on that floor in her first nursing job. I had not seen Rachel in a while but counted her as a good friend, so it was fun catching up. Also, Tom, who had spent all his spare time during his shift visiting his mom, sent an amusing text:

"Now we got badge readers that tell how much time we spend in each room. They'll look back and say Tom did really well on that patient in room 9. He never took breaks and spent all night helping patients."

By Thursday, May 12, Liz had stabilized with regard to her two new drains, so we thought she would be transferring back to Mary Free Bed. I rushed over at 1:00 p.m. to help her move, but, because she had received intravenous morphine that morning, Mary Free Bed deferred, preferring that Liz be taking only oral pain meds when she was readmitted. On Friday Liz had early Dialysis, so I was able to arrive at 3:00 p.m. to assist with her move back to room 3122 in Mary Free Bed, making sure her tube feeds were not stopped during the move. It was very good to be back, and we received several celebratory texts from our kids.

It was now only a week before our fortieth anniversary, an occasion that, up until six weeks earlier, I had thought we had little chance of seeing together. Now the date loomed before us, and I was beyond excited to be within striking distance. Maybe some would think that, in reality, this was just another day in the course of Liz's long hospital journey. But to me, having been so devastated for such a long time thinking we were going to fall just short of that round number, it represented a mark of God's great blessing on our marriage. The closer the date got, the more excited I became.

CHAPTER 23

With Mark and Tamara's wedding less than three weeks away, I joined the "boys" for an all-day bachelor party, since I had the day off. Mark was required to wear a ball-and-chain apparatus to all the festivities, which included the following: a round of golf, lunch at Buffalo Wild Wings, a round of target shooting, a venison grill at Brek's house, and a Whitecaps baseball game. At the game Mark got to throw out the first pitch, still carrying the ball-in-chain that had been strapped to his ankle all day.

Liz had a lighter day of therapy, and I didn't want her to feel abandoned for the day, so I managed to visit her in the early morning and again when I sneaked away from the target shooting to visit her. The contrast between the pre-wedding merriments and Liz's ongoing residence at Mary Free Bed made me melancholy about Liz's likelihood of having to miss her last child's wedding. She tried to maintain a brave front about that prospect, but I suspected it was bothering her as much as it was me.

Monday, May 16, was another eventful day for three generations of our family, a day that had my emotions pulling me in three different directions. Jamie finally had his knee surgery, a repair that included his ACL and a "bucket-handle" tear of his meniscus. Halle was told in the recovery room that Jamie would have to be non-weight bearing for eight weeks. He would have to learn to be creative to perform eye surgery within that limitation once his pain had subsided enough for him to discontinue pain meds. Apparently his nausea was getting the better of Jamie.

"Go ahead, make fun of the eye doctor," he texted out. "But I have quite a stash of 25 mg Phenergans dating back to 2007; are they still good?"

Tim was trying to take care of his Grandma Marie, who had shown signs of steadily increasing paranoia and anxiety for the past week or two, to the point that this was inhibiting her ability to care for herself. Her physician's recommendation was in-patient admission and electroconvulsive therapy (ECT) at our local mental health institution, Pine Rest Hospital.

Tim called me from the Saint Mary's emergency department, where he was obtaining the necessary medical clearance for that admission. I stopped down to see them, but Tim declined my help and insisted I stay with his mom, who had dialysis—her most despised treatment—scheduled for that afternoon. Tim, never one to have much discretionary time, spent most of that day getting his grandma situated at Pine Rest. My diary note acknowledged, "Very kind and patient—a real hero."

Liz extended that praise as well to Laura, who soldiered on alone on a day on which she usually shared duty with Tim; anyone with autistic kids would understand. Tim texted out a progress report that night, indicating that the plan for Grandma Marie was two to four weeks in Pine Rest, but with plans for Marie to attend the wedding if at all possible. Tim also asked his siblings to visit Marie whenever they could.

Meanwhile, Liz and I were forgotten in Dialysis for forty minutes after her run was finished. When we finally did get taken back to Mary Free Bed, Liz's feeding tube inadvertently got pulled back right after she had received her nightly insulin. I readvanced the tube and taped it in place but didn't dare allow it to be used for feedings without an X-ray check. Liz managed to drink a milkshake prepared for her by her nurse and kept her blood sugar above 300 all night long.

That evening I noticed what looked like frank blood coming out of Liz's ostomy, as well as a pattern of prominent engorged veins over her abdomen and chest. This constellation, in the face of Liz's known liver disease, was very frightening to me. I was concerned that the cirrhosis might have gotten acutely worse, affecting blood flow through her liver. My inherent tendency to think the worst until proven otherwise was running strong; I solicited a lot of prayers that night.

The ileostomy bleeding continued on Tuesday, seemingly worse. Liz's abdomen seemed to be getting bigger, indicating an increase in ascites (fluid); along with the prominent venous pattern, this frightened me. Our friend Sue Elenbaas sat with Liz that evening, allowing me to go to a bonfire in Brek's back yard that night with kids and grandkids as we celebrated Brek's birthday.

On Wednesday morning the ileostomy bleeding continued, and by evening it had accelerated, the nurse reporting at one point that Liz had lost 800 milliliters (about 27 ounces) throughout the day of mostly frank blood. I was more and more concerned about this bleeding, especially as our wedding anniversary grew closer.

Our neighbor Sue Host had kindly volunteered to sit with Liz that evening while I went to play softball. This was a special treat for me. I've never been a softball fanatic, but this was a fast-pitch team on which I got to play with Brek, Tom, and Mark (and, some years, Jackie). The other bright spot in the day was heralded in a text I sent out early that morning: "After numerous attempts to pee last night, Mom finally got catheterized and had 500 mls of urine." I had never given up hope that her kidneys might yet start to function again, and it now seemed ever more likely that God was about to answer all those prayers in a mighty way.

Thursday, May 19, was one of those days we have sometimes when the whole day is focused on the day after. Laura had gone into "organize mode," as only an elementary teacher could do, putting together a master plan for our fortieth anniversary celebration. She somehow managed to reserve a private recreation room at Mary Free Bed on a Friday evening, a day the room would normally have been quite busy. She arranged for a table with some games and elegant decorations, many in an owl motif, per our now famous connection to the Blandford Nature Center owls.

She made sure there was a cake (owl-themed, of course) and plenty of other refreshments but kept the guest list conservative, as she didn't want Liz to be overwhelmed. Laura's invite list consisted of a small group of close friends, as well as all her Paauw siblings. She and Tim also created a secret Facebook post so that many other friends were able to send cards—of which, again, many were owl-related—and to contribute to a memory book Laura had created. I think Laura's goal was to have a happy, if muted, celebration of a truly noteworthy milestone that had seemed impossible less than two months earlier.

Liz spent Friday afternoon having her hair done professionally for the first time in five months. Of course, as debilitated as she was, this had to be done in a wheelchair at the bathroom sink in her room. Later that afternoon our close friend Meridell Gracias came with her daughter Nicole. Liz loved these visits from her faithful friends, even though they tended toward being one-sided conversations, as she was, even after weeks of therapy, still quite weak.

I arrived around dinnertime, about the same time Tom stopped by before his night shift at Saint Mary's. I was greatly relieved to hear that there had been no bleeding observed from her ileostomy that day, as I had begun to be convinced that the bleeding was a result of worsening liver disease, that black cloud that always hung threateningly over Liz's rehabilitation.

Jamie called that evening to check on his mom and to let us know that he had started physical therapy for his knee that day. Although his knee was still quite painful, Jamie thought he might try to return to his ophthalmology practice the following week. That night as I went to bed, on the doorstep of marking forty years of marriage, I was moved to raise up a David-like offering of praise to God for his great faithfulness to Liz and me. Words from Psalm 103 spilled out of me: "The steadfast love of the LORD is from everlasting to everlasting on those who fear him, and his righteousness to children's children." For moments I lay quietly, watching for my digital clock to turn to 12:00 before thinking to myself, "We made it!"

Friday, May 20, was a long and tiring day for Liz; she had multiple therapies before finishing the afternoon in Dialysis. I didn't make it back to Mary Free Bed until 6:00 p.m., as I had to stop at home after work to pick up the dress Laura had instructed me to bring. It was a very fashionable, long blue-and-white dress that Liz had purchased on the cruise my mother had arranged for her kids just two months before Liz's accident. Liz had never had a chance to wear it . . . until now.

As I arrived to Liz's room, she was just getting back from hemodialysis, which always tired her. That, combined with her long day of therapy, left her noticeably wiped out, yet she was excited to make it to the festivities. It took four of us to dress Liz on the side of the bed because she had no strength yet to hold herself up. After we had placed her into an electric wheelchair, one of Liz's nurses curled her hair, and we happily motored off to our fortieth anniversary celebration, like the owls—two star-crossed lovers who wouldn't be kept apart.

The room was perfect, down to the pink and white carnations like those we'd had at our wedding so many years earlier. All of our in-town kids and grandkids were present, and Jamie, still very sore, called to extend congratulations from Virginia. Our close friends the Hosts, the Elzingas, and the Vander Werps also brought greetings and presents, including a touching gift from Sue Host. Sue had found a pair of handcrafted owls at the Blandford Nature Center itself and, even though they were part of the Nature Center decor and therefore not for sale, had succeeded in talking the manager into selling them to Sue with an impassioned story about Liz and me. Those owls still sit on Liz's bedroom dresser to this very day.

When the cake was cut, Liz deferred, as I had known she would. She ate very little yet, surviving almost exclusively on her nightly tube feeds. I thoroughly enjoyed that party, but my eyes were constantly drawn to my wife, her wheelchair tipped back to keep pressure off her bottom, her body not moving except for her eyes. Liz was still so weak and frail that it was an effort for her to even turn her head from side to side, much less move her arms or legs. There she sat, gaunt and motionless except for her smile, looking for all the world as though she were paraplegic.

Her ileostomy, which had been bleeding heavily again all during that day, was bulging under her beautiful dress. Two drains were hanging from her right foot, which was partially hidden by a dainty white slipper. And her tracheostomy—now capped—sat prominently in the center of her neck, framed by a necklace that Laura had bought to draw attention away from it. And yet I couldn't help but cherish one thought while watching her: *I don't think I've ever seen anybody more beautiful in my life.*

My text to the kids that night included the following:

"Thanks so much. This was a strange day, full of the joy and thanksgiving you would expect on a 40th wedding anniversary yet overshadowed by fear . . . We had a very blessed time, and, amazingly, Mom was able to make it for more than an hour despite her long day. On returning to her room, we were reminded that she had been having quite a bit of blood from her ileostomy all day, certainly dampening our mood. She was able to make it through almost an hour of a movie before tiring.

"Our devotions led us to reflect not only on all the blessings by which we've been flooded but also on our current circumstances, aware as we are that her very life remains threatened. We discussed how faithful God has been to us so far—our Ebenezer—and renewed our trust in Him who has done so much for us, knowing that, whatever happens, we have already won. We are ready to accept this adventure the way we always have, hand in hand, trusting in his mercy."

CHAPTER 24

I had to work on Saturday, May 21, but planned to interrupt my work at 11:00 a.m. to see Liz at Mary Free Bed. We spent the better part of an hour going through the memory book Laura had made and had presented to us the evening before.

"Mom and I just went through the memory book," I texted the family. "It's so awesome; very touching and emotional. We've had such great family and friends. Can't believe you got so many to contribute; it looks like a ton of work. Not much we would change in those 40 years. When we finished, Mom asked when we could look at it again. Thanks for blessing our celebration in such a meaningful way."

I had to leave at noon to head to Mark's house to get ready for his college graduation. I sat with Tamara in the stands and felt bad that Liz was missing another life event—and, even worse, that she would soon miss her son's wedding. After the graduation, I hurried back to finish work by 7:15 p.m., so I didn't see Liz again until 7:30. It was a day that made me acutely aware of how much time juggling I was doing throughout Liz's hospitalization. I tried not to focus on that too often, as it made me tired to just think about it. Sunday was a quieter day, notable only for a comment I wrote in my daily journal: "Dinner of potato chips and peanut M&Ms—pretty common."

By the following Monday, I was able to text out some positive news, the kind of report an army likes to receive, reporting progress on all fronts.

"Mom has had no ileostomy bleeding since Friday. Dr. Randy Baker thinks it's gastritis from the feeding tube, not varices from the liver disease. He's adding Carafate, a stomach lining coater she was on before. Also, they catheterized her Friday before our anniversary celebration for 300 mls of urine. She got cath'ed again last night and had 450 mls more. Steady progress on eating more each day—she especially focuses on her protein drink. The staff is now trying to avoid moving her by mechanical lift and just having her stand and pivot to move from bed to chair and back. Oh, and she's had the tracheostomy completely capped for 48 hours. They may be able to remove it this week, but Mom is very anxious about that. God is answering our prayers generously."

This was followed by a round of excited replies from several of our kids. Jamie's enthusiastic response, however, came with a caveat: "Please put me on the prayer list as I'm having foot drop. It's likely not permanent but can be. Very scary for my career!"

Tom, who worked on a Neurology floor, strongly encouraged Jamie to see a neurosurgeon, as he had seen several "horror stories" regarding that entity. When Jamie saw his orthopod later that week, he was pulled back off work after having experienced too much pain during a half-day back.

My daily journal noted that Liz and I napped together in Dialysis after work before I cut her fingernails. I had to go back to work but was able to return that evening to cut her toenails. She was very appreciative of this and told me that it made her feel loved. Maybe so, but I was her husband, and it needed to be done—of course I'd do it. We were up to Psalm 21 together that evening in our recently renewed joint devotions, and my entry noted, "Really sweet communion—indeed, the best days of our lives."

I had one more surprise that evening on my way home. The city had resurfaced our entire street since I had left that morning. Tim immediately stepped up to take credit.

"Nice! That was our whole family finale surprise gift for your anniversary!!"

"I'd rather have the cash," I replied.

With apparent sadness, Jamie retorted, "Now you tell us. No refunds!"

Apparently my progress report was glowing enough that the next day, for the first time, someone mentioned what had been to that point unthinkable.

"Also, is there a determination about whether Mom will be at the wedding?" Emily asked. "I have asked several times but have not received confirmation one way or the other. There are many things that go into her being there that we should probably work on if that is to be the case."

She, Laura, and Jackie had shared a conversation about having Liz's hair colored (by Laura) and going for a cut just down the street on June 2, since commercial hair professionals were not permitted to come into Mary Free Bed. But these events were not specifically in preparation for the wedding.

"Either way, she desperately needs it colored," Laura observed, "so, that's what I'm going to do tonight."

The June 3 wedding was now about ten days off, but until this conversation it had been assumed that Liz could not make it. I spent that evening with several of my kids at a newly established Gravel Bottom Bible study, a Bible study over beer and pizza at the Gravel Bottom microbrew, upholding the tradition of living in Beer City.

The leader pulled me aside with tears in his eyes and surprised me by telling me I was a hero.

"No, just a husband," I corrected him.

On returning to see Liz, I found her to be wiped out, so we had, as my entry noted, "brief but sweet devotions. I can't imagine loving her more."

The following day, Wednesday, May 25, was again a very busy one of juggling time for me. My entry noted that Liz's friend Sue Host relieved my bedside vigil in Dialysis so I could get in a workout at Snap Fitness before catching my grandson Breky's T-ball game, and then off to my own fast-pitch game. Devotions that night included Psalm 22, the "crucifixion Psalm," after which Liz and I talked about how great God's love for us really is.

Liz's primary physical therapist, Sean Murphy, first approached me with a plan to somehow transport Liz, as debilitated as she was, to Mark and Tamara's wedding in some kind of Mary Free Bed vehicle. I was stunned but delighted that this might even be a possibility, having assumed it to be a foregone conclusion that it was not. Sean had become a good Christian friend with whom I had a lot in common. He hated to think that a mother would miss her son's wedding day, so he had begun to scheme with Ashley, a recreation therapist, to see if it could indeed happen.

Wednesday was the day Liz's entire Mary Free Bed team would meet to discuss her progress and the plan for the next week. Apparently Liz's therapists were persuasive because on Thursday Dr. Sam Ho, Liz's rehab physician, informed me that he had officially approved Liz to go to the June 3 wedding—just eight days in advance.

There were a few caveats attached to this approval. Liz's dialysis would still have to be done that day but could be moved back to the morning. Also, Dr. Ho felt that three hours was too long of a time for Liz to be gone; Liz agreed that she just wanted to be there for the ceremony and then leave. Then there were some physical needs to be taken care of: since Liz would go with a manual wheelchair, someone had to be responsible to do "pressure relief" every 15–20 minutes, as well as monitor and possibly empty her ostomy bag during the adventure.

I was designated to do both tasks. We also had to complete the Off Grounds Checklist the morning of the wedding. Originally, plans called for a family member to take Liz to the wedding, but none of us had ever done this before. Indeed, Liz had not traveled outside the hospital at all yet. Thankfully, her recreational therapist, Ashley, followed through with an earlier plan to load Liz into a Mary Free Bed van with Sean Murphy's assistance and drive her to the wedding herself. There was some question as to whether Liz would be better served with an electric wheelchair than a manual one, but the weight of the electric wheelchair mitigated against using it in the van. However, Jamie graciously volunteered.

"I'll use the motorized; she can use the manual."

Dr. Ho had to chuckle when he himself hobbled in that morning on a cane after having sustained a foot injury, only to have Liz volunteer to loan him her motorized wheelchair.

Our family "prepare-Mom-for-the-wedding" team immediately rolled into high gear, with texts flying back and forth about nails, hair, dress, and other details. Emily volunteered to take care of Liz's nails; I had to admit to her that I had just cut them a few days earlier, so there was going to have to be some "damage control," to which I received the exasperated hands-to-the-face emoji.

Katie, Liz's recreation therapist, had taken her outside in a wheelchair and explained to Liz that they were going to borrow a Mary Free Bed van the next week to take her to the wedding. To say that Liz was elated would be an understatement. I don't think any of us had realized how desperately she wanted to go to the wedding until we saw her reaction to that approval.

This turned out to be just the beginning of a red-letter day for our family—and even a red-letter week. As if in response to the wedding news, Liz took five steps on the parallel bars, her best effort so far. We told her, "Now you're just showing off," which drew a proud smile from her. I texted our kids that day.

"Her mind is clearer, and the speech therapist says her short-term memory is improving dramatically . . . Best of all, she's smiling and has her sense of humor back."

Later, when they catheterized her bladder, 350 milliliters of urine was drained off, again her best so far. A respiratory therapist came to remove her trachea cannula, the first time since her tracheostomy had been done back in January (17 weeks!) that she was free of any apparatus there. (We were told that the residual hole would gradually heal up on its own over a week or so, but the reality was that she would have to undergo surgery months later to accomplish this.)

While I had dinner at the home of Duane Bras, a close Christian brother from my men's Bible study, Liz, who had at last been advanced to a general diet, finally got the watermelon she had been begging for since January. That day we also heard good news on the Jamie front. He had continued to experience a lot of pain in his surgically repaired leg, and his surgeon had thought he might have had a deep vein thrombosis in that leg, so there was a lot of family prayer being raised on his behalf. His study that day came back negative for a clot; Liz and I had an awful lot for which to be thankful that night during our devotions.

More of the same on Friday, May 27, when my entry started out, "Great day!" Of course, a day off is almost always a great day. I had breakfast with my pastor, Rev. Corey Dykstra, who was checking up

on me specifically, which I appreciated. I stopped by to see Liz briefly
and learned that she had a long day of therapy planned, followed by
dialysis later in the afternoon. I met Mark to go mountain biking late
that morning on a local course before stopping at a nearby microbrew
for a burger and a beer, one of my favorite ways to spend a morning
with one of my kids.

I spent the afternoon in Dialysis with Liz before joining Mark,
Tim, and his boys at the nearby food court for dinner. After dinner
Mark and I stopped at the home of our church friend Dave Mast to
sample his latest home-brewed beer effort before we both returned
to share evening devotions with Liz. My entry finished with, "Such
a good day. And she was cath'ed of 250 mls!" Indeed, after what we
had been through, these did indeed seem to be some of the best days
of our lives.

The weekend came and went quietly, marked by visits for Liz
from two different sets of grandkids. The pictures texted out on Sunday
of Liz with these little ones, and especially baby Isaiah (her fellow
"sleeper"), were sweet, as were our evening devotions covering Psalm
27 ("very appropriate") on Saturday and Psalms 28–29 ("very sweet
discussion") on Sunday. Also, urine production for those two days
was 350 milliliters and 500 milliliters, respectively, ever increasing our
hope that Liz might someday be free of dialysis.

The following day, May 30, Memorial Day, brought a visit from
my sister Joan and her daughter Kita, the first of a parade of extended
family visitors in town for the upcoming wedding. It also brought an
excited note of urine production of 550 milliliters, continuing a slow
but steady increase, giving us hope that, after four months, maybe,
just maybe, those kidneys were finally recovering.

Tuesday brought a litany of visitors for Liz: me in the early
morning and my mother (Edna) and my sister Joan with her daughter

at lunch, followed by Liz's close friend Sue Elenbaas, me again, and finally Emily to do her "damage control" on Liz's nails. Tom stopped in for dinner at 6:00 before his night shift at Saint Mary's, following which I came back again later on for devotions. I noticed that the full day of therapy, in conjunction with a host of visitors, had greatly tired Liz, who still told me it had been one of her best days since the accident.

CHAPTER 25

Our entire family began to gear up with final wedding preparations on Thursday, June 2. Liz's mom, Marie, had suffered from significant paranoia as a manifestation of Alzheimer's disease and had spent several weeks at Pine Rest Mental Health Services for treatment, including electroconvulsive therapy (ECT) but was now deemed ready to be discharged. I was tasked to bring her from Pine Rest to, not her home in independent living at Breton Woods, but a temporary room at a nearby assisted living unit.

Unfortunately, Marie's short-term memory had been temporarily affected by the ECT, and no matter how many times I explained the plan to her, she kept slipping back into thinking she was going home to her Breton Woods room. When my mother and I picked up Marie, I thought I would soften the blow for her by taking these senior ladies to meet Jamie's family for lunch at a restaurant near the hotel at which they were staying, before we all went over to Mary Free Bed to visit Liz.

The trouble began when I left with my mom to bring Marie to her new temporary "home," which Marie was simply not having. I remember having to stop on the side of the road by the Wealthy Street bridge for twenty minutes trying to calm down this usually mild lady before we ultimately brought her to her new room at Raybrook Manor. Even then, it required an extra hour more to get Marie to move into that room; it broke my heart to see this gentle lady so stirred up by the confusing agenda of events that culminated in her being deposited in unfamiliar surroundings.

Fortunately, Liz's sister Maria, in town from California for the wedding, arrived to help settle Marie into that strange room, allowing my mother and me to make it to the wedding rehearsal just in time. Marie soon settled back into her usual sweet demeanor and never remembered that episode, but I was shaken by the experience. It made me acutely aware of families who have to deal with mental illness on a long-term basis and the trials they must go through. If you know a family like that, I encourage you to be in regular prayer for them.

The wedding rehearsal went off without a hitch until Mark "practiced" wheeling his mom down the aisle, at which I immediately lost my composure and wept. I was fearful that, in my ongoing broken emotional state, I would not be able to maintain my self-control for the real thing the next day. This made me remember something my son Tom had shared with me several months after Liz's accident: "I don't think I ever in my life saw you cry before the accident but now you cry all the time."

This would be one of the first lessons I learned from my experiences. Even though men by nature seem to fight it, it was okay for me to cry. To this day certain things people might say or things I might see or remember can instantly leave me in an emotional struggle. Even as I read notes and try to record these experiences, my tears well up. I guess I'm never going to be "normal" again.

Rather than hiring a caterer for the rehearsal dinner, to which we had invited all of our extended family members and any out-of-town guests, we turned to our friend Gary Schutten, Brek's dad, who lived in our basement, to take care of the meal. Gary had quite a bit of experience preparing meals for large groups of hungry people from his work with Project Serve in the past. In fact, when I and several other leaders had taken our church youth group on a two-week mission trip to British Columbia in 2004, we had invited Gary along as our chef, so it was only natural that we would turn to him again.

Gary did not disappoint. The dinner was held in the large fellowship area of the church, where we feasted at a carving station with ribs, bacon, chicken, brisket, and ham, along with pork-and-beans, noodle salad, potato salad, fancy peppers, onions, and mushrooms, all topped off with a homemade chocolate/cherry cake.

I would be remiss if I didn't note the exceptional decorations that Emily, who comes from an innately artistic family, had prepared. All enjoyed that fellowship and the occasion. But conversely, a feeling of depression that had been lying latent within me for a week or so began to grow. I missed my wife, knowing she would so much have loved to attend this event. After dinner, Mark came down to Mary Free Bed with me on the eve of his wedding to spend some sweet time with his mom, who had missed all of the day's activity.

I arose quite early on Friday, June 3, the wedding day, to spend a few moments with Liz before I returned home to have breakfast with Mark. From there I took Mark to the City Flats Hotel to drop off his luggage; it was the weekend of the Grand Rapids Festival of the Arts, an art, music, and food extravaganza in downtown Grand Rapids, making it hard to navigate due to closed off streets. Ordinarily I would have spent at least some time on that weekend perusing the art and music, while enjoying some of the varied cuisine at one of my favorite Grand Rapids celebrations.

After dropping off Mark at home, I quickly hurried back to Liz's room. From there we brought her down to the Mary Free Bed van, where we used the liftgate to move Liz, in her wheelchair, into the back of the van and secure her there with four straps, each reaching in a different direction to immobilize that wheelchair. I was very nervous as I closed the back doors, but if Liz was she didn't show it. She was almost giddy at the prospect of being somewhere other than a hospital for the first time in almost five full months.

I waved as Sean and Ashley headed out for the drive to Redeemer Church in Ada, about a 15-mile distance. I followed the van in my own car and was present to help unload Liz from the back of the van at the front door of the church. On her face was the biggest and happiest smile I think I had ever seen.

We didn't have a lot of time before the processional, as we had timed her arrival closely due to concerns about her ostomy bag and the need for frequent "pressure relief" in her wheelchair. This last issue was especially critical, as Liz was just getting over a months-long pressure sore on her bottom that had been the bane of her existence— if any readers have ever experienced this, you will know what I'm talking about.

Arriving at the church, Liz had just enough time to duck into the restroom with the bridal entourage to put the finishing touches on her hair before being wheeled to the back of the sanctuary for the processional. Mark, heretofore against all human odds, came back to "process" his mother into the ceremony, with me following closely behind.

While Liz could not have been happier, smiling and waving from side to side like a pageant princess on a parade float, among the rest of the guests present there was not a dry eye in the place, including my own. As I sat next to Liz, where Mark had parked her on the end of the front row, I struggled mightily with a Kleenex trying to control my tears, but they only got worse when Liz's hand found my own to give me a reassuring squeeze, she smiling at me and having no idea how truly heroic she was.

The wedding itself, maybe as most weddings tend to be in retrospect, is a blur to me at this writing. My only real memories are of a beautiful young woman radiantly walking down the aisle and of my telling myself, "Wow—she's going to be our daughter now."

My journal entry for that day simply described the event as "a beautiful, God-centered wedding." We had prayed for months that Liz might make it to this moment, never once thinking this was humanly possible—and maybe it wasn't—but now it was over, and there she was, happily posing for pictures and receiving innumerable greetings and well-wishes. So many people came by to tell her they were praying for her! I was overwhelmed. *This indeed is the family of God*, I thought. But like Cinderella, her time limited, we soon had to load this princess back into her carriage for the trip back to her humble home at Mary Free Bed.

The wedding reception at City Flats was elegant and beautiful. The Paauw brothers (Brek included) carried on the tradition of singing a toast comprised of a knockoff version of a current song favorite with appropriate lyric changes to reflect the newly married couple. They serenaded Mark and Tamara, who both were infamous for their inability to make a decision, by turning to the movie *Frozen* and conveniently adapting the words from the song "Let It Snow" to their own rendition, "I Don't Know."

For me, this was a very hard time. Mark had been born to Liz and me when we were forty years old, a late comer who had become my buddy and kept me young. For years we had done everything together, a host of activities from mountain biking to luging and backpacking to cross-country skiing. He had often made the cross-town trip home from his studies to spend a weekend with us; I had really enjoyed some special time with him during the two weeks he had lived at our house after graduating from Calvin College.

I couldn't have been more excited about the beautiful Christian woman he had made our daughter, but there was another side to my emotions that evening. I struggled at that reception; my entry reflected that, since the accident, this was the time I had most missed my wife. I knew I would see Mark considerably less often, but I didn't have a wife at home to share that with.

"Tough evening," my journal summarized.

My despair deepened as a "couple's dance" was announced, but suddenly there was Halle, seemingly aware of my depression, beckoning me to join her in that dance. This gesture was so touching to me. I don't think I will ever forget her kindness at that moment.

The next day, Saturday, was a flurry of post-wedding activities, with out-of-town family stopping to bid Liz goodbye while I shared a breakfast with Jamie and Halle's family at their hotel before they returned to Virginia. At noon I texted out a "State of Liz" message to our kids:

"As you know, Mom made it to Mark's and Tamara's wedding yesterday, thanks to the generosity of two therapists, Sean and Ashley. It was so emotional for me and everyone else to see her coming down the aisle with Mark, but Mom herself was just excited to be there. She told me she was not emotional, just happy and excited. I told her she made everyone else cry.

"It was a very sweet experience to be out of the hospital with Mom for the first time in 5 months. I couldn't let go of her hand. Other news: they downsized but left the abdominal abscess drain in place yesterday but did discontinue the antibiotics. She's getting steadily stronger and is almost independent in turning herself—she needs help tucking pillows under her to avoid pressure sores.

"This Tuesday she will be brought home for a few hours to assess her needs in preparation for a 3 or 4 day visit home in a few weeks. She will have round-the-clock assistance during that future visit home. On the kidney front, she was cath'ed of 275 mls before the wedding and another 275 at bedtime, for a total of 550 mls yesterday. I read her this text; she wants you to know how much she appreciates your prayers."

This note prompted several excited responses from our kids, as well as comments on "the most epic toast ever known."

We started to get back to our routine that day, as I spent three hours with Liz, keeping her company in Dialysis before going to a baby shower at Jackie's house for my nephew and niece, Matt and Julie Brouwer—ordinarily an event Liz would have gone to "with bells on." But now she could only enjoy it vicariously, when, returning for devotions, I told her all about it.

My journal entry that night reflected that I was still very depressed: "a black time feeling lonely and seeing happiness all around." I kept playing in my mind an old Simon and Garfield song in which I took comfort, and I finished my note late that evening with the words, "I am a rock; I am an island."

CHAPTER 26

By the time I swung by early Sunday morning to visit Liz, things had begun to settle down for both of us. Liz was still recovering from the effort of going to the wedding, so, when I came back to spend time with her after church, she slept most of the afternoon. After I left for our afternoon church service, her spirits were lifted by visits from her sister Maria and from Tim's family. I came back in time to field a call with Liz from Mark and Tamara in Hawaii, checking in on her. *How thoughtful. A small gesture for these kids, but so meaningful to their mom.*

On the way back from church, I was deep in thought about Liz's kidney function. I was disappointed that Dr. Ron Hoffman, her nephrologist that weekend, had been unimpressed when I told him Liz was making 500–550 milliliters of urine each day. Ron was a friend of mine, and I think he wanted to avoid setting me up for any false expectations.

"Her kidneys have taken a lot of insults," he replied.

He clearly did not have a good feeling about Liz making it off dialysis, but as a physician who works frequently with patients who have acute kidney injury (AKI), much less the end stage renal disease

275

(ESRD) Liz was now classified as having, I also knew well that the chance of Liz regaining adequate kidney function to come off dialysis after four months was very small.

I prayed a very specific prayer on that drive back to Mary Free Bed that Liz would produce 600 milliliters of urine that day and 700 by the weekend, so we could see the momentum continue. Having told Liz of my specific prayer request, we were amazed when the staff catheterized her that evening of 325 milliliters, for a total of exactly 600 milliliters of urine for the day. God answers prayer, for sure.

On the same day our son Tim, a godly man always looking for a way to honor his Lord, began to work on a project to share Liz's video testimony of God's grace and mercy. Tim texted me that he was creating a plan to work with his friend Ryan Faber, a marine veteran disabled in the Iraq war, to create a video of Liz's story.

"It's an interview of sorts for her testimony, along with photos," he explained. "She is known by so many people because of their prayers, and this will be an opportunity to shine Christ's healing power and the power of prayer around the world in a visual way."

Tim's plan was to have Liz and me interviewed together at Mary Free Bed for the video, as well as to record Tuesday's upcoming "home study." I was excited for the opportunity to thank so many unknown people for the prayers that, I was sure, had been instrumental in saving Liz's life, but also because I realized for the first time that we were all finally confident that Liz was actually going to survive and make it home at some time. And the preliminary to that homecoming was only two days away.

A funny vignette occurred earlier that day at our home with one of our grandkids. Liz and I have a digital frame in our living room that our kids load up with photos of themselves and their families. My four-year old Virginian granddaughter, Lexie, was still in town from the wedding when she happened to see a picture of her Uncle Mark with a buck he had taken the year before.

Lexie: "What's that?!"

Me: "Mark with his deer."

Lexie: What happened to the deer?"

Me: "Mark shot it with his bow."

Lexie, looking horrified: "That's mean! Why did he do that?"

Me: "So he could eat it."

Lexie, looking even more horrified: "You don't eat deer!"

Me: "You wouldn't eat a deer?"

Lexie, pulling a face: "NO! You don't eat animals."

Me: "Would you eat a cow?"

Lexie: "No!"

Me: "Would you eat a pig?"

Lexie: "No!"

Me: "Would you eat a chicken?"

Lexie: "No!"

Me, smugly: "Where do chicken nuggets come from?"

Lexie, confidently: "McDonald's."

I had nothing.

When I arrived to see Liz early Monday morning, June 6, she told me that she had been cath'ed of another 375 milliliters at 3:00 a.m. When I had mentioned to my kids that I was praying for 700 milliliters by the weekend, Jamie had volunteered, "Is that enough? I've been praying for 1000."

Hmm, maybe I was praying with too little faith, I thought.

By the end of that day I was sure I had been, as the grand total for the day reached 875 milliliters! Liz had had a long day of therapy and dialysis, but the ordeal had been offset by her sister Maria sitting with her for several hours that morning before heading to the airport to fly back to California.

Making it an even better day, our good friend and neighbor Jane Elzinga had joined me in sitting with Liz in dialysis that afternoon. That evening the staff made last minute preparations for Liz's "home study" the next day. As I lay in bed that night, I was too excited to sleep for several hours. After almost exactly five months, my wife was actually coming home! I knew it would be for only a few hours, but the thought of that homecoming gave me great hope that this was just a pledge of something much more substantial to come. I finally fell asleep with sweet praises in my mind.

Tuesday, June 7, was the day we had been anticipating for five months. I had a noon meeting at work and hurried over to Mary Free Bed as soon as it was done. Three therapists—Sean, Katie, and Nick—loaded Liz into a Mary Free Bed van and followed me to our home. After we had driven at an exaggeratedly slow pace to make sure I didn't lose them, they lifted Liz out of the van and wheeled her up the newly constructed temporary ramp. Kendra, our insurance liaison superstar, waited in the doorway with an excited grin. Also there was Ryan Faber, Tim's friend who had interviewed us on Sunday and was creating a video account of Liz's story. I think my summary text to our kids that night best describes that scene:

"On the Mom front we had another red-letter day. Mom got loaded up into a MFB van by three therapists and followed me home. Yes—home! We were met there by Kendra to see what it would take to get Mom home for a short stay (3–4 days) and a long stay (hopefully for good).

"One dark night several months ago, when Mom appeared to be dying in the ICU, she opened her eyes to me and mouthed the words 'Let me go.' I told her she had a home and that I was going to take her there. I promised. With eyes closed, she had shaken her head no. At that moment I believed—no, I knew—that she was right. It wouldn't matter, I had thought; she'll never remember that conversation anyway.

"Today we found out that I was wrong—but so was she. When she was wheeled into our home, Liz looked at me and said, 'You kept your promise.' We embraced and wept for several minutes, while the staff waited respectfully for us to have our moment before getting on with the job at hand. They took a lot of measurements and pictures.

"A lot of work needs to be done making ramps, moving furniture, widening doorways, and remodeling the shower. For today, it was enough to have Mom home, beaming in her favorite recliner. We thank God for delighting in giving good things to his children."

That photo of Liz in her recliner has become one of my all-time favorites. After an all-too-short stay, her therapists loaded Liz back up to be returned to her other home at Mary Free Bed. But we had a very blessed time together in devotions that evening.

The next day Liz was back to her routine, with therapy all morning and dialysis in the afternoon. It was the same, yet it was different now. There finally seemed to be a purpose to all of this, a light at the end of the tunnel. I stopped in early for a few minutes on my way to work, in time to meet with Dr. Ho, her attending physician. He told us that his plan was to send Liz home overnight for a trial run in a week or two, and then maybe for several weeks after that, depending on how Liz did with the overnight.

I made it back from work in time to sit with Liz in dialysis, joined there by Sue Host, another close friend and neighbor. Liz's attending nephrologist that day was Dr. Mark Boelkins, a longtime friend of mine and very conscientious. Mark pored over Liz's recent records before coming over to tell us his thoughts: "I think your kidneys are coming back."

He cut her dialysis from four hours to three that afternoon. This was the first indication from a nephrologist that they thought there was kidney recovery. I texted our kids and other prayer supporters that evening.

"Thanks for your continuing prayers. We know each and every prayer has been instrumental in her recovery . . . Dr. Boelkins's report was only 7 simple words but electrifying to us."

During devotions that evening, Liz and I talked about her upcoming birthday on June 19.

"I'm looking forward to my birthday," Liz told me. "This is the first one in a long time that I didn't *not* want to see."

On Thursday, June 9, Liz had a long day of therapy, punctuated by my bringing her in the afternoon across the walkway to see Dr. Sandman, only to find that her appointment had been scheduled for the morning. I took her down to Interventional Radiology instead, where she had a "drainogram" study of her abdominal drain, which we were anxious to be rid of. Later, I met our son Tom in his mom's room at 6:00 for dinner before the start of his night shift at St. Mary's. There we also met our pastor, Rev. Corey Dykstra, who had stopped by for a visit. Corey stayed for two hours, and we had a great chat with this godly young man.

The following day, Friday, was another red-letter day in what had become a week of them. Liz worked on walking between what we called "the parallel bars" and was able to reach five steps each time, for five times. This was a marked progression from what she had been able to do up to that point and was duly noted by Jamie, who texted, "What? Mom is more weight-bearing than me?! No fair!"

During dialysis, Dr. Boelkins told us, "We'll get a 24-hour urine collection from Sunday to Monday, and, pending the results of that study, we possibly won't have to do dialysis on Monday—in fact, we might be able to discontinue dialysis."

I texted our prayer group: "So awesome! And I think Dr. Boelkins had a lot of fun telling us."

Liz made remarkable progress on the parallel bars on an otherwise quiet weekend marked by several visits by kids and grandkids. I also noted that her foot wounds were finally starting to heal up nicely.

On Monday, June 13, we finally got the word we had waited four months to hear: "No dialysis." It would be hard to overstate how remarkable this event was, coming at least four months after her having started dialysis and two months after Liz had been diagnosed with End Stage Renal Disease (ESRD). Humanly speaking, the odds of kidney function recovery at that point were miniscule, but through the prayers of the saints and a merciful God answering those prayers, all things are possible. Just to prove the point, Liz had produced over 1400 milliliters of urine by dinnertime.

"Now you're just showing off," I told her.

This day Liz also took her first steps with a walker, which she found to be much more difficult than the parallel bars—three steps three different times—and noted that her right ankle hurt—remarkably, the first sensation she'd had below her knee since the accident.

On the family front, we had all been praying for Laura, who was having surgery to remove her thyroid that day. Thankfully, late that afternoon Tim was able to report successful surgery for Laura. This reinforced to us that, while Liz was monopolizing our prayer attention during her months-long ordeal, other family needs requiring diligent prayer were regularly popping up, and our family could not be slothful in lifting up those issues as well.

As though to emphasize this point, our friend Gary, who lived in our basement and took care of cooking, cleaning, and laundry for me

during this busy time, was admitted with heart issues requiring him
to undergo a cardiac catheterization, which got delayed several times.

"We've lost our home support," I wrote in my entry that day.

Wednesday, June 15, was one of those days when progress on
all fronts made us feel that we might be on the homestretch of this
seemingly endless ordeal. I had been having great concerns about Liz's
blood sugars, which had been wildly uncontrolled for several months
and were a matter of specific prayer by our family. I stopped by early
that morning to see Liz and happened to catch up with Dr. Kim
Turke, her primary internist while she was in Mary Free Bed.

We had gotten to know and appreciate her bright and positive
personality and always looked forward to her visits. This day was no
exception, and Dr. Turke was excited to tell us the good news of how
much better controlled Liz's blood sugars had become ("Thank you,
God!" I wrote in my note).

Shortly thereafter, Liz traveled to Interventional Radiology,
where she waited 3½ hours to have her abdominal drain checked,
only to find out that it could not yet be removed; on the other hand,
she finally had both her dialysis catheter and PICC line removed after
several months. That afternoon we were told that, at the Wednesday
morning providers' meeting the team had changed course, given Liz's
steady progress. I texted our kids and other supporters:

"The care team has decided she will not get an overnight home
visit, as previously planned, but instead will go home for good in 4
to 5 weeks, if all goes well. I can hardly imagine it. Obviously a lot of
work has to be done with Liz and our home in the meantime."

When I happened to walk out of the building with Dr. Ho the
next day, he told me what he had said at that staff meeting: "If a cat
has nine lives, Liz has fifteen."

Earlier that day the Wound nurse had shown me that all three
remaining wounds on Liz's left foot and ankle were contracting and

"granulating in," so much so that Plastic Surgery had decided Liz likely wouldn't need surgery on that foot, as had previously been planned. Further, that terrible coccyx pressure sore that had been so painful had finally healed up. More answers to prayers.

Prayers were being lifted up in many more places than even we were aware, as we found out almost daily. I had become friends with Bobbie, a Liberian man whom I had met at the Snap Fitness Center where we worked out together. In conversation with Bobbie that day, I confirmed that he was a brother in Christ and had been quietly praying for my wife for several months. We had a touching conversation that day about faith in the midst of suffering.

A few days later, in church on Sunday, where a former pastor and his family were visiting from Canada, the pastor's son told me that his church north of Calgary in Alberta had been praying weekly for Liz since she first had been in the accident. As I said, similar revelations happened almost daily, and I developed a tremendous affinity for the family of God.

Steady progress didn't mean that all was rosy and that there wouldn't be more challenges. Gary had finally gotten his cardiac catheterization on Thursday, June 16, with a report that his coronary arteries were normal, but now they had to figure out why his heart had been acting up. At least he got to come home, a great support for me.

On Friday, Liz had to cut short her therapy at 10:00 a.m. because of persistent nausea and retching, which, ominously, did not improve with Zofran or Phenergan. She slept from 11:00 a.m. to 6:00 p.m. and really had me worried. Was this from a recent change to a fiber-containing tube-feeding formula or due to a viral gastroenteritis? Or, heaven forbid, another peritonitis that would lead to septic shock and a transfer back to the ICU? As I have said before, my OCD mind always went to the worst possibility until proven otherwise, and septic shock is where my mind went now. I was very anxious about the latter and prayed, "Please, no sepsis; her kidneys just started to work again."

At about the same time Jamie, still recovering from his comprehensive knee surgery, texted to tell me that his lower back, which had started to act up over the past week, had gotten much worse, essentially disabling him. His situation was coming to a head, and he was trying to decide if he might need to have major surgery and file for disability. As the junior (and very recent) partner in his ophthalmology practice, Jamie decidedly did not want to be a financial burden to his practice, especially after having already been off work for an extended period from his knee surgery. Jamie was scheduled to see a physiatrist the following Monday, possibly for a back or sacroiliac injection. He had been lying flat in bed all weekend but still was in exquisite pain. He even confided to me that he was concerned he might lose his house.

"We're very troubled," I wrote in my journal.

When I told Jamie how worried his mother and I were, he texted me this: "Jeremiah 17:7–8 describes my (and Mom's) year, but also our position with God." I forwarded that "sweet verse" to his siblings with the following request.

Please pray for Jamie.

"Blessed is the man who trusts in the LORD,
whose trust is the LORD.
He is like a tree planted by water,
that sends out roots by the stream,
and does not fear when heat comes,
for its leaves remain green,
and is not anxious in the year of the drought,
for it does not cease to bear fruit."

This day was also the twin's sixth birthday, and after her long nap Liz "roused from her sickbed to enjoy the birthday kids." We took a precious picture of Kathryn and Nolan climbing up into that bed to get a birthday hug from their grandma.

By the next day Liz felt even a little better and was able to achieve twenty steps with her walker for the first time. She also successfully used the bedpan once, saving herself at least one catheterization. This may seem a small thing to the reader, but it had occurred to me that one of the most likely sources of her recent fever was infection from the repetitive urinary catheterizations she was undergoing. Any movement away from those procedures was important.

She was also "eating like a pig," I wrote happily, and maybe heading toward finally getting off the tube feeds that had sustained her for months. Her close friend Meridell Gracias brightened her day further when she stopped by to deliver an early birthday present.

Sunday, June 19, brought not only Father's Day but another milestone for Liz that earlier in the year we had thought she had little chance of making: her 63rd birthday. Tim, always the organizer, had arranged to pick up something at the local Panera and Applebee's for a birthday (and Father's Day) dinner at 6:00 p.m. in Liz's room. Moreover, I finally gave her the present she had been pressing me about for some time.

Months earlier, with Liz in and out of consciousness and telling me that she wanted to die, I was desperately trying to encourage her to keep fighting. Finally I had resorted to the one thing I knew she most wanted from me (and which I least wanted to give her)—a cruise. We had only ever been on two Caribbean cruises, with my siblings and their spouses when my parents, and then my mom, had paid for us all to be together.

Liz had long wanted to go on another cruise with just me (or with all our kids and their families), but this kind of getaway wasn't my favorite thing. In that desperate time, however, I had needed something reliable to try to lift her spirits. The reader may recall, one late evening hour, as I sat by her bedside holding her nonresponsive hand, I had fatefully murmured my deal with her: "If . . . no, *when* you make it home, I'm going to take you on a cruise."

Liz had not been interactive at all that day, so I was not surprised when there was no response from her to my promise.

About two months later, when I was sitting with Liz in dialysis and it was starting to look as if she might even make it home eventually, she had turned to me and stated, "You promised me a cruise."

I tried to deny the fact, but she insisted I had made the promise. *She had actually heard what I told her.* I was baffled. "How can you possibly say you remember that? You were in a coma!"

We had been bantering about that for several weeks before I actually made the promise official with a credit in a birthday card, good for me to take her on that cruise. I also read her the lyrics and personal notes from eight cards that had come in the mail from our church family that week, and then seventeen more that I had found in our box at church that morning—Liz was thrilled to be assured that the church family remembered her.

I did spend some time in the afternoon in our pool with Tim and Laura's family before we headed over to join the rest of our in-town family for the combined Father's Day/birthday party at Mary Free Bed. Liz's floor had a family lounge with kitchen facilities where we settled to observe Liz's birthday, as well as to honor the multiple fathers present. This was a remarkable time of remembrances and thanksgiving for all the events we had been brought through since January. When I left Liz that night, there were more than thirty cards taped to her closet door.

"They still love me, don't they?" she asked with a satisfied smile.

"Of course," I replied. "You know you're some kind of a hero, don't you?"

She looked perplexed. "I haven't done anything but survive."

"But you've done it heroically," I noted. "More than that, your story is an example to many people of God's mercy and faithful answers to prayer. A lot of people have told me it's been a privilege to pray for you and that they've been blessed by the experience."

"Well, anyway, I'm not a hero," she concluded.

As I drove home a few minutes later, I reflected on the day and all that we had negotiated together to make it to that birthday.

You are *a hero, Liz. You're my hero.*

CHAPTER 27

After Liz passed the birthday milestone, we all began to feel secure that she was on the homestretch, that she might finally make it home. On Monday the most notable thing I recorded was, "She made me watch The Bachelor tonight—terrible!" Yet little things continued to be magnified in my mind, conditioned as I was from months of progress curtailed by terrifying setbacks.

On Wednesday, June 22, Liz's long-tenured abdominal drain finally fell out. Her physician staff conferred and decided to leave the drain out but to follow up in a week with an abdominal CAT scan to assess the status of the abscess for which the drain had been placed. It didn't help my mental state at all when, at about the same time, Liz developed a fever with an elevated heart rate and blood pressure. As she began to feel ill, my mind, of course, immediately went to the worst-case scenario, an uncontrolled abdominal abscess leading to sepsis and impending shock. I immediately texted out to our kids and supporters an urgent request for prayers, as Liz was placed back on antibiotics.

My relief was palpable when cultures proved her urine to be the source of an infection that quickly responded to the antibiotics. I gratefully texted that information to our children and supporters, adding to our kids, "Your mom is fragile." Indeed, the term Dr. Randy Baker had coined for Liz way back in February came back to me often: "The tigress of fragility." And tigress she was, as she progressed quickly from 25 steps with a walker to doing that twice, and then 30 steps on consecutive days.

Liz performed well on "reasoning games" with the speech therapist ("they were hard!"), as well as stringing beads with the occupational therapist, who noted good function of her reconstructed right hand. Tim brought Liz's mom, Marie—along with his own twins—to visit her on Thursday evening, for the first time in almost a month. I texted a picture that evening of Liz's "birthday card hall of fame," now grown to 38 cards taped to the closet door as a result of what we now referred to as our church's "birthday conspiracy."

Ryan Faber continued to piece together a video story of Liz's long climb back from the portals of death. He captured a segment in the gym of Liz reaching 32 steps with the walker, then a long interview with Tim and me, followed by another with Randy Baker. Curiously, to this day neither Liz nor I has seen that video story in its entirety, but it was not created with us in mind. It is a story to tell others of fervent prayers and merciful answers, of God's faithful kindness to his children—a story we had already lived together. That story had plenty of downturns mixed in with the progress, events that served to heighten our desperate dependence on God's mercy.

Interestingly, several years later that video reconnected me with a church friend from my high school years in California, Dick Klaver, who had gone on to be a pastor in West Michigan. We had not seen each other more than once or twice in those intervening years, and he had since "retired," although, as is the case with a lot of retired pastors, Dick was functioning as an interim pastor for a church, this one in Colorado. Somehow Dick had come across that video and was moved to reach out by way of a card to me, prompting me to respond with a letter in return (yes, people still do write letters on occasion). This was family-of-God stuff.

While Liz now was making steady, if slow, progress, we continued to have issues, although not all on Liz's part. Jamie finally had a back injection, which did not bring the immediate relief for which we had hoped and prayed. After months of ongoing pain and multiple injections, Jamie eventually had to undergo a lumbar decompression surgery the next March that disabled him for eight weeks.

And though I have had plenty of sports injuries and procedures over my lifetime, I considered myself to be nearly invincible, an attitude that got me into trouble that week. It was fast-pitch softball season, and, as it was unseasonably warm that week, I violated one of my cardinal rules—never play softball without sweatpants on. Choosing to wear just shorts on that muggy Wednesday evening, I tore open the skin of my left knee while diving back into first base because of a fake throw-down by the catcher. Looking down at the now muddy mixture of blood and dirt on my knee, I remember admonishing the first baseman: "Not cool! You don't do that to the old guys." I was one of the oldest players in a young man's league and thought I deserved better than that.

Unfortunately for me, our team congregated after the game for some appetizers and a craft beer at a local restaurant, and, of course, I had to go, what with living in "Beer City." Several hours after the injury I finally hopped into the shower and washed out the wound with soap, dressing it with antibiotic ointment and a Band-Aid. A day later, when I noticed a red streak traveling up my leg, I began to mark its progress with a pen, somewhat in disbelief as the marks steadily advanced up my thigh. I started taking oral antibiotics on Friday, but by Saturday I texted our kids:

"I'm going to have to go to the ER. My knee is infected, and it's gone up to my thigh. My attempts at self-treatment are not going the best. I have a red cord up the upper part of my leg. Can't ignore it much longer. Plus, Mom is on the warpath and being very insistent."

"Yikes, Dad!" Tom replied. "Go in you punk."

Laura added, "And you call yourself a doctor—go get it taken care of!"

In my defense, I was worried about Liz that day, as she was dealing with a sore throat as well as residual effects from the urinary tract infection. But I knew the jig was up, and as my daily entry recorded, "I spent Sunday afternoon in the ER getting an antibiotic shot. Worst shot I ever had."

I think that this, too, was a consequence of my being a physician. The nurse administering the shot, assuming that a doctor would have a clue, asked me if I wanted the three- milliliter injection as one shot or two. Contrary to what people may think, most physicians don't routinely give injections, so to me, three milliliters seeming like such a small number. *Why would I want two shots if I can have it in one?*

Why, indeed. That injection was extremely painful, and I literally couldn't sit down for a day and a half. Jackie, my nurse daughter, chided me, "Why would you let anybody give you a three-milliliter shot . . . that's huge." Who knew? Oh, and my friendly ER physician colleague informed me that, for this type of cellulitis, the oral antibiotic dose was twice that which I had put myself on. Maybe there's some truth in the old adage that a physician who treats himself has a fool for a patient.

Scarier were our concerns for our little grandson, Isaiah, born just that February, and, along with Liz, one of the two "sleepers" who had together been comatose in Critical Care more than four months earlier. Brek and Jackie had noticed that Isaiah had an unusual, slowly growing forehead ridge representing premature closure of the frontal skull suture, commonly known as "the fontanelle." The pediatrician gave his parents the impressive sounding term "metopic craniosynostosis."

A CAT scan was ordered for Wednesday, June 29, to be followed by an appointment with a craniofacial expert to determine if surgery was indicated. Brek, always trying to add a little levity to a situation, texted out a picture of a Star Trek character labelled with the following: "Believe it or not, this is not a recent photo of Isaiah. We knew it was bad when we couldn't tell him apart from a Klingon . . ."

Of course, Isaiah's mother felt differently—"That's so insensitive!"—and that put an end to the levity. But a lot of prayers were offered on behalf of that precious little guy, who eventually saw a long-time colleague of mine, Dr. Bob Mann. He had reassuringly emailed me a couple of weeks before Isaiah's appointment to say, "Quite often no treatment needed."

I joined the parents in taking Isaiah to that visit; we were delighted that the craniofacial doc was not only a known entity to us but a good Christian friend. In the end Dr. Mann determined that the process was stable and that no treatment would be needed other than periodic observation. Check: prayers answered. An interesting side note to this episode is that Jackie, serving as a surgical recovery unit nurse sometime later, worked alongside Dr. Mann's son, Sam, developing a collegial friendship with him.

For her part, Liz was putting in long, hard hours in therapy every day and making measurable progress. As she became more energetic, many of our friends who had prayed so faithfully for Liz came by to see this miracle lady.

On Monday, June 27, sandwiched between visits from Meridell and our close neighbors the Vander Werps, an emotional Dan Door stopped in. Dan was a former classmate of our kids and a close family friend; you may recall that it was his mother, Kathy, who like an angel had, unsolicited, brought lunch to feed our entire family in the "war room" on a January afternoon when Liz was undergoing a critical emergent abdominal surgery, and then quietly slipped away.

Dan had been in daily prayer for Liz and wept to see how well his "other mother" was doing. Indeed, that week was a happy blur of steady progress and new milestones for Liz. Her abdominal CAT scan on Monday showed the abscess regressing, so there was no need to have the drain replaced.

Thursday, June 30, started out with very good news on the Laura front in that the results of her thyroid surgery were revealed to contain no cancer, a cause for great rejoicing by all of us on behalf of this young mother of three. That afternoon also brought a huge milestone, as part of Liz's therapy included my bringing Liz to Johnny Bs, a nearby restaurant, under the watchful eyes of Sean and Ashley, two of Liz's regular therapists. This trip was meant to be a trial run, not only to see how well Liz would do but to test my own capability to load her into and out of a car, as well as transport her from car to table and back again.

As with many homemakers, Liz had always loved to eat out at restaurants, so to say that she was excited would be an understatement. After Mark and Tam's wedding and our brief home visit, this was just the third time Liz had been out of the hospital in nearly six months.

Of the two of us, I was definitely the weaker link. The therapists went on ahead to the restaurant, as this was to be a test of our independence. I proudly followed my training in successfully transferring Liz from her wheelchair to the passenger seat of our Toyota Matrix. As I opened the hatchback of that car, though, it suddenly dawned on me that I had no clue how to fold up that wheelchair to fit it into the back of the car. I had to run back into Mary Free Bed, where I found a therapist working with a patient at a brace shop and with embarrassment asked her for help. She graciously came out to the parking lot to show me how this was done—a simple maneuver I've done thousands of times since, but foreign to me at that time.

The restaurant was only about a mile away, but I think Liz must have commented on a dozen things we passed on the way: "Oh, look at that dog . . . The flowers are out; they're beautiful . . . I love the trim on that house . . . ," and so on. Sean and Ashley were waiting expectantly for us at Johnny Bs, along with Sean's wife, Wendy, who had joined us there.

Again, it was up to me to pull the wheelchair out, set it up. and transfer Liz into it. I was glad that Sean was hovering over us like a mother hen over her chicks, because as I was transferring Liz, the surgical scrub pants she was wearing slipped off right down to her ankles, right there along Wealthy Street. Sean quickly pulled them back up, but all Liz and I could do was laugh. After "the best dinner" Liz had ever had, we returned uneventfully to her "home" at Mary Free Bed.

A few evenings later, on Saturday, July 2, after Liz had spent some time outside pushing her own wheelchair around, we were able to watch the Grand Rapids city fireworks right from the window of her room. The next day she was finally able to get from a sitting position up to her walker on her own for the first time, an accomplishment that had been several weeks in the making. That evening Mark and Tamara came over to share their newly obtained wedding pictures, again bringing tears to my eyes as we shared memories of that first time Liz had finally made it out of the hospital.

On Monday, the Fourth of July, the staff set up a "carnival" on an outside patio, where Liz rolled out like a queen, spun the "Wheel of Fortune," and played Plinko and other games. She relished that experience with an innocent excitement, oohing and laughing at each new experience. For me it was immensely heartwarming, and I praised God for having allowed us to reach that simple moment.

"Mom broke her personal record today; she walked 30 feet with her walker," I texted the next day. "Yesterday I took her out on the balcony for the Fourth of July Carnival, where she played Wheel of Fortune, Plinko, and some other games. She earned enough tickets to buy a lava lamp for her granddaughter (yes, they apparently still make those!). She was so excited and happy, almost childlike enjoying those games. It was so much fun for me to watch her, it brought tears to my eyes. Currently, we think she might be coming home in early August; I'm working with an insurance guy to see what has to be done to our house to get ready. This Friday will be 26 weeks since her accident—half a year. A testimony to God's faithfulness; He would not let my bride go."

The next week was a blur of steady physical progress, along with a regular stream of visitors who had been praying for Liz and were blessed to see their prayers answered. Liz began to work on steps—first a three-inch step, then graduating to a four-inch step, which was particularly difficult for her in that she had to drag up her reconstructed left foot; it was painful for her to bear much weight on that side. She wheeled outside by herself, all the way from her fourth-floor room. She reached 40 feet with the walker and did this three times in one day. She changed her own ileostomy for the first time on Saturday, July 9.

Liz was working very diligently on her therapy, determined to convince the staff that she was ready to go home. In the meantime, she enjoyed welcome breaks in the monotony of therapy when visitors came to see her. There was an emotional visit from Marla Roedema, a close friend who saw her for the first time since the accident but had been much in prayer for Liz.

Friday, July 8, turned out to be a family day, with visits from Jackie and her boys, Mark and Tamara, and then Tom and Emily in the evening. This day was noteworthy in that it marked exactly six months since Liz had been in the accident. We reminisced about the six months and remembered Randy Baker telling us that first week not to get hung up with looking for daily or even weekly progress but to be ready to endure months and even a year to recovery—I don't think any of us at that time knew how prophetic those words would be in the end. The next day I texted a summary of those six months to our kids and other prayer supporters:

"26 weeks yesterday, exactly half a year. A good time to take stock:

At least five times we thought we might be saying goodbye to Mom . . . but didn't.

Deadly heart arrhythmias, including 'flat line' three times . . . prayed for and resolved.

Unresponsive respiratory failure . . . prayed for and resolved (also, to date, her pre-existing autoimmune respiratory symptoms).

Deadly liver disease . . . prayed for and significantly improved.

End stage kidney disease . . . prayed for and resolved, against all human expectation.

3 large open wounds on her foot and a painful pressure sore over her tailbone . . . prayed for and resolved.

Disabling anxiety . . . prayed for and resolved.

Massive deconditioning . . . prayed for tolerance of and response to therapy, with dramatic progress to date.

The most beautiful 6 months of marriage we have ever shared.

I love this God; can't wait for the next six months."

As if to prove that point, the next day, Sunday, my entry noted, "A light day with therapy; heavy day with visitors," including Meridell Gracias with her husband, Dr. Vince; Liz's cousin Ginny; close friend Betty Bouwman; and, finally, Tim and Laura with their kids. I concluded, "As usual, I was swarmed by people at church asking about Liz."

That week was also significant because of the wedding anniversaries of three of our children and their spouses. Tim offered Jamie and Halle congratulations on theirs on the 15th, to which Jamie replied, "Yes, thanks for remembering. 15 years. During that time we have now seen all our siblings get married. Mostly to OK people." Laura added, "It's actually quite impressive: a 40th, a 15th, and a wedding. Oh, and those random (two) 6-year anniversaries." Blessed indeed.

But, as had always been the case during those six months, amid all that progress there was always some need that kept us focused on prayer. This time during which we approached Liz's anticipated return home proved to be no exception. As Liz progressed with walking and climbing, the pain she was experiencing in her left foot was escalating as well. On Monday, July 11, Liz was fit for orthotic shoes.

"These are not going to be very fashionable; they're ski boot shoes," she demurred.

But wearing them, she managed to stand at a table and color some pictures without a walker for an extended period. However, afterward her left foot was quite a bit sorer, and one of the wounds that had been nearly healed up began draining again. Because her blood sugars also were very poorly controlled, the medical staff began to have concerns about a deep bone infection, an osteomyelitis. This would have been catastrophic, as it would have required exploratory surgery on Liz's ankle and deep bone cultures, which, if positive, would likely have required removal of all of that bone hardware with which Dr. Geoff Sandman had so meticulously repaired her ankle. This could possibly even have led to amputation. An appointment with Dr. Sandman couldn't be scheduled until the following Monday, July 18.

In the meantime, Liz continued to push through the pain in her ankle, reaching 40 feet multiple times daily, and finally 50 feet. Her therapists would often combine her physical, speech, and occupational therapy, having her walk up to and stand at a table to play mind-challenging games like Connect 4 (speech therapists are involved in more than just speech and swallowing therapy, also assessing and promoting brain injury recovery).

Despite her painful ankle, Liz was able to reach 60 feet of walking by Sunday, and then—just showing off, I suspect—did it two more times that day. Also that week, she was finally able to hold Isaiah, now five months old, for the first time, resulting in a beautiful picture that was sent to all our supporters. Mark and Tamara visited that day, and we noted that the Scripture "call to worship" for our evening church service had been from Psalm 107, the same psalm that Liz and I had reached in our devotions. Coincidence?

On Monday, July 18, I wheeled Liz across the walkway to see Dr. Sandman. After examining her foot, he scheduled Liz for surgery the next afternoon. This was something we had been praying would not have to happen, so it was a disappointment. Despite that, she walked 60 feet once and 50 feet twice more that day, as well as negotiating six-inch stairs for the first time.

The following day Liz was not allowed to eat until her surgery, which wasn't scheduled to happen until 5:20 p.m. During that surgery Dr. Sandman "debrided" (cleaned out) the bone and took out some "heterotopic bone" (abnormal new growth bone), as well as some screws from the talus and tibia bones. He left a VAC dressing on the wound, a dressing hooked to vacuum suction to remove drainage fluid from the wound as it formed. Dr. Sandman seemed to be quite upbeat about the surgery results, noting that the bone cultures would take several days to finalize. Liz was quite sore afterward, and we spent a quiet evening watching a movie on TV.

By Wednesday Liz was told that no bacteria or white blood cells (indicative of infection) were seen in the preliminary look (gram stain) of the deep bone cultures from the previous day. We were told further that it was now unlikely that Liz would need six to eight weeks of intravenous antibiotics.

"A very beautiful answer to prayer," I texted our kids. "Also, at the weekly staff meeting today, they set August 5 as the day she will finally come home, exactly 30 weeks after her accident. I was emotional when I heard; I can hardly imagine having her home after everything we've experienced. God's ways are mysterious and wonderful."

CHAPTER **28**

The next week passed quickly, with a parade of milestones marching through my daily entries: "Walked three times, 60 feet—40 feet—40 feet . . . 60 feet twice . . . 60 feet, 50 feet once . . . 75 feet, then 60 feet twice . . . 4-inch stairs x 4 . . . 6-inch stairs x 3."

The ever-increasing physical success was, however, taking a toll on Liz, as I recorded:

"Lots of pain . . . with much agony."

The feeling was definitely back in Liz's left foot, and this was not entirely welcome, especially with the progressive walking she was doing. There were still a lot of little victories to celebrate, however. Liz was also progressing in her occupational and speech (cognitive) therapy. She spent an afternoon "bedazzling" her orthopedic shoes with sparkles and small doodads, and she worked on crossword puzzles with Tom, who was very impressed with the cognitive progress she was making. Liz worked daily at the difficult task of standing up on her own, following a pattern of "stand up—march—sit down" over and over again. Therapy was challenging for her, but the motivation of finally going home drove her forward relentlessly.

Fortunately, a steady stream of visitors helped to lighten that load: Sue Host, Pastor Corey, Liz's sister Sue and family, Jackie and

301

Brek with their boys. Tom stopped in regularly on his way to his night shift on H3. One day Liz and I joined Tom in the St. Mary's Café for dinner before going with him to H3, where, as you may recall, she had spent the better part of a week as a patient. The care staff was excited to see the progress Liz had made in the weeks since that stay, but not nearly as much as the staff on H2 (ICU), where we visited next. Liz had been a critically ill patient in that unit twice, for the better part of a month each time, in February and again in March/April. The ICU staff members were astonished to see how far she had progressed, and a number expressed their amazement that she was even still alive.

On another evening Liz and I went out on our own to pick up her mother and take her to dinner at Chili's. This was challenging because Liz was in a wheelchair and Marie was using a walker, but we managed. We had been practicing car/chair transfers a lot, which helped immensely. We did have a scare that week when Liz found a breast lump. A few days later she was seen by Dr. Jamie Simon, a surgeon I had worked with when she was a resident. She suspected the lump was just a calcifying bruise from Liz's original trauma but ordered a mammogram and ultrasound to be sure.

On Wednesday, July 27, I flew out to California for a week to visit my family, after making sure I had Liz's full approval when she was in a state of normal cognition. The reader may recall my ill-fated trip to Florida in March, preapproved by Liz with that approval quickly forgotten afterward. I certainly didn't want Liz telling visitors she was "going to get a divorce lawyer" again. I don't think I've ever been more torn about making a decision to travel.

Late July was a traditional time for me to visit my California family, a vacation I looked forward to all year, but I was desperately reluctant to leave Liz at that particular time. Our children all encouraged me to go, telling me that I needed the restorative downtime and promising to redouble their efforts to visit their mother while I was gone. Thankfully, they upheld their part of the bargain, starting with that very day when Mark and Tamara came by in the evening to visit and share devotions with Liz. In the meantime, I called Liz at least three times a day, anxious to hear whether her admirable progress was continuing.

The next day we had very good news when Liz, after spending several hours in Radiology for her mammogram and ultrasound, was informed that the breast lump was a resolving hematoma (bruise). What an answer to prayer this was, relieving our anxiety in a way with which I imagine a lot of readers can identify. Tim dropped by that evening to direct devotions with his mother and offer prayers of thanksgiving.

In my absence Liz continued to push herself despite the pain in her left ankle, reaching 110 feet and 80 feet on Friday, 120 feet and 80 feet on Saturday, and 160 feet and 120 feet on Sunday. I realize that "absence makes the heart grow fonder," but I was tremendously proud of Liz for pushing through the pain to achieve those marks. She desperately wanted to come home.

Liz also spent a lot of time practicing transfers: bed to walker, walker to commode, walker to chair and back. My entries document a litany of visitors as well, as our children coordinated their efforts to maintain the promised schedule of visits. On Friday, Brek and Jackie came in the evening, joined soon afterward by Tim and Laura's family. Liz told me it was a "rowdy night," but Tim stayed to share some quiet devotions with Liz.

Saturday was somewhat of an aberrancy, in that Liz got sick and vomited late in the morning, took a Phenergan, and then slept all day. She had no visitors that day and went to bed early. I barely had time to worry because she felt better by Sunday morning. Brek and Jackie's family joined her for lunch after church, followed by Tim and Laura and the kids and cousin Ginny after that. Monday, after our good friend Betty Bouwman stopped by, Mark, Tamara and Emily took Liz to dinner at Chili's again. This was the first time she had been out without me hovering over her.

The following day two staff members unexpectedly brought Liz for an ophthalmology appointment off site, but there was no knowledge of that appointment in that medical office, so they turned around and brought her back. On returning, Liz took the two therapists to lunch at the St. Mary's Café before talking them into bringing her to the hospital gift shop to buy—what else?—gifts. Liz had discovered the gift shop a few weeks earlier, and this had turned out to be one of her favorite diversions. This development turned out to be somewhat stressful on our pocketbook, but it was hard to restrict her after all she had been through.

Tim came by again that evening for devotions with his mom. These frequent visits by our children and their families certainly eased the guilt and stress I was experiencing away from Liz that week. After a quiet day Wednesday, August 3, which Liz spent mostly practicing car transfers with her therapist Sean, I arrived back to her room in the evening to find her sharing stories with our neighbor Sue Host.

Liz and I used most of the following day to pack her personal belongings and get ready to leave. It was a surreal day, the 210th she had spent being hospitalized. After seven eventful months it hardly seemed possible that she would be coming home at last. Staff members from both Mary Free Bed and St. Mary's wandered into her room off and on throughout the day to congratulate Liz and offer her well wishes.

I think that day may have been one of the more emotional we experienced—certainly, at least, since coming to Mary Free Bed in April. After four months, albeit interrupted by a few panicked transfers back to St. Mary's, that room had begun to feel like home to Liz. Now that she was leaving that safe place to go to her real home, her feelings were understandably a mixture of excitement and apprehension.

Mine were, too. I had grown accustomed to balancing the hours of my days between being a practicing physician and being a patient's family member. Gradually weathering that early role confusion, I had become something of a hybrid, seamlessly slipping between roles. My role as family member had changed the way I approached my own patients . . . a lot. I realized that, in my physician function, I was more patient, spent more time sharing small talk, and was certainly more emotional than previously.

I was better. This is not to suggest that I had not manifested these traits before the accident, but just that they were more prevalent in me now. If I had to sum up the situation with few words, I guess I would say I had achieved greater empathy. *Maybe,* I thought, *every physician would benefit from experiencing something similar.* However, as Liz and I shared again with each other that afternoon, our experience was something we would never want to give up—but also one we would never wish upon anyone else. And yet . . .

Tim joined us that evening for some emotional devotions, during which we read "Liz's Psalm," Psalm 30, yet again. Saying goodnight to my wife, hopefully for the final time during this long ordeal, I joined Tim for a craft beer at Harmony Hall, a place that had become an occasional refuge for us over the past months, especially on particularly anxious and emotional nights.

I stayed up late that night, going through our house, checking, rechecking, and triple-checking to make sure everything was ready for my homecoming bride—her favorite recliner in place with her favorite comforter on it; her hospital bed plugged in and working, the one railing down so she could easily get in and out; her favorite snacks in the cupboard; even down to a clean new toothbrush in the holder she had last used on a wintery January day. Lying in bed that night, I said a long prayer of thanksgiving for all those answered prayers, all those remarkable blessings that had kept a dying wife alive and now on the verge of returning home . . . at last.

Friday, August 5, was a typically hot and humid summer day in Grand Rapids, but I hardly noticed. I had woken up early and couldn't get back to sleep, so I finally got up and busied myself moving and straightening stuff for the umpteenth time. Although I was early, I thought it odd when I arrived at Liz's Mary Free Bed room that morning that she was still sleeping soundly—if she was as anxious as I was, she was not showing it. But then her room got busy with the preparations of going home . . . *Going home.* We kept saying it to each other over and over again, as if this were the last part of a dream . . . and the only part one would really remember.

Staff kept coming in and going out, with lots of instructions I was furiously trying to keep up with on a notepad, but some just to say goodbye and wish Liz well. Ryan Faber was there to video-record the moment. Liz was presented with a green Mary Free Bed shirt covered with numerous signatures, well-wishes, and verses—the shirt traditionally given to patients who were "graduating." And then it was time to go, really and truly time to go.

As I had been trained to do, I assisted Liz with her transfer into her wheelchair and headed to the elevator, with five of her most regular caregivers serving as an escort to our waiting car. As Liz prepared to transfer into the front seat, she shared abundant hugs and tears, tears of sad separation but also of joy. I must admit that my eyes were not dry, either, that morning. When the time came to fold her chair and place it into the back hatch, I did it like a professional, with pride but also some mirth, remembering that day five weeks earlier when I'd had to run back into the orthotic shop to solicit help from a handy therapist.

As we rolled out of the parking garage, Liz was waving excitedly to the Mary Free Bed send-off party. She was the only one with dry eyes. Then it was just the two of us, out for a drive together on a sunny morning, as we had done a thousand times before . . . yet unlike any other time. It was a quiet drive, with both of us lost in a myriad of thoughts of the last seven months and what it would be like to have Liz home once again, for good.

As we turned off onto Lake Michigan Drive to head into the West side, I glanced at her, surprised to see not a smile but a pensive look on Liz's face. Of course, she was nervous about the prospect of being home, away from the security of her nurses and aides. But we did have the consolation that she would have in-house aides, at least for now, to help her through the day.

As we turned down Covell Road, I finally spoke. "I'm taking you home, babe."

She was smiling again now as she reached for my hand. "You promised you would."

I nodded. "I did and I am."

Turning up Elmridge Drive from Richmond Street, I pointed to a towering telephone pole. "That's where I see the owl sometimes."

She just smiled and nodded, her face beginning to show the emotion bubbling up inside. Then we were turning on to Glencairin Drive and pulling into our own driveway. Tim and Laura and their kids were waiting there, waving excitedly and yelling, "Welcome home, Grandma!"

Still holding her hand, I told her quietly, "This is our home. Owls do mate for life."

AFTERWORD

I'd like to say that we lived happily ever after, but anyone who has experience with major trauma knows that couldn't have been the case. We started out fine. My notes record that Jackie brought her kids over that afternoon. Our faithful friends and neighbors stopped in that day, first the Elzingas and later the Vander Werps. We had a family dinner to celebrate the homecoming and welcomed the first of numerous home health aides.

"Liz gets up twice during the night—settles in well," I wrote. The next day, Saturday, we tried to develop a routine. "Restful day—family in and out. We go to Culver's in the evening with family." We had our first Sunday family dinner in over seven months. Monday, we had the "first of many trips for doctors' appointments." But there was never again going to be a routine.

We didn't anticipate the later difficulties that would result from Liz's accident, significant complications with her left ankle, her eyes, her kidney function, and others. We together weathered numerous additional hospitalizations, tests, surgeries, and therapies, because that's what owls do. But those are not a part of this story—maybe another sometime.

When I retired at the end of September 2023 (the accident had happened in 2016), Liz had already planned two long-awaited "retirement" trips to Orlando theme parks with various family members. Liz and I made it to Florida with Tim's family just after Thanksgiving later that fall, a dream trip for her that we had often doubted would ever happen. It was a wonderful time of celebrating with her kids and grandkids, with lots of photo memories.

A second dream trip was planned with the families of four of our children just after Christmas that same year, but, sadly, Liz did not make that adventure. She had not been eating well for several months and had lost significant weight. Her body was worn out from months and years of injury and illness.

I was not surprised that Liz developed a respiratory illness upon returning from Florida, and she was admitted to the hospital a week later with bilateral pneumonia. She survived a crisis on the fifth day and seemed to be slowly improving for several weeks. However, her body had suffered more than a body can reasonably endure. After two and a half weeks in the hospital, she unexpectedly developed an abdominal catastrophe related to her original accident, necessitating emergent surgery, following which she passed into arms of the Savior to whom she had dedicated her life.

Before that last surgery, Liz and I had an hour-long wait for surgery escort to come take her to the operating room, during which she and I had a very intense and intimate conversation, knowing that she was likely not going to survive that operation. I told her that, if the surgery proved unsuccessful, she would go to be with Jesus and Miles (a beloved lost grandson) in heaven.

"I would get to see Miles," she confirmed. "I want to go be with Miles."

"No fair!" I chided gently.

She followed by giving me a smirky smile as if to say, "I'm going to beat you."

We were able to express how much we loved each other, and we gave each other one last kiss as she rolled out of her intensive care room on her way to surgery, knowing that we were unlikely to see each other again on this earth.

As she had requested, the gospel was preached at her memorial service, and I was able to tell all who were there, and those online as well, that, as she had expressed throughout her life to everyone close to her, Liz would have wanted to tell them to love Jesus and join her in heaven someday.

At the time of this writing, a month after Liz's passing, I remain brokenhearted, the grief only bearable because I know that she has at last received the complete healing for which so many family members and friends had prayed over the past eight years. Her body is finally whole, and she will never again have to experience the physical and emotional suffering she endured for those eight years.

I want to emphasize that this is a story of heroic perseverance by a godly lady against overwhelming odds, not because of her own strength, as she would have been the first to tell you, but because of God's sovereign will.

This is a story of a physician husband who quickly learned that his status and skills as a physician meant very little in this situation, and that his main—maybe his only—responsibility in bringing healing to his wife was to do everything possible, for seven months, to make sure she was covered at all times with a blanket of prayer.

This is a story of family, friends, and brothers and sisters in Christ across the country and beyond who were not willing, when this lady hung between heaven and earth, to let her go, tirelessly praying for her throughout that long journey.

This is a story of Psalm 30, of faithful Christians lifting a loved one in fervent and enduring prayer and a merciful God faithfully answering those prayers.

www.ingramcontent.com/pod-product-compliance
Lightning Source LLC
Chambersburg PA
CBHW062043080426
42734CB00012B/2547

9 781625 862792